Performing

10-Minute Plays

with Friends

A guide to do-it-yourself theater

David K. Farkas

V.12-31-20

ISBN
Paperback: 978-1-7367012-1-8
Ebook-Kindle: 978-1-7367012-0-1

Dedication

To the enthusiastic theater-goers and emerging backyard performers, Jonah (age 8) and Hazel (age 6), our beloved grandchildren.

Acknowledgments

I wish to gratefully acknowledge the current and past members of the Goat Hill Living Room Theater Group: Jeff Altman, Judy Altman, Charles Anstett, Bill Baron, Deana Baron, Bob Boiko, Rick Ells, Gary Elmer, Jean Farkas, Jackie Gardner, Tyson Greer, Jim Halliday, Doug Hennick, Kitty McKoon-Hennick, Dennis Moore, Kristine Moore, and Jean Reid. Also, my thanks to all those who watched us perform, energized us, and offered all manner of helpful suggestions.

In writing this book I benefited greatly from the insights of Charles Blank, Susan Blank, Michael Davis, Jean Farkas, Bob Herman, Donna Hoke, and Marty Levine.

I also wish to thank the many playwrights with whom I've exchanged reviews of our 10-minute plays on Trade a Play Tuesday (#TAPT), Donna Hoke's weekly 10-minute play exchange. I've learned a great deal about theater from you folks.

Finally, the infinitely helpful Ziaul Haque contributed his expertise in graphic design, book design, and digital publishing in the conversion of my MS Word manuscript to digital and print Kindle publications.

—DKF

Table of Contents

Preface

This book is based on my experience organizing and managing the Goat Hill Living Room Theater Group, centered in the suburbs just north of Seattle, Washington (USA). We began performing in June 2019. From the outset of our project, I took detailed notes, both to have a personal record of what we were doing and to be able to share what we learned with others. We suspended our activities due to the Covid-19 pandemic, just as we were planning our April 2020 performance and as we were organizing a traveling troupe to perform at senior centers and senior residences. My notes, therefore, became a book earlier than I expected because of the enormous amount of extra time I had on my hands.

Before television and before the Internet, friends and family members spent sociable evenings singing together to a piano in the parlor or on the porch to a banjo. The aim of this book is to encourage a similar kind of fun and camaraderie with a do-it-yourself approach to theater.

Although the history of the Goat Hill Theater has been short, it was long enough for us to learn how to do living room theater. We were up and running. We made mistakes, we fixed them, we established best practices. I am now finishing this book without changing—except at moments—the exuberant, optimistic tone of my pre-pandemic notes.

Our group resumed in a limited way in the Farkas backyard in September 2020, when the Covid-19 infection rate temporarily decreased. As I write this in November 2020, cold weather and a spiking infection rate will preclude further outdoor performances for 2020. I deeply hope that sometime in 2021 we will be able to resume our regular living room theater performances, which had been taking place in the Farkas living room and in the community rooms of the Shoreline, Washington, public library.

A Second Book: Writing the 10-Minute Play

My second book, *Writing the 10-Minute Play*, will appear in 2022. It is a start-to-finish guide that covers brainstorming, structuring the plot, developing characters, writing dialogue, formatting the script—absolutely everything. I am writing it primarily to encourage and help folks write 10-minute plays for the living room theater group they are part of. By way of establishing my qualifications for a book on writing plays, especially because I don't have a history of having my plays produced, I'll mention that I am a life-long theater-goer, hold a Ph.D. in British literature, enjoyed a long career teaching university writing courses, and (before turning my attention to writing books about theater) I wrote fifty 10-minute plays in a 15-month period. My plays are not remarkable literary works, but I believe they fall well within the level of quality that we see in 10-minute play festivals.

A Note on the Appendices

This book has four appendices that need to be explained.

Appendix A: Summaries of the Plays Used as Examples

Throughout this book, I illustrate ideas with examples. Very often these examples are drawn from my own 10-minute plays, and in those instances I do not identify myself as the author. Therefore you will see many sentences that begin like this: "In "Flames" the protagonist . . . " I've tried hard to make all my examples completely self-contained. However, because some readers may want to know more about a play than what is explained in the example, I have summarized, in Appendix A, every one of my 10-minute plays used in an example. In addition, I have summarized the 10-minute play "Black Box," by Bob Boiko, which is discussed in the book.

You can read this book productively without looking at a single summary. But for those who do decide to look at the summaries, I've tried to write them in an entertaining manner—as 2-minute short stories. Finally, these summaries collectively suggest the enormous variety we find in 10-minute plays and may help you think of events and ideas that you can dramatize in your own 10-minute plays. With very few exceptions, all my other examples are drawn from Shakespeare. This is because Shakespeare's plays are likely to be familiar to readers of this book and because plot summaries (and the full texts) of his plays are readily available on the Internet.

I should point out that I depart from many authors of 10-minute plays in favoring multiple short scenes rather than the more typical single scene. Therefore, most of my examples come from such plays. Very briefly, I explain this preference: To write a one-scene play, the playwright must depict a very special 10 minutes in the lives of the characters—the 10 minutes when a relationship dissolves, the ten minutes when a lonely person is prevented from committing suicide, a very humorous misunderstanding in the waiting room of a doctor's office, etc. Therefore, with just certain exceptions, none of the events leading up to this special moment and none of the consequences are shown on stage. Rather, they are revealed in dialogue that looks backward and forward in time. Although multiple scenes interrupt the momentum of a play and add to the complexity of the staging, they allow a more natural kind of storytelling—depicting a succession of events—and make possible a broader range of subject matter.

Appendix B: Finding 10-Minute Plays in the Public Domain

The goal of this book is to promote living room theater. One way to do this is to direct you to scripts of 10-minute plays that you can perform without paying a royalty or making special arrangements. In Appendix B, I list and briefly describe a good selection of such plays. Most are old plays that have passed into the public domain. Because they are in the public domain, you can use them in any way you want, including re-writing them. A few of these plays, while royalty-free, are not in the public domain and bear certain legal restrictions. Copyright issues are discussed in Chapter 2.

Appendix C: Nine Complete Scripts You Can Use

Because I am committed to living room theater, I have placed nine of my own 10-minute plays in the public domain. The full scripts of these plays comprise Appendix C. I call these nine plays the Jumpstart Collection because they enable any reader of this book—and anyone else—to immediately get started performing some contemporary 10-minute plays. I've also made them downloadable from the Internet so that each cast member can have their own script to work from.

Appendix D: References and Resources

This appendix contains the full bibliographic references to works cited in this book, plus some helpful resources.

Chapter 1

Living Room Theater

This book explains how to perform 10-minute plays with your friends in a non-theater venue such as someone's living room or backyard or in a church basement or the community room of a library. These are very informal performances you can call "living room," "do-it-yourself," or "home brew" theater. You can say we do a recreational form of "flash drama." Whatever name you choose, it's highly creative and great fun. The first time I reserved a community room at a local library, I found that the online reservation form required a name for the group. Without much thought, I typed in "Goat Hill Living Room Theater Group." (My neighborhood was once called "Goat Hill.") Folks in our group are barely aware that we have an official name, but having an official name is at times necessary or at least convenient. So, if you start a living room theater group, you might want to give it a name.

Kristine and Dennis Moore, "in bed together," as they perform Dennis' sexy 10-minute play "Unlikely Event."

I need to emphasize that this is very informal theater. We perform script-in-hand—no memorizing lines. Our plays have small casts, ranging from one actor performing a dramatic monologue to a cast of four or five. Our sets and props are basic, minimal, or non-existent. Our costumes generally come out of the actors' closets, although some folks do get more serious about their costumes (as shown by the cover photo of me costumed to perform in "Gawain and the Green Knight").

We communicate by email. We don't have a website or a logo. But our performances are not sit-down readings. They are action performances. We enter, we exit, we move around, we hug and kiss, we shoot guns, and more. Only two people in our group have training or extensive experience as actors. I myself am untrained—although I've begun attending acting workshops sponsored by the As If Theatre Company in Kenmore,

Washington. Because of the relaxed mood of our performances, there is very little in the way of stage fright.

Here in three sentences is the point of this book:

- There's a sweet spot between sit-down readings and more professional productions at community theaters.

- This sweet spot consists of friends who informally perform 10-minute plays for themselves and some guests.

- This do-it-yourself theater is still more fun if some of the folks are willing to take a shot at writing 10-minute plays for the group.

Program and Audience Size

The Goat Hill group typically performs a program of three 10-minute plays. Actors sometimes perform in two plays, but they take a minor role in one of them. Each play has a director. If the play was written by a group member, the playwright usually directs the play. The director may also be one of the actors.

When we perform in our library's community room, we usually have 15 to 20 people in the audience, but audience size is not a goal. I am perfectly happy if an audience consists of 7 or 8 people. But I will explain why 15 to 20 is a likely number for the size of the audience. Let's say that one particular program of three plays has a total cast size of 9 (an average of three actors per play). At any one time, there will be 6 "off-duty" actors watching 3 onstage actors. Let's assume that 6 of the 9 actors bring a single guest— perhaps their romantic partner, a child, or a friend. With these 6 "bring-alongs," the audience at any one time during the performance now grows to 12, who are watching three actors on stage.

In addition to our off-duty actors and their "bring-alongs," we are apt to have a few true guests. These are friends and neighbors who, when told about our living room theater project, were curious enough to want to see a performance. Perhaps they are potential recruits who have shown up to check us out. Let's say, then, that we have 3 guests. So for this performance the total audience size at any one moment is 15, and there will be 18 folks eating pizza when we all socialize after the performance.

If we perform in an actual living room, we need to limit the number of attendees. The Farkas living room is not large, but when we carry out our coffee table, an end table, and a big potted plant, we can bring in enough extra chairs to seat 12 people.

Our group has both core and occasional participants. Some folks have very busy schedules or travel a lot. Folks drop out and new folks join us. Some folks have been with us since the beginning. Note that we do not publicize our performances or hold auditions for actors. Everyone is part of a circle of relatives or friends or is welcome to join our circle. Below I preview the various roles people take on.

Roles

- The **Organizer** keeps the project going. This means scheduling the performances and doing the overall planning—a big part of which is choosing the plays, directors, and venues. The organizer (or organizers) works with the director of each play to choose and invite actors from our pool of actors, although directors may certainly recruit their own actors.

- The **Director** of each play guides the actors in performing that play and takes charge of obtaining set items and props. As noted, if the play was written by a group member, the playwright is likely to direct the play.

- The **Stage Manager** handles much of the logistics for the performance, coordinating closely with the organizer and directors. The stage manager has special responsibility for tasks that span the three plays making up the performance—for example, deciding what part of the venue will be used as the acting area, what part for seating, and how the chairs should be arranged. If the three plays making up the performance collectively require a lot of set items, the stage manager decides where these set items will be placed so that the stage hands can quickly and efficiently carry them on and off the stage. During the performance, the stage manager might deal with sound effects and lighting. It does not hurt if the stage manager happens to live with the organizer so that they have lots of opportunities to coordinate. Jean Farkas, my wife, is more interested in pen-and-ink drawing than theater, but she has very graciously been serving as stage manager.

- **Stage Hands** carry set items on and off the stage and perform related tasks. Cast members typically perform this function because they know the play intimately and because they are already standing on the stage ready to carry something.

- The **Actors** and the **Audience** are what the whole thing is about.

How the Group Functions

The Goat Hill Theater has so far only performed plays written by our members. Initially we performed plays that I wrote, but increasingly members of the group are contributing their own plays. Many people with a love for theater and an interest in creative writing discover that with a little practice and perhaps some guidance they can turn out a good 10-minute play. If you decide to perform plays written outside your group, you will have no trouble finding very suitable plays, as explained in Chapter 2.

An important issue is rehearsals. We started out doing only a brief walk-through of each of the plays just before the performance. These days we are more likely to schedule one or two rehearsals—although sometimes the cast of a play decides to forego rehearsals in favor of the pre-performance walk-through. Although results vary with the particular cast and script, some performances go off quite well with just a walk-through.

Even with a rehearsal or two, you should not expect professional quality. Just the fact that you are performing script-in-hand detracts from the audience experience. Audiences, however, are more engaged and more generous in their judgments when they are personally acquainted with the folks putting on the play. Living room theater is as much a social activity as an artistic endeavor. Before electronic and digital entertainment, when friends spent sociable evenings singing together at the parlor piano, not everyone had a good voice. Finally, discussion and socializing are integral to living room theater. This includes a talk-back (question and answer period) directly after each performance.

Theatrical Readings as an Alternative

As noted, this book is about action performances, not theatrical readings. However, there is nothing wrong with a theatrical reading in any of its forms. For many years Jean Farkas and I occasionally hosted sit-down readings of plays by Shakespeare and other playwrights. Theatrical readings require a lot less planning and rehearsing than action performances. Because there are no sets or stage actions, is it easier to perform full-length plays. Retirement communities favor sit-down readings because they are physically less demanding for the actors. Here are the familiar forms of theatrical readings:

- **Sit-down readings.** Sit-down readings call for the full use of facial expressions and as much gesturing as one can do sitting down. Because the script is on a table or one's lap, the actor's hands are free for gesturing.

- **Cold readings.** A cold reading means that the actors have not previously looked at the script. Actors often perform cold readings as part of an audition, but there are theater people, such as Cold Reads International (www.coldreads.wordpress.com) for whom performing scripts they have not yet read, typically seated together at a table, is part of the fun.

- **Stand-up readings.** With a stand-up reading the actors are fully visible, head to toe. This encourages body movement. Gesturing becomes easier if the scripts are on music stands. For many years, the Wild Geese Players of Seattle have performed stand-up readings of a chosen chapter of James Joyce's *Ulysses* on or around Bloomsday (June 16). Actors can sit to indicate that they have exited the stage.

- **Closet dramas.** These are stand-up performances of plays that were written to be read. The cast performs only minimal actions. The plots of closet dramas emphasize dialogue rather than stage action.

- **Radio dramas.** Radio-dramas, like closet dramas, are written to be read. But it is understood that the actors—and the audience—will only think about voice. Facial expressions are not part of the job. True radio dramas flourished during the era in which radio was the only broadcast medium. Podcasting is a contemporary medium akin to the radio drama.

Here I need to clarify some confusing terminology. Theater people use the term "staged reading" to describe the kind of full-movement, script-in-hand performances that we do in living room theater. I prefer to reserve the term "reading" for performances in which there is no significant action. Note that with theatrical readings, it is often necessary for someone to read the stage directions, perhaps modified in certain ways, so that the audience fully understands the actions that are taking place. In other words, the narrator needs to tell the audience that someone has just pulled a knife unless this action is revealed by the dialogue. If you do decide on a theatrical reading, this book will still be helpful. However, you will need to make some obvious mental adjustments as you proceed, and you may want to skip certain parts of the book.

Finally, while I have often enjoyed attending and acting in theatrical readings, my commitment is very definitely to action performances. I believe that if you accept the steeper challenge of an action performance, the more complete theatrical experience will surpass, both for performers and the audience, what a theatrical reading can do. You might begin with theatrical readings and then, as you gain experience and confidence, move up to action performances.

More Terminology

Before moving on, I want to explain how some other theater terms are used in the book:

- Although living room theater rarely takes place on an actual theater stage, I often use "stage" as a convenient synonym for the more precise phrase "acting area."

- I use "professional" with reference to both individuals and theater groups, and by "professional" I mean a professional level of quality, not whether the individual earns a living in theater or whether a theater group brings in much revenue or turns a profit.

- I use "mainstage" for big-time theater. The largest, most established theater companies in medium and large cities are mainstage, as are the major productions of well-funded colleges and universities. Mainstage theaters seat something like 200 or more people, have high-quality lighting, audio, and special effects, and are fully capable of mounting productions with elaborate costumes and sets.

- I use the word "performance" both in reference to a single play and to multiple plays (in our case, usually three) performed together as one event.

- "Theater tech" and "stage craft" are theater terms that describe the creation and handling of sets, scenery, sound, make-up, and more. I use "theater tech," but my big point is that in living room theater there isn't a lot of theater tech, and you are unlikely to have theater tech professionals helping you. The very simple theater tech will largely be the job of each play's director with help from the stage manager.

A Long Tradition

Living room theater has a long history. Western theater evolved from the theater of Ancient Greece, which has its origins in religious ritual rather than professional entertainment. Medieval mystery plays (also called miracle plays) and, later on, the more secular morality plays were performed largely by non-professional actors in the towns and cities where they lived. In *A Midsummer Night's Dream,* Shakespeare gives us an uproarious picture of unsophisticated townspeople who get together to rehearse and perform a play for Duke Theseus and his court (Act I, Scene 2 and Act III, Scene 1). Both before and after professional theater became well established in England, short, often musical plays called "masques" were often performed *by*—not just for—courtiers and royalty. The great 17th century poet John Milton, most famous for his Biblical epic *Paradise Lost,* wrote the masque *Comus* to honor an important individual, John Egerton, 1st Earl of Bridgewater. The man's children were the principal actors. When you perform with family and friends, you are carrying on a long tradition.

In the midst of the Covid-19 pandemic, Jean Farkas and I, along with our daughter and son-in-law, performed "Bitter Cantaloupe" as a Zoom play. This was pure family theater (my birthday present), not part of the Goat Hill group. Jean and I performed at our home, in front of a PC. Our daughter and son-in-law played their roles from their home. The only live audience consisted of our two young grandchildren (8 and 5 years old), who were with their parents. A few months later, our daughter, son-in-law, and the grandchildren (in the starring roles) performed a very simple 5-minute play ("The Robin") in their backyard, with Jean and I as the socially distanced, mask-wearing live audience. In this age of digital games and social media, I very much want these kids to grow up with both professional performances and do-it-yourself theater as part of their lives.

Chapter 2

Obtaining Scripts from Outside Your Group

You can't perform plays until you have plays to perform. In this chapter I talk about obtaining scripts written by playwrights outside of your group. You will readily find a great many good plays to choose from. Some can be performed without cost; others may require a royalty payment. In the next chapter, I suggest that you and others in your group write your own 10-minute plays.

Before discussing copyright law, I state the following caveats. Although this chapter has been reviewed for accuracy by intellectual property attorney Francisco Cabrera, member of the Washington, DC, bar, the legal information in this book is not legal advice. Furthermore, each individual's legal circumstances are unique. Therefore, for any but the most straightforward situations, you should consult an intellectual property attorney. Here is the starting point: By default, literary works are the intellectual property of their author.

Performing Plays Without Charge

In most cases, the authors of 10-minute plays are not paid when their plays are staged, or else receive a nominal payment. If a community theater is well funded, one or two of the plays that are performed in its 10-minute play festival may be awarded a cash prize, which can be substantial—perhaps $500.

The vast majority of playwrights have day jobs, and many playwrights do not regard their plays—especially their 10-minute plays—as a significant source of revenue. Therefore, many playwrights will grant you permission to perform their 10-minute plays without charge, especially because you are a very small, entirely non-profit, zero-revenue group that is very likely planning a production run consisting of just a single performance.

If you know the author of a 10-minute play, perhaps someone whose play you saw and enjoyed, you can ask for permission to perform the play. Many playwrights will be pleased by your interest in their work. If the playwright is local, they will probably want to attend. They might ask to direct their play. They might join your group. If they cannot attend, you might offer to make them a simple smartphone video of the performance. Playwrights learn a lot by seeing one of their scripts performed, and, in addition, they may regard your production as a professional credit, although certainly a small one.

If you don't have any plays or playwrights in mind, there are many ways to find scripts—as I explain later in this chapter. Regardless of how you find your script, be open to paying a royalty. The fee will almost certainly be modest, and you are helping to support theater as an art form.

When you receive permission to perform a play—whether or not you are paying a fee—you are being licensed to perform the play on a specific date (or dates) and possibly with further stipulations specified by the playwright. Legally, permission to perform is separate from permission to reproduce copies of the script for the actors and director. If a play you are interested in has been contracted to a publisher, the publisher may require that you purchase a copy of the script for each actor.

Plays for Which Payment is Expected

There are definitely playwrights who have an interest in making money from their plays—including their 10-minute plays. Some people are trying to make a living as playwrights. Others are hoping to recoup the money they spend on the submission fees that most festivals charge and on the money they spend traveling to see one of their plays performed. Others want to be paid at least a nominal sum as a matter of principle.

The best way to cast a wide net in your search for 10-minute plays is the New Play Exchange (NPX). The New Play Exchange (www.newplayexchange.org) is "the world's largest digital library of scripts by living writers." With a Reader Pro subscription at $12/year, you can search by author or title, and you can perform highly sophisticated searches with such parameters as genre, cast size, gender presentation, and whether the full script is available for download. Furthermore, there is very often a link through which you can inquire about licensing rights.

The Playwrights' Center (www.pwcenter.org) is an active theatrical organization, physically located in Minneapolis, Minnesota (USA). The Playwrights' Center offers online and face-to-face events such as performances and workshops. It also lists submission opportunities. Members, who pay $75/year, can upload scripts, a bio, and show their agent representation. Scripts can be accessed and downloaded by members and non-members alike, using an unstructured search facility. Because the search facility is unstructured, to find 10-minute plays you should search separately on the search terms "10-minute play," "10 minute play," "ten-minute play," "ten minute play," or (the broadest search) "minute."

In addition, many playwrights maintain their own websites with lots of information about themselves and their plays, including licensing. If you don't have a particular playwright in mind, you can type search queries such as "playwright 10-minute play" into your favorite search engine and click persistently through the many results that the search engine will return. Some of these results will be playwrights' personal websites. You can also find published collections of 10-minute plays. These collections most often include the playwrights' contact information, and you deal directly with the playwright or the playwright's representative in regard to licensing. Most theatrical licensing agencies don't bother with 10-minute plays. However, 10-minute plays are a staple of some smaller agencies that focus on the school and community theater markets—for example, Big Dog Publishing (www.bigdogplays.com) and Pioneer Drama Service (www.pioneerdrama.com). Note that Big Dog Publishing and Pioneer Drama Service require the purchase of a copy of the script for each cast member.

In 2020, $40 is a typical royalty fee for a single performance by theater groups, such as a living room theater group, that are at the bottom of the fee scale. When you request performance rights, these factors are relevant:

- The number of performances (probably just one).

- The expected and maximum audience size.

- That there are no tickets or any kind of revenue (including institutional funding).

- That no one involved in producing the play is receiving any kind of payment or remuneration.

- And, if this is indeed the case, that the play will be performed privately—without any kind of public advertising or public notification and before an invited audience consisting of family, friends, and acquaintances. (As discussed later in this chapter, you are not legally required to pay a royalty fee for a private performance.)

A key point is that playwrights and theater people generally struggle to get any reasonable return on their creative work and that it is good behavior to facilitate their desire to be paid. Indeed, it is in everyone's best interest to support theater and the arts in every way possible.

The Dramatists Guild's Bill of Rights

The Dramatists Guild is a trade association and quasi-union for playwrights. They strive to make playwriting a viable career and to protect the right of playwrights to exercise artistic control over their plays. What is most relevant here is their Dramatists Bill of Rights. This document, available at http://wwww.dramatistsguild.com/rights is a set of principles and best practices. It is by no means law. Rather, the Dramatists Guild promotes the bill of rights and strongly encourages playwrights to include its provisions in the contracts they sign with those who will produce their plays.

My two big points are (1) that anyone who stages plays at any level should be aware of the Bill of Rights and recognize that it is wrong to abuse playwrights either financially or artistically and (2) that key provisions of the Bill of Rights, such as those listed below, seem to have been written with mainstage productions in mind. Consequently, they are not a good fit with the vastly more informal practices of living room theater:

- No one (e.g., producers, directors, actors, designers, dramaturgs) can make additions, deletions, alterations, and/or changes of any kind to your script—including the text, title, and stage directions—without your prior written consent.

- You have the right to mutually approve (with the producer) the cast, director, and designers (and, for a musical, the choreographer, orchestrator, arranger, and musical director), including their replacements.

Probably, living room theater doesn't even appear on the radar of the people who formulated The Dramatists Guild's Bill of Rights. In any case, some flexibility is appropriate and necessary in lightly rehearsed theater performed largely by and for friends and acquaintances. For example, it may be necessary to make small script changes on the fly: If you find yourself substituting a shorter actor for the tall actor specified in the script, you may need to change a line such as "My, you are tall!" to something like "My, you look strong." Re-arranging the chairs in your venue may require changing a stage direction that specifies how an actor exits the stage. Certainly, however, living room theater groups should attempt to get clearance for any significant changes in a script by a living playwright unless that playwright has explicitly waived the provisions of the Dramatists Bill of Rights.

Scripts in the Public Domain

There are many scripts of 10-minute plays that are in the public domain and therefore can be performed without cost and without asking anyone's permission. You will find lists of such plays on the Internet, often with links to the full scripts. Type in search-engine queries such as "10-minute plays public domain" and "short plays in the public domain." Pay attention as you scroll through the search results: Not everything you see listed will actually be in the public domain or royalty free. Most often, but not always, public domain plays are old plays. Later in this chapter, I explain in detail how to determine whether an old play is old enough to be in the public domain.

There are 10-minute plays in the public domain written by such classic authors as Anton Chekhov, August Strindberg, F. Scott Fitzgerald, and John Galsworthy. There are also many public domain plays that were popular in their day but are by no means classic theater. Appendix B lists some resources for finding 10-minute public domain plays and briefly describes some plays that are promising candidates for your productions. Living playwrights will sometimes place their plays in the public domain, as I have done with nine of my 10-minute plays (Appendix C).

When plays are in the public domain, you can reproduce and distribute the script freely. Furthermore, you can stage the play in any way you like. For example, you can update obscure words and add topical references to contemporary events. You can also make major changes in the script. If your changes are sufficiently large, it is both legal and ethical to copyright the play and bill yourself as the author. You should acknowledge the original work on which your play is based with phrasing such as "freely adapted from . . . " Your copyright, of course, applies only to your new content, not to the original public domain text.

Special Copyright Provisions and Creative Commons

You may find scripts or published collections of scripts with copyright notices that permit you to perform the play without charge under certain conditions such as these:

- The play is being performed by a non-profit organization.
- The play is being performed without an admission fee.
- No one involved in the production of the play is being remunerated.
- You have purchased the script or a collection of plays in which the script appears.

For example, if you purchase a copy of Laurie Allen's *22 Comedy Ten-Minute Plays: Royalty-free Plays for Teens and Young Adults* (2019), you are licensed (on the copyright page) to perform these plays without paying a royalty or notifying the copyright holder, provided you fit within the broad designation "amateur group." The copyright page also allows groups to "make small changes to language or abridge the plays for contest purposes provided that the playwright's intent remains intact." In other words, playwright Laurie Allen is partially waiving the Dramatists Bill of Rights. The overall quality of Allen's plays is high, and there are plays in the volume (for example, "The New Meteorologist") suitable for audiences and performers well beyond their teenage years.

Furthermore, you may encounter scripts that bear one of the carefully written copyright licenses (each with a distinctive logo) made available by Creative Commons. For example, if a script bears the "Attribution-ShareAlike CC BY-SA" license, you can perform and also modify the work (giving credit to the original author), even for commercial purposes—all without paying a royalty. However, if you modify the work, your modified version must carry the same license and grant the same rights to someone who wants to use your modification. By choosing this Creative Commons license, the original author has sent the work into the future in a way that prevents it from ever being locked up by someone else's copyright, even if it is modified. You may also find scripts with one of the other Creative Commons licenses, such as a license that prohibits anyone from distributing an altered version of the work. If you are interested in performing a script that carries a Creative Commons license, visit their website (www.creativecommons.org) and carefully study (perhaps with legal assistance) the provisions of each of their licenses.

Copyright Law and the Public Domain

Here I provide more detail on how to determine if a script is in the public domain. A modern work is in the public domain if the copyright holder has added such a declaration. Literary works also pass into the public domain with the passage of time. For many years, works entered the public domain only if they were copyrighted before 1923. Now, because of revisions to United States copyright law, works published prior to or during 1925 enter the public domain in the United States on January 1, 2021. Works published in 1926 enter the public domain in 2022, and on into the future. However, if the play has been translated, the translation may well have an active copyright. Similarly, if an old novel or short story has been adapted for the stage, the publication date of the adaptation is the date that matters.

All works created and published between 1925 and 1978 have a 95-year protection term. However, works published during this period may be in the public domain because of technicalities in copyright law. Works published between 1925 and 1963 will have fallen into the public domain if they didn't bear a proper copyright notice or if the copyright was not renewed. Works published between 1964 and 1978 are in the public domain if they did not bear a proper copyright notice. These days there is no need to renew a copyright. Furthermore, a script is automatically copyrighted even if it does not bear a copyright notice. You should consult an intellectual property lawyer if you want to ascertain whether a work published after the ever-moving public domain date may be free of copyright protection.

The rule of thumb for any work created on or after January 1, 1978, or created earlier and published in 1978, is that the duration of the copyright lasts the life of the author and an additional 70 years. However, this rule may vary according to a wide range of factors. Regardless, the duration of these copyrights will, in all circumstances, extend decades into the future.

There are many relatively understandable websites that explain the fine points of public domain status and other aspects of copyright law. See, for example, www.publicdomainsherpa.com. If you are inclined to research copyright on your own, you can download, at no cost, the complete text of U.S. copyright law (U.S. Copyright Office, 2020) and the *Compendium of U.S. Copyright Office Practices* (U.S. Copyright Office, 2017). The *Compendium* interprets copyright law and reviews legislative history and legal precedents. These are the respective URLs:

www.copyright.gov/title17/title17.pdf
www.copyright.gov/comp3

This final comment is for playwrights: Once you place a play in the public domain or assign a Creative Commons license to a work, that decision is permanent—no backsies.

Copyright Law and Privately Performed Plays

Because living room theater very often qualifies as a private rather than a public performance, you may be legally entitled to perform copyrighted plays without paying a royalty. My own view is that living room theater groups should willingly pay the royalty fee, which, as I have noted, will almost certainly be modest. If your intention is to pay the royalty, you can skip the rest of this section, which is legalistic and complex. Read on if you want to investigate whether the performance you have in mind might qualify as private.

Whether or not a particular performance of a copyrighted work is public or private is determined individually in court where specific facts and circumstances will be considered. Also note that if the performance is recorded or transmitted, the law becomes much more complicated and is outside the scope of this discussion. Section 101 of US Copyright Law ("Subject Matter and Scope of Copyright") states that

> To perform or display a work "publicly" means—
> (1) to perform or display it at a place open to the public or at any place where a substantial number of persons outside of a normal circle of a family and its social acquaintances is gathered.

Section 1908.3 of the *Compendium* interprets "private" with less focus on family:

> A performance or display that occurs at "a gathering confined to [an] individual's social acquaintances would normally be regarded as private." Id.

Thus, while a performance of a living room theater group may well be more than a *family* activity, it is nevertheless private if it is performed at a residence or other private place, and the audience consists almost entirely of friends and social acquaintances as well as family members. Note that the law allows for a small ("not substantial") number of people to attend even if they are not part of the circle of family and social acquaintances. Perhaps you have invited the owner of a local business who loaned you a prop.

The *Compendium* also draws a distinction between a private place and semipublic places such as a "club, lodge, factory, summer camp, or school," and discusses performances at semipublic places as public. However, a performance at a business meeting or government meeting, while taking place in a semipublic place, is normally regarded as private because of the small number of people involved:

> A performance or display that occurs during "[r]outine meetings of businesses and governmental personnel" would be normally considered private "because they do not represent the gathering of a 'substantial number of persons.'" *Id., reprinted in* 1976 U.S.C.C.A.N. at 5678. Likewise, "an entity does not transmit [a work] to the public if it does not transmit to a substantial number of people outside of a family and its social circle." *American Broadcasting Companies,* 134 S. Ct. at 2511.

Therefore, if a play is performed for recreational reasons, by and for a limited number of individually invited guests largely known to one another, then performance venues such as the community room of a library, a church basement, the back room of a tavern (all semipublic places), and a park (a public place) might well be regarded as an extension of or equivalent to a private performance at a residence. But, of course, an attorney seeking damages will examine the circumstances surrounding the performance and seek to make a different argument. Was the performance held in a secluded area of the park or in everyone's view? Perhaps a living room theater group consists of highly social people, and they filled a venue with, say, 100 personally invited friends and acquaintances. An audience of this size certainly moves the event in the direction of a public performance.

Note that in all these situations the minute you put up a poster in a coffee shop or send out a broadcast email to some large group you're in, you've gone public. Furthermore, it does not matter that admission is free, that you are performing for a school group, or that you're performing at a senior center or a house of worship. Nor does it matter that the actors are amateurs or that it's just a sit-down reading. So, while your performance may qualify as private, for both ethical reasons and perhaps prudence as well, it is best to license the play and pay the modest royalty. If the copyright holder or publisher is being difficult, there are a vast number of other 10-minute plays to choose from.

Music

Music, in all its forms, can enhance a 10-minute play. Here I explain the fundamental intellectual property issues, which in their full detail are beyond the scope of this book. First, if you are staging your play as a private performance, you can use any and all forms of copyrighted music, but you should still consider the ethical dimension of using music for which the creators wish to be paid.

If you compose the lyrics (words) and melody, you have no concerns whatsoever, even if you perform the play publicly and charge admission. You own the copyright. Nor do you have concerns if the music (including an old recording of the music) is in the public domain. For example, George Gershwin's *Rhapsody in Blue* (including an early recording) has just entered the public domain. The laws regarding expiration of copyright and public domain status are essentially the same for music (as well as graphics and cinema) as they are for text. Websites such as www.songfacts.com and www.publicdomain4u.com can help you find public domain songs and recordings that fit your needs. For example, Songfacts explains that Bobby Day's original 1957 version of "Rockin' Robin" has slipped into the public domain because the copyright was not renewed. If contemporary music (including the lyrics and the performance itself) carries a Creative Commons license, you must examine the particular license. It may well be that you can use the music, but not modify it for public performance.

What follows applies to living room theater performances that are public and therefore not covered by the private performance exemption of copyright law:

- If you include in your script either the melody or lyrics to a copyrighted song, you face copyright infringement issues. Even more so if you include a full recording with voice and instrumentation. I know an intellectual property attorney who negotiated a $1.5 million dollar settlement for a client who had aired television commercials using a hit song that the client had not licensed. Doing living room theater, the odds are very small that a copyright holder will learn about and then take action against you. But you will be breaking the law.

- Under certain circumstances—most obviously, parody—including a copyrighted song in your 10-minute play could qualify for the Fair Use exemption in copyright law. Fair Use is complex. For example, the fact that you are not planning to charge admission does not in itself constitute Fair Use.

- It is false that you can legally include copyrighted music if the duration is less than 30 or 15 or 10 seconds.

If you are determined to legally include a hit song in your performance, you can license it, but this will cost significant time and money. You can obtain a "sync" license to just the lyrics and score (so you can make your own cover version) or license the actual performance (a "master license"). To get sync licenses, you should search for the song at the websites of SESAC, ASCAP, BMI, and Global Music Rights. To get a master license, you need to contact the record label. A simpler and much cheaper path is to license "generic" music. For example, $29 at AudioJungle.net will buy you a permanent license for a track of "modern funky hip hop," which may well be fully adequate for your play:
www.audiojungle.net/item/modern-funky-hip-hop/28807762

Chapter 3

Performing Plays Written by Your Group

There is a lot to say for performing plays written by members of your group. Audiences like watching plays written by people they know. Your familiarity with the playwright adds to your understanding of the play, and seeing the play deepens your understanding of the playwright, sometimes in surprising ways. Some people are better able to share events of their lives in a play than directly. In addition, you may see plays that address a common experience the group is sharing or has shared—the closing of the community's only nearby hospital or an act of intolerance or violence that shakes a community.

In some respects, theater is an artistically limited medium. Theater, especially the low-budget staging typical of 10-minute plays, cannot begin to compete with film (not to mention 3D and virtual reality) in regard to visual richness and impact. Furthermore, unlike the novel and short story, plays are largely restricted to what characters say to each other. Except for the occasional soliloquy and aside, we have no direct access to the private thoughts of the characters. Finally, in novels and short stories the reader's experience is continuously filtered through some kind of carefully crafted narration—a first-person narrator, a third-person narrator, an ironic narrator, an unreliable narrator, etc. (Abbott, 2002). But there is none (or very little) of this in theater.

What is unique and irreplaceable about theater is its highly social nature. People gather together to be part of a communal experience, created and shared by the audience and never to be repeated in exactly the same way. This communal experience is powerfully enhanced in living room theater because the audience and the cast are well acquainted. The playwright too may be part of the group or may be attending the performance. It's very possible that these plays will be lower in quality than plays you obtain outside your group—especially if you obtain outside-written plays that have been voted the winner of a festival or which have had many productions. But audiences are engaged and generous when they are participating in a communal event. In this context, I'll mention here that we ask each of our playwrights to briefly introduce his/her/their play. Audiences will enjoy a play more and will be more engaged when the playwright has just stood up and spoken personally about the play.

Reasons to Become a Playwright

Writing plays provides many benefits. Most obviously, you will, I predict, hugely enjoy those creative moments when everything comes together in your mind, and you know you will soon have a finished, ready-to-stage script. Even if there are flaws in your script, the creative experience is itself worthwhile. There are any number of very happy painters who know they will never create a great painting. Furthermore, "finished" doesn't have to mean truly finished. You can always keep working on a script. Many of my better plays were not at all good when I first wrote them. I keep my "not good enough" scripts along with those I could not finish at all in a folder on my hard drive. Periodically, I revisit them to see if I can finish one or make one better.

Another reason to write your own plays is that doing so will enrich your experience as a theater-goer for all the plays you will ever attend. I guarantee that you will notice much more about entrances and exits, about lighting and scenery, about the interactions among the actors, and more. I have attended theater regularly since childhood, but I never paid proper attention to some significant aspects of theater until I began writing and staging plays. Finally, writing plays for a living room theater group is an important way to participate in and strengthen the group you're in.

How Hard Is it to Write 10-Minute Plays?

Easier than you think! You are not dealing with complex plots and subplots. Rather, you are dramatizing a meaningful but necessarily simple story. These scripts are short. Even following the very spacey format of standard script formatting (lots of blank space per page), the script of a 10-minute play runs only 8 to 12 pages. If someone suggests that you completely rewrite the middle of your play, the middle is just 3 or 4 pages long. I have written two full-length plays, and I can attest that these are very big projects compared to writing a 10-minute play, which you may well get to the first-draft stage in an evening or two. Actors in our group who were initially skeptical have written 10-minute plays. I heartily agree with folk singer Carrie Newcomer, who in her song "Angels Unaware" (2005) wrote, "I have never met a person yet without a tale to tell."

Ideas for plays may come directly from events in your own life or from family stories. In the summarized plays (Appendix A), "Bowling with Tape" (and others) come directly from my life; "Regional Distributor" is a story my father used to tell about his days as a traveling salesman; and "Nationalities" is loosely based on my Uncle Joe's first job working for a Mafia family. Plays may come from your fantasy life. "Walkers" is a dramatization, with just a few modifications, of my long-standing fantasy of how my wife and I might die. Bob Boiko, an information scientist, wrote a play that is both suspenseful and highly conceptual (see "Black Box" in the summaries).

Alternatively, you may have no direct relationship with your story. You just read or think about something and say to yourself, "Hey, that might make for a good play!" "Horizons" comes from this kind of artistic calculation—although I've come to feel sadness for Richard Russell, the emotionally confused airline employee who stole and fatally crashed a commercial airplane. You may base a play on a historical figure who interests you. "First-Rate Man" is a mini-biography of workplace efficiency guru Frederick W. Taylor (1856–1915). "Baucis and Philemon" is an expansion of a story in Ovid's *Metamorphoses*. For a full discussion of getting ideas especially suited for 10-minute plays, see *Writing the 10-Minute Play* (Farkas, forthcoming 2022).

Of course, thinking of a plot does not get you a finished play. You need to plan out and write the play line by line. However, writing stage directions to indicate actions and then writing dialogue for your characters are simpler tasks than describing a character's inner life in a short story or novel. Writing dialogue is especially easy when your characters are based on actual people you know well. Dramatic monologues are built around a single character. Many dramatic monologues are first-person narratives about events in the author's own life.

There are, of course, a great many books and websites on every aspect of writing a play. However, your skills will develop steadily if you do nothing more than participate in living room theater. As you rehearse and perform, and as you watch and discuss 10-minute plays, you will gain a good sense of what does and what doesn't work.

A Note on Quality

I have referred to the quality of 10-minute plays. But let's step back. First, any judgments about the quality of plays are necessarily subjective. In fact, simply defining quality is tricky. Different plays are intended to achieve different impacts on different audiences. How do you compare a realistic play to an absurdist play? What about a play that is little more than the vehicle for witty dialogue and jokes—but the dialogue is very witty and the jokes very funny? Let's say that one play tends to evoke divided judgments in an audience. Two thirds love it, one third doesn't care for it. Is this a "better" play than a play that gets a modestly favorable response from the entire audience?

I have seen or read several hundred 10-minute plays, including many prize winners and those selected for published collections. But while there are many very good 10-minute plays, I have yet to encounter one that I would call truly great, a transformative theater experience, or a literary landmark. This judgment encompasses Strindberg's "The Stronger" and Chekhov's "The Swan Song" (which actually runs 15 minutes), even though Chekhov and Strindberg, in their longer works, are among our greatest playwrights. There are truly great 30-minute plays, such as J.M. Synge's *Riders to the Sea* (1904) and Elaine May's *Hotline* (1996), but there seems to be an upper limit on what can be achieved in just 10-minutes. Here is one implication of this idea. Let us assume that your living room theater group is performing plays by folks in the group, folks in your community, and other unheralded playwrights. And let us assume that these plays are interesting and engaging—you think you've found good plays to perform. If so, you are not likely—in my judgment—to be missing out on truly magnificent 10-minute plays being written elsewhere by more celebrated playwrights.

There are also 10-minute plays that will be markedly more successful when performed before friends than before an audience of strangers. Although John Milton's *Comus* is a fine literary work, we cannot begin to experience it as Lord Bridgewater and his family did. So, for example, you might celebrate someone's many years of service to a volunteer organization in a home brew play intended to be performed only on this one occasion. Given all these issues surrounding the idea of quality, perhaps it is best not to talk much about quality. Perhaps we should just say that each person has their own voice, that every voice has value, and that some people write most meaningfully for specific audiences and communities.

Submitting Your Scripts (Preview of Chapter 16)

Ultimately you may find yourself wanting to submit your scripts to 10-minute play festivals and the like. You will find that even the smallest community theater that accepts submissions from the public is inundated with scripts—many of which are very good. In most cases there is a $10 to $20 dollar submission fee. So, unless your work is remarkable, you may find yourself paying numerous submission fees, waiting a long time to see one of your plays selected, and boarding a plane to see your play performed. When you get to the show, you may find a surprisingly small number of folks in the audience—many of whom are attending because they have some personal connection to one of the playwrights, directors, or actors who are part of the festival. I am a great fan of community theater and 10-minute play festivals and will always attend performances when I can. But, from the perspective of the playwright, there is something to be said for bypassing the script submission system and simply writing and staging plays for an audience of friends.

Group-Written and Outside-Written Scripts. Longer Plays.

My discussion of whether to obtain scripts written outside your group or to perform group-written scripts concludes here with the idea that you can do both. Perhaps you will rely on outside-written scripts when your living room theater group first gets going. Then, over time, your members will hopefully start contributing their own scripts. A group that is writing their own scripts might still want to perform outside-written scripts that folks in the group especially like. Or, let's say that you have two inside-written scripts that address a particular theme (perhaps technology gone awry or spiritual growth), and you're interested in staging a thematically unified program of plays. You can do so by finding a thematically compatible outside-written play or even inviting an outside playwright to contribute such a play.

Finally, you can always perform longer plays—perhaps a program of two 20- or 30-minute plays or one full-length play. My caution here is that longer plays are harder to do well and need to reach a higher level of writing and performance quality to satisfy an audience. A not-so-great 10-minute play is OK. If nothing else, it will soon end. However, sitting through a seriously unsatisfying 30-minute or full-length play is an ordeal. You don't want living *tomb* theater.

Chapter 4

Selecting Your Venue

Much of your theatrical decision-making will be driven by five considerations: (1) The pool of scripts you have to choose from, (2) the venues you have available, (3) your pool of actors, (4) what you expect to be the size and preferences of your audience, and (5) your specific goals for each program of plays. Here we focus on venue.

Your play will necessarily be performed in some kind of venue—perhaps a living room or den or backyard. Perhaps a church basement, the community room of a library, a martial arts studio, or the back room of a tavern. Some venues charge a rental fee. Certain coffee shops and taverns are happy to provide a performance space because they will sell food and beverages to those who attend. What I want to talk about are the key differences among venues and how the characteristics of the venue influence what plays you can stage and how they will be staged.

Big Rectangular Spaces—and Blocking

Let's begin by imagining a totally flat, bare, rectangular room of ample dimensions. It is well supplied with chairs that you can move easily. Let's say you set up chairs all around the perimeter of the space (along all four walls), in one or more rows. Now you've created an arena theater or theater-in-the-round (although it's not truly round). There is no backstage and no obvious upstage or downstage, just performers completely surrounded by the audience. You will quickly encounter problems with this arrangement. First and foremost is blocking. Blocking, at the rudimentary level, means making sure that everyone in the audience will see the actors' faces most of the time. With seats placed all around the acting area, blocking becomes complex. Your actors are always shifting around to provide views from all sides.

In direct contrast, all the seats of an old-fashioned proscenium theater face the front of the stage. Now blocking is largely reduced to ensuring that no actor stands directly in front of another actor. The two community rooms of the Shoreline Library, like a great many public spaces, are rectangles that can be set up in various ways. Because our audience size is small and we don't need many rows of seating, we like the simplicity of the proscenium approach. However, if the audience size is large enough that we want to reduce the number of rows, we can set up one or two rows of seats on each side of the stage, approximating a thrust theater. Side seating does make some demands in regard to blocking. We don't want audience members spending too much time looking at the sides of the actors' faces.

You are unlikely to have line-of-sight problems—where the audience members block each other's view of the stage—unless the actors are seated. But whenever you set up multiple rows of seats, you can improve the line-of-sight situation by offsetting each row of chairs so that audience members are looking past the shoulders of the people in the row directly in front of them rather than sitting directly behind someone's head.

The Backdrop

When we perform in the Shoreline Library, we set up a portable, inexpensive 10-foot photographer's backdrop screen as the stage backdrop. This is what the audience sees as the wall hiding the backstage. To exit (or enter) the stage on either side, actors simply disappear behind (or appear from) the backdrop. The screen, plus an imaginary line extending outward a few feet on either side of the screen, is the upstage boundary of the acting area. In other words, not everything has to happen in the 10 feet directly in front of the screen. Actors can stand a few feet beyond the screen on either side.

The screen is a sheet of black fabric which is clipped by two hefty alligator clips to a horizontal metal bar (assembled from three shorter pieces) that is held up on both ends by two tripods with adjustable vertical posts. The posts can be extended so that the screen will fully hide the head of the tallest actor. We bought our screen from the Tablecloths Factory (www. tableclothsfactory.com) for a (perpetual) sale price of $40 ("8 Ft x 10 Ft Adjustable Portable Photography Backdrop Stand"). The whole apparatus is easy to deal with and can be carried in the sturdy sack that comes with it.

You can purchase two big bags that you can fill with sand to hold the screen in place during a mildly windy outdoor performance. For more money, you can buy a bigger, heavier backdrop screen that can stand more jostling and more wind. For any kind of bare rectangular venue, a backdrop screen is very useful.

Entrances, Exits, and Crossovers

Theater people speak of stage left and stage right (often abbreviated in scripts as SL and SR). Stage right is the right side of the stage as the actor faces the audience. Stage right is also "house left," and stage left is "house right," except that theater people don't often talk about house left and house right. As noted, our portable backdrop screen enables actors to enter and exit the acting area from either side of the screen. This roughly approximates entering from and exiting to the "wings" of a proscenium theater. As an extremely general guideline, actors most often enter stage right (house left) and exit stage left (house right), which, from the audience's perspective, corresponds to the left-to-right reading direction of English and other languages. Here is a convenient mnemonic: Your good guys, the "righteous," most often enter stage right, and your bad guys, who are sinister (the Latin word for left), most often enter stage left. Note that with an arena configuration and also with a proscenium/thrust configuration but no backdrop, there is no obvious way for actors to exit the stage and disappear from the view of the audience.

A cross-over is a means by which an actor can exit stage right (or left) follow a passage behind the stage and re-enter stage left (or right). This provides a lot of flexibility in staging. Backdrop screens not only allow actors to enter and exit on either side, but provide a cross-over. In addition, the cross-over passage is a good location for the narrow "prop table" that is at times provided to enable actors to conveniently grab any props and costume accessories they need between scenes or within a scene. That is, Deirdre may exit and then re-enter with a tennis racket in her hand. The actor playing Deirdre gets the tennis racket from the prop table, possibly from a basket on the table marked "Deirdre."

Living Rooms

A living room (or den or basement) may be a more complicated performance space than a bare rectangular room. Although the room may be rectangular, the usable dimensions are constrained by the sofas and other heavy pieces of furniture that you are not likely to carry out. In the Farkas living room, we carry out the coffee table, some end tables, the big potted plant, and the rocking chair. But we leave the big sofa that faces the stage (equivalent to the first row of a proscenium theater). We then place some compact chairs on either side of this sofa, so that seven people will be seated directly facing the stage. We can seat four more people along the stage right side of the acting area (two of whom sit on a smaller sofa that we also leave in place), and we can seat another four on the stage left side. If necessary, some audience members can stand through our relatively short performance, just as "standees" do in mainstage theaters. For the social time after the show, we use the living room, the dining room, the kitchen, and the back deck.

When we started the Goat Hill Theater, Jean Farkas and I realized that our living room has a built-in cross-over. It is a partial brick wall that separates the living room from the dining room and kitchen. An actor can exit stage left, step through our kitchen, continue through the dining room, and re-enter stage right (or the reverse). Many living rooms let you exit stage left or stage right and disappear from view. But you must re-enter the same way you exited.

Size of the Acting Area

How large an acting area do you need? The 10 feet provided by the screen is too narrow, but if you allow 3 feet on either side of the screen, your acting area is wide enough (16 feet) for the modest staging requirements of most 10-minute plays. It's still better to have a width of 18 or 20 feet. If you have 6 to 8 feet between the back of the stage and the front row of seats, you have a workable depth for your acting area. But remember, if you are using a portable screen as a stage backdrop, you need at least three more feet *behind* the screen to serve as the bare-minimum backstage area and cross-over passage.

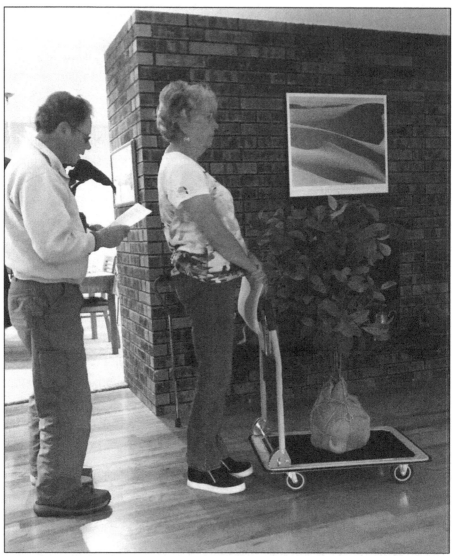

Gary Elmer and Jackie Gardner in the Farkas living room performing "The Horse and the Sparrow." They are positioned stage right and face stage left.

Portable Stages and Traditional Raised Stages

Portable stages, which typically can be elevated either 8 or 16 inches off the floor, improve the audience's line of sight in venues in which the floor is flat. This improvement becomes significant if you have more than a few rows of seats. Many small theaters keep their portable stage set up all the time. You can set up your own portable stage on a flat floor, although you are not likely to do so because of the extra work and expense. If you are up for the task, there are many event- and party-rental businesses from which you can rent portable stages, and they can be purchased from businesses such as school supply companies (www.schooloutfitters.com). Portable stages differ considerably in construction. Many come in modular units that can be latched together to create stages of any size. One issue to keep in mind is whether the echoing sound of footsteps on the portable stage will be annoyingly loud.

The traditional raised stage very definitely improves lines of sight but creates a kind of emotional distance between audience and performance. You probably want 30 or more people in the audience before a traditional elevated stage provides a meaningful benefit in regard to lines of sight.

Lighting

Ideally, you would have highly flexible lighting options including the independent control of the stage area and the house. With really good theater lighting you can:

- Emphasize, via "spot" lighting, particular people and actions.
- Illuminate one entire area of the stage (where things are happening), while obscuring another part of the stage until things start happening there. This contributes to the effectiveness of "split sets," discussed below.
- Create moods, especially with colored and mottled light.
- Differentiate day and night.

- Signal the beginning and ending of plays and scenes within plays.

There are few living rooms in which the acting area can truly be lit or dimmed independently of the room as a whole. This is also true of many non-residential spaces. The two Shoreline Public Library rooms are lit by big fluorescent light fixtures that provide little control over the lighting—it's pretty much lights on or lights off. Furthermore, the lights flicker for an annoyingly long time when they go on or off. Finally, the room is never truly dark or even dim during the daylight hours when the room is available, because some daylight shines through the large windows, even with the shades pulled down. Therefore, we keep the lights fully on the whole time we are in the room, and we use other means—mostly having the actors freeze—to indicate divisions within and between plays. (See Chapter 10.)

The windows of the Farkas living room allow for a light-filled mid-day performance, and various floor and table lamps light the room adequately for a dusk or true evening performance. The season of the year is also a factor. We can get considerable light through our windows for a 7:00 pm performance in July, but not so in December. Remember that lighting is a consideration for the cast as well as the audience. With script-in-hand performing, the actors need enough light to read from their scripts, unless everyone agrees to read from a digital script displayed on their smartphone or tablet.

Our lighting includes two table lamps with fully controllable Philips Hue light bulbs that enable us to project colored light sufficiently strong to create compelling lighting effects, especially during an evening performance when there is no competition from the light that makes its way through our window shades. In a performance of "Echoes of the Professor," it would be a nice touch to project warm yellow lighting in the outdoor scenes.

Finally, I'll point out that there is much to say for performing in a finished basement, the back room of a tavern, and other venues where sunlight can be blocked out, making it possible to plan the lighting without thinking about the time of day and season.

Outdoor Performances

Outdoor performances are a good daytime option, although they may be subject to street noise, airplane noise, gusts of wind, and other distractions. If you perform in a park, folks may wander right into your performance, and there may or may not be a convenient toilet or porta-potty. If you schedule an outdoor performance, you should probably have a backup date or an indoor alternative in case of bad weather. If the ground is sloped, you need to consider whether the acting area should be at the downslope or the upslope. But when all goes well, outdoor performances are delightful.

During the Covid-19 pandemic we managed to stage a single performance of four 10-minute plays in our backyard. However, because of the need for social distancing, we restricted the attendance. Also, our scripts were either dramatic monologues or scripts performed by co-habiting actors. Despite the significant restrictions, it was great to be doing recreational theater once again with some good friends.

Venue and the Choice of Plays and Staging

In some cases, the venue very directly influences what plays you can perform and key decisions about staging. An effective staging of "Kalalau Trail" requires a traditional 3-foot (or higher) raised stage. The best comic moment in the play is when Laurie tries to step on the fingers of Sam, who is trying desperately to claw his way back to the trail after Laurie has pushed him off. The scene should be played with Sam crouching on the theater floor (audience level) with his fingers on the edge of the raised stage, while Laurie, looking downward, is kicking and stepping on his fingers. "Solo to Tandem" absolutely requires a cross-over because actors repeatedly exit on one side of the stage and re-enter on the other side. "Engagement" benefits greatly from actual darkness in the opening scene. "Stripes" requires a sophisticated theater projection set up, well beyond what I am able to achieve.

It is often possible and very desirable to set up two entirely separate "split sets" in your acting area and have your actors simply switch from one to the other. For example, your characters meet in a bar—perhaps represented by just a table and two chairs—and in the next scene appear in a living room— just a sofa and a floor lamp. Both the bar and the living room can be set up on stage as a split set. Along similar lines, mainstage productions sometimes use a revolving "lazy Susan" stage that rotates to show only the set that the audience needs to see. A split-set arrangement, of course, requires a large enough acting area to fit both sets and, ideally, lighting capabilities that enable you to dim whichever set is not in current use. Some plays require split sets because both sets are being used at once. In "Good-bye from SILVE" we see George and Martha speculating about Skip's late arrival for dinner while we watch Skip lying on his chaise lounge sipping beer and swallowing pills.

Special Rules

Public venues have their particular rules and regulations—for example, a posted occupancy limit set by the fire marshal, a rule against serving alcohol or perhaps any kind of food or beverage. In the case of the King County Library System (serving the suburbs surrounding Seattle), you cannot charge any admission, and all events are open to the public. Although this is unlikely, anyone can walk in and take a seat.

Time Needed

Even if you are performing in someone's home, you should have a good idea how long the entire event will last. But it's important to calculate the time requirements carefully when you are reserving a block of time in a public venue. Don't under-estimate. You might need four or even five hours. Why so long?

Set up

You may need 45 minutes to do the following: (1) Fold up and carry off the tables and chairs that the last group using the room were *supposed* to have stowed away, but did not. (2) Arrange the seats, presumably following a general plan that you worked out in advance. (3) Assemble your screen and carry in your set items and props. (4) Prepare the set for the first of your plays. (5) Find good offstage places for the set items and props for the subsequent plays making up the program. (6) Prepare whatever refreshments you may have for serving.

Walk-throughs, performances, and introductions

You may need 90 minutes for the following: (1) Last-minute walk-throughs or mini-rehearsals for the plays—about 30 minutes. (2) The curtain speech that kicks off the event—about 5 minutes. (3) Running times of the three plays—30 to 40 minutes. (4) Playwrights' introductions (which provide set-up time for the second and third of the plays)—about 15 minutes. The walk-throughs, curtain speech, and playwrights' introductions are further explained in later chapters of this book.

Talk-back and social time

You may need 90 minutes because of the following: (1) You almost certainly want to do a talk-back, which might take 30 minutes, and (2) you may be holding your social period in this venue (rather than at someone's home or another location), which could take an hour or more.

Take-down and clean-up

You will need about 45 minutes to do the following: (1) Take down and stow the screen. (2) Carry the screen, set items, and props back to your vehicle (or vehicles). (3) Restore chairs and tables to the venue owner's specified locations and clean up, especially if you have served food.

If you are renting space at an hourly rate, try to find out whether the renter is strict and wants to charge you from the moment you enter to the moment you exit and lock the door, or whether they charge you only for the core activity and don't charge for your set up and clean-up time.

Virtual Performances—Zoom Theater

The closing of theaters due to the Covid-19 pandemic has led to many Zoom performances. Indeed Zoom theater can be regarded as a new medium that may endure and evolve even after healthy times have returned. There is certainly value in a medium that enables actors who are physically separated to perform together. Joshua Glassman and Karen Vuranch offer excellent, wide-ranging guidance for staging Zoom productions (Pioneer Drama Service, 2020).

One practical problem with Zoom performances is the latency and occasional visual glitching. A more fundamental problem is creating the illusion of one physical space when each actor appears in that actor's individual Zoom window. There are scripts that in their natural staging call for the characters to be physically separated. Consider, for example, a script that consists entirely of two characters talking by phone. Or, a script in which the three characters are an astronaut in a damaged space capsule, another astronaut on a rescue mission, and a support engineer from Houston Control. Individual Zoom windows work well in these situations. The challenge arises in the much more typical situation where the script calls for the cast to share a physical space. Sometimes, however, you get lucky and manage to partly simulate a shared physical space in a Zoom performance.

During the Farkas family performance "Bitter Cantaloupe," held during the Covid-19 pandemic, my daughter and son-in-law, from their home in West Seattle, played Stevie and Mr. Damerst, who mostly appear at Mr. Damerst's table in a small café. From our home in Lake Forest Park, Jean Farkas and I played the supporting roles of Rose and Mr. Johnson, who mostly appear seated together at another table. This is certainly more effective than performing the play in four separate Zoom windows. We were even able to momentarily bridge the gap between the two Zoom windows when Stevie held a carafe of coffee close to the video camera on her computer, and Mr. Johnson lifted his coffee mug close to the video camera on his computer to be served the coffee.

None of this, however, gets around the fundamental truth that theater is, at root, a face-to-face encounter between performers and audience. The celebrated video-captured performances of Great Britain's National Theatre are not viewed live, but at least the remote audience is aware of the live theater audience. The Goat Hill folks toyed with the idea of a Zoom performance but never quite mustered the enthusiasm to do it.

Chapter 5

Planning a Program.
Casting Your Actors.

This chapter explains how to plan a program of plays. Our working assumption is a program of three 10-minute plays to be performed at a public venue. One very important part of planning a program is casting, and this is treated in one lengthy section of this chapter.

Choosing the Scripts

Early on, you choose your scripts. You want scripts that you like individually and that collectively make up a good program. I would prioritize scripts written by a member of your group and by local playwrights who will participate if you stage one of their plays. Furthermore, you may well have found suitable public domain scripts or those bearing a Creative Commons license or similar broad permissions. But you can enlarge your pool of scripts infinitely if you go to NPX, the Playwrights' Center, and elsewhere on the Internet (Chapter 2).

Cast size, set, costumes

Some scripts will require a larger cast than is feasible for your group or a larger acting area than you have available. Other scripts will require sets and costumes that are beyond what you can do. Also check that the script doesn't require an excessively time-consuming costume change between two successive scenes.

Pleasing your audience

A key consideration is pleasing your audience. What are their backgrounds, their values, their taste in theater? You will be well acquainted with the members of your living room theater group, and you can easily get their input on specific plays and issues. But you also want to please your bring-alongs and guests (discussed in Chapter 1). In my experience, most 10-minute plays, especially those performed at festivals, are comedies or at least have some comic elements. To be well accepted, entirely serious plays must be really good. I will report that, whether the play is comic or serious, sex engages audiences.

Both in regard to the members of your own group and to outsiders, one good strategy is to hedge your bets. You might decide on two scripts in which you have a lot of confidence in order to balance out a script that looks risky.

Your own vision—and moral standards

There is also your own artistic vision. What do you really want to do? Where do you think your living room theater project is headed?

There are important considerations regarding immorality, bad taste, and other forms of unacceptability. When our group performed and then discussed "Graduation," several people I greatly respect judged it degrading to women. Had I thought so, I would not have written the play. I considered it "sex positive." To allay objections, I made significant revisions. Even so, the play perhaps teeters at the drop-off into unacceptability.

Amateur actors may have objections to eroticism on stage that almost all professional actors have long stopped worrying about. This became an issue when we performed "Gawain and the Green Knight," which calls for kissing and some degree of undress. (I also wrote a kid-friendly version of this play.) In "Mordecai in the Time of Plague" an anti-Semitic character says ugly things about Jews. Indeed, the play is very much about anti-Semitism and intolerance, but I—a Jew—do not believe the play is anti-Semitic. If anything, I've made Mordecai too virtuous. However, audiences don't always understand context. If some folks hear anti-Semitic dialogue, it's an anti-Semitic play. In my view the play is ethically problematic for an altogether different reason. Father Grigori, the play's bad guy, is included in the act of reconciliation that ends the play, even though his stable and loving relationship with Marius apparently began when Marius was a choir boy in Grigori's church. The ethical quandary, then, is whether the play is too relaxed in regard to pederasty. My broad point here is that there are many directions from which objections may come, and you need to be alert and thoughtful in this regard.

Choosing Performance Dates and Times

When you select your program, you also need to choose a date and time of day for the performance. Perhaps you want evening performances, perhaps weekend days. Recall that in living room theater the time of day may well have implications for your stage lighting. Consult one of those special calendars that lists holidays and other special events. I happily cast a play in the large community room of the Shoreline Library (I was surprised that it was available for the entire day), sent out all the invitations, and was informed immediately by an invitee that I had scheduled the performance for Super Bowl Sunday. I had to find another date and reschedule.

I suggest setting your next performance date quite comfortably into the future—perhaps three months after your previous performance. Your personal schedule may get unexpectedly busy, and there may be other delays. To keep the whole thing fun, don't schedule too many performances and don't create schedule crunches for yourself.

Sequencing the Plays

You should consider the sequence in which your plays are performed. Perhaps you want to start with a low-key, whimsical comedy, proceed to your serious play, and finish with your uproarious comedy. Keep in mind that sets and perhaps costuming may constrain the sequencing. If one play has significant requirements in terms of sets, you might want to perform that play first so that you have a lot of time to put up the set, rather than having to do it in the limited time between plays. If an actor will appear in two plays, the sequencing should allow time for any significant costume change.

Substitute Plays

You may also want to have an easy-to-stage alternative play, perhaps a dramatic monologue, ready as a backup in case you have a last-minute actor cancellation that necessitates scratching one of the plays on your program.

For example, my friend Jim Halliday, if given the script, can perform one of his dramatic monologues on the spot. Therefore, if I know that Jim will be present at a performance, I can print a copy of one of his dramatic monologues so that, in an emergency, I can hand Jim the script and say, "Hey, I need you to perform this. You have 15 minutes to get ready."

Casting Your Actors

A central consideration in planning your program is casting each play from your pool of actors. I speak here of the "pool" of regular actors, but a director might cast their play with folks from outside the group. Actors will vary along such dimensions as their natural styles of acting, their acting abilities, their preferred onstage genders/sexual orientations, their height and body type, their ages, and much more. Careful casting enhances performances.

Age

Age is a huge consideration in professional theater. Actors fret about "aging out" of certain roles. Age is a much smaller consideration in the Goat Hill Theater. We routinely play characters much younger than our actual ages.

Cast size, multiple roles, and doubling

If you are short on actors, choose plays with small casts and perhaps ask certain actors to perform in more than one play. Typically, this means giving the actor a major role in one play and a smaller role in the second. There is also doubling—having one actor play two (or more) parts in one play. Doubling roles effectively, however, requires skilled acting. It is perfectly OK if the audience knows (as will almost certainly be the case) that one actor is playing two roles. What is crucial is that the audience should not be confused as to which character they are watching. Note that differences in costuming, even if this is nothing more than two different hats, can do much to disambiguate characters. Professional actors relish doubled roles as a means to show off their range. Untrained actors, on the other hand, may be intimidated by the prospect of a doubled role.

Many scripts indicate the likely possibilities for doubling. In "First-Rate Man," the initial stage directions indicate how the 12 roles can be performed by a cast of five. In some cases, doubling is integral to the play and is specified in the script. A. R. Gurney's full-length play *Dining Room* is notable for specifying a cast of six actors for over 50 roles. A well-funded theater company with a plenitude of actors would not dream of increasing the cast size. In "Solo to Tandem Canoe Club," a wacky comedy, six actors play 26 roles—all but one of whom paddle (virtual) canoes. In this play the doubling is necessary to limit the cast size, but it is also part of the fun. Here is the big picture: If you have a lot of eager actors, choose plays with larger casts, avoid or minimize doubling, and perhaps even add an extra play or two to your program. If you are short on actors, do the opposite. Furthermore, everyone should recognize that there will be times when those who would like to act will need to sit out a performance.

Casting procedures

The Goat Hill Theater does not audition people for roles. Leaving aside auditioning, here are two very different options for casting your program of plays. One option, the "boutique" approach, is for each director to individually invite folks to take a specific role in a play. This is a highest quality approach because you are fitting actors to roles in a very personal way. But it is time consuming, and you may find some of your actors becoming fussy about which roles they prefer. Furthermore, directors may be competing with each other for certain actors.

A more efficient alternative is the "one-shot" approach: The organizer sends a broadcast email to the full list of potential actors inquiring (with a deadline for responding) who is interested in performing and what their preferences are (e.g., a large or a small role; serious or comic; is doubling OK?). Then, when responses have come from the actors, the directors, consulting among themselves, fit the willing candidates to the roles in the plays comprising the program. Not only is this approach faster, but it is flexible because the program can be changed in response to the actors who have volunteered. (An even faster but distinctly lower-quality variation on the one-shot approach is for the organizer to fit all the volunteering actors to the roles.) If you are directing a play or if you are the organizer of the group, resist the temptation to cast yourself in the biggest or the best parts.

Music and dance

A surprising number of folks can sing, play an instrument, and dance. Therefore, don't immediately dismiss a script that requires music or dance. In the case of a public domain play or if you have the permission of a living playwright, you can perhaps add your own musical interlude. Two short songs, sung acapella, give extra meaning and impact to "Stones and Rope," even though they are not integral to the plot.

Aging through the play

Some plays call for a character to appear in two (or more) different stages of that character's life. Here I exclude child roles. Very likely the character will be depicted in early adulthood and then in maturity, or else in maturity and then in old age. However, to fully examine the problem, we will consider "The Expulsion from Eden." This play calls for characters in three stages of life: An unfallen Adam and Eve in their early adulthood, a mature Adam and Eve (their sons Cain and Abel have reached adulthood), and an aged Adam and Eve.

In a professional production, there might well be two actors cast as Adam and two as Eve. Focusing on Eve, one actor might play Eve in early adulthood and maturity, while the other plays the elderly Eve. Or, one actor might play Eve in young adulthood, while another plays the mature and aged Eve. By the way, it's easier for an actor to play a character older than their actual age (aided by a little white powder in the hair, etc.) than for an older actor to play a much younger part.

In professional and especially mainstage theater with open auditions and therefore a very large acting pool, directors casting the Eve role can find two actors who differ markedly in age but who bear a generally similar appearance (height, etc.). Plus, professional-level makeup can make a big difference in an actor's appearance. Therefore, it should be easy to find two actors who can jointly do a good job performing Eve in all three stages of life. Perhaps one highly skilled actor can do this persuasively.

However, in living room theater with its much smaller pool of actors, you may have difficulty finding two actors that differ markedly in age but who are otherwise similar in appearance. If you don't have such actors available, it may be better to cast the same actor for all three stages of Eve's life. Alternatively, if you do cast two not-so-similar actors as Eve, the most important consideration is not to confuse the audience: The audience must know that the actor with gray in her hair and a halting walk is the aged Eve and not some new character.

Casting actors who live together

I have had good success casting people who live together (or who otherwise associate closely) in the same play and, beyond that, casting them in roles in which they interact extensively. Actors who live together have many opportunities to rehearse with each other and likely have a personal chemistry that will contribute to their performances.

Backups

You should have some plan to go forward with a play even if one of the actors can't start their car, goes into labor, or is otherwise forced to cancel at the last minute. Take note of people who have schedules they can't control—for example, people who might be called into work or need to travel at a moment's notice. Fortunately, when your cast performs script-in-hand, it's feasible for someone to fill in on very short notice. I attended a full-length play at a professional (Actors' Equity) theater company in which an actor was called upon to substitute in a major role for that evening's performance. (Understudies are more prevalent in musical theater.) This last-minute substitute delivered an effective script-in-hand performance.

Cross-gender casting

These days there is a lot of cross-gender performing. Actually, Sara Bernhardt starred in an acclaimed production of *Hamlet* in 1899, and in an informal "living room theater" performance a young Ulysses S. Grant took a shot at Desdemona in Shakespeare's *Othello* (Chernow, 2017, p. 43). Here again, the key issue is that the audience knows the gender of the character being played. A more radical possibility is changing the gender of the character. Increasingly, scripts indicate those characters who can be played as any gender. If, however, you change a character's gender from what was specified in the script, you should, if at all possible, contact and get approval from the playwright, in accordance with the Dramatists Bill of Rights.

Reaching out for actors

You may need to take extra steps to cast actors with backgrounds your group does not have. Unfortunately, given the racially segregated patterns of neighborhoods and social interaction in the United States, a group centered in a white locale, may not have a person of color to perform a particular role. And, of course, we should strive for more overall diversity in the membership of a living room theater group.

"Baucis and Philemon" includes the roles of Damien and Sylvia, a young, newly married couple. In this play, the contrast between youth and age is highly thematic. To get youthful actors for this role, I'd be tempted to recruit high-school students or university theater majors if I had no youthful actors in my living room theater group.

Your guest actors may have no interest in being paid—or very much the opposite. It is unfortunate, but true, that very few actors command high salaries. Even in mainstage and near-mainstage productions, many cast members work for the minimum wage or not a whole lot more. I make this point only because I don't want folks to give up on the idea of hiring a professional actor because they fear the cost would be prohibitive.

Involving Audience Members in the Performance

Some scripts, typically comedies, specify or at least allow for audience participation. At the end of "Close Encounters of the Talkative Kind," the main character entreats the audience to help him make a key plot decision. I saw a Shakespeare-in-the-park performance of *A Winter's Tale* in which the actor playing the picaresque thief Autolycus roamed through the audience, found a group with a picnic spread, called out "Oh, that looks good!" and snatched up and ate a slice of their pizza. Everyone was startled—and then delighted.

Audience members can also be recruited for bit parts. Doing so adds energy to a performance and can reduce cast size. In a performance of "Kalalau Trail," it is easy to recruit someone to read the narrator's introductory speech and, later, the one-line part of the backpacker. In "Milton Amid His Enemies," two or more audience members might play the brief, non-speaking roles of the courtesans who are trying to entice King Charles.

Most likely you will recruit your audience-actors on the day of the performance. You might do this as part of the curtain speech, so everyone sees that these folks are last-minute volunteers. Because this is living room theater, you know who will be attending. Therefore, you know who are your likely prospects. You can also recruit folks in advance (in which case they are sort of ex-officio cast members). If recruited in advance of the performance, your courtesans might choose to dress for the part and rehearse just a bit of seductive, courtesan behavior. Improvisation and audience recruiting—as long as you are careful not to embarrass anyone—engages the entire audience and contributes to the success of a performance.

Chapter 6

Script-in-Hand Acting

The living room theater model calls for script-in-hand acting. This is a major difference between our very informal, recreational theater and professional theater. Because our actors don't need to memorize their parts, preparation time is vastly reduced. I don't think the Goat Hill Theater model would work if actors were asked to memorize. However, script-in-hand performing (which professional actors call "on-book" rehearsing and performing) has drawbacks that lessen the impact of the play. These are (1) less eye contact with the audience, (2) encumbering the hands of the actor, and (3) the visibility of the script to the audience. The challenge is to find ways to minimize these drawbacks. To counterbalance this chapter's claim that script-in-hand performing is a significant drawback, I will cite a much more positive assessment by long-time acting coach Fran Montano (2019). Montano says that if the performance is really good, he soon forgets that the actors are holding a script.

Less Eye Contact

Some day actors may wear augmented-reality eyeglasses or implants that project their upcoming lines right before their eyes. But right now the need to look down at a script is a big problem. The most effective way to address the problem is good preparation. Script-in-hand reading is not the same as cold reading. Ideally actors will "half-memorize" their lines so that they need do no more than peek at their next speech, hold that speech in short-term memory, and then deliver the speech entirely or largely from short-term memory. If the speech is lengthy, the actor may need to peek at it several times to put separate pieces of speech into short-term memory. Peek-and-speak acting is a skill that improves over time.

In addition, you can optimize your personal, onstage script (discussed below) for peek and speak. For example, you can apply a yellow highlight to your own speeches and a light blue highlight to stage directions that pertain to you. You can even add little notations to remind yourself about special pauses, changes of volume, etc. Peek-and-speak works best if you choose the right moments to peek, which generally means that you peek while the audience's attention is on another actor. Let's say that Actor A is speaking to Actor B, who is exhibiting a strong emotional reaction to the speech. This is the perfect moment for you, as Actor C, to peek at your script.

Encumbering the Actor. Visibility of the Script.

Encumbering the actor and the script's visibility to the audience are closely linked, and so I treat them together. It is difficult for the actor to realistically carry out many actions while holding a script. The script also limits your range of hand gestures. While preparing, each actor needs to think about which hand will hold the script at each moment, and when and how the actor will transfer the script from one hand to the other. Just a bit of memorization can make a big difference. For example, a director might request that the actors in an action-packed scene memorize just a few crucial lines—so that, for example, no one needs to look at their script while threatening another character with a gun.

The Physical Form of the Onstage Script

I attended a workshop performance of a full-length play that was well acted, well directed, and well staged, except that the actors held loose-leaf binders. The binders encumbered the actors and were very noticeable to the audience. There are better ways to take a script onstage.

Actors should make their own decisions about the physical form of their onstage script. One of our actors performed her large role holding a deck of 3 x 5 cards with one or two speeches on each card. After finishing with a card, she would deftly slip it to the bottom of the deck. Not everyone, however, has the physical dexterity to do this, and the process of creating the deck of 3 x 5 cards was time-consuming. I have seen palm-sized editions of Shakespeare's plays printed on very thin high-quality paper so that one page could be flicked to the next by an actor's thumb. I have performed with 8-1/2 x 11 inch sheets with the script printed on both sides of each sheet and each sheet folded in half horizontally. Using only one hand, I read from the top half of Side A and then flipped the half-sheet to display the dialogue on the bottom half. Furthermore, with just a momentary assist from my second hand, I turned the sheet over to read from the top half of Side B and then from the bottom half of Side B. If there are two or more scenes, I bring a new sheet on stage for the next scene. If a scene is long and my role large enough, I carry two sheets on stage and switch from one to the other. Sometimes I have the second sheet waiting for me, perhaps on a table or some other set item. There are also script-in-hand performances in which music stands are set out strategically on the stage so that actors can step up to one of the music stands, read their script from the stand, and leave their hands unencumbered (Newman, 2019, p. 48).

By long-standing convention, standard script formatting calls for placing the character's name on a separate line above the character's speech. However, when scripts are published in print books, where reducing the page count saves money, character names generally appear on the same line—like this:

BEN: We're not exactly strangers. We've spent some time together.

I prefer the more compact print publishing convention for onstage scripts because onstage scripts also benefit from reduced page count.

You can much reduce the total length of your onstage script by deleting the middle portion of the lengthier speeches of your scene partners. This technique does require you to take some care that you don't lose your place in the scene. You may want to highlight the last sentence of the truncated speech, because it is your "cue line."

If you are going to truncate speeches or otherwise make a customized onstage version of the script, you want to receive your copy of the full script as a word processing (probably DOCX) file rather than as an uneditable PDF file or on paper. However, if you do receive the script in PDF form, you can convert it to a DOCX file using a version of Adobe Acrobat or free services available on the Internet.

Digital Scripts

I have been experimenting successfully with digital scripts, and think this is the future of onstage scripts. I modify the full script in any way I choose, send it to my iPhone as an email attachment, and then open it on my iPhone in the Kindle app. So far at least, I need to add my yellow and blue highlighting in the Kindle app, because the highlighting I apply in the original DOCX file on my PC is lost in the conversation to the Kindle file format. The Kindle app, however, gives me control of the font size, and I like the ability to flick from page to page rather than scroll. I lock the orientation of the display to "portrait," so if I happen to tip my iPhone horizontally while carrying out some action on stage, the orientation doesn't suddenly change to landscape and make me lose my place. This is certainly not the only technique. In fact, you can simply open the script as an email attachment and scroll through it.

The 5.5 inch screen size of my iPhone works well for me. I can move the iPhone freely as I gesture, and with the font size somewhat enlarged, I can read the text even at arm's length. Also, I can easily flick from page to page with my thumb. Certainly, there is less to draw the eyes of the audience than a sheet of paper. The Pulp Stage (2020), a theater company based in Portland, Oregon, performs in various venues (theaters, bars, living rooms) using tablets to display the scripts. Cold Reads International (2020) advocates reading from tablets. However, in my experience some actors find that tablets are too heavy or too clumsy. Whatever digital script technique you try, check to see that all the formatting in the original script survives its journey to your mobile device. For example, let's say the director or playwright sends you a DOCX script that uses a two-column table to show two characters speaking simultaneously (a standard technique in script formatting). There's no guarantee that this table formatting will survive when displayed on your smartphone or tablet.

"Off-Book" Performing—with a Safety Net

Performing without holding a script is a big jump upward. One compromise between script-in-hand performing and total off-book performing is to tell your actors that they are expected to perform off-book but that they can carry a script to peek at in case they suddenly forget their lines. Another safety-net procedure, which is sometimes employed in professional theater, is to have a human prompter standing just offstage ready to feed an actor any lines the actor has forgotten. In professional theater, the audience never sees the prompter. At the compromise level I am speaking of now, it would not be so bad if the audience were to see the prompter occasionally rescue an actor, as long as the whole prompting process were carried out smoothly.

Chapter 7

Sets and Props

Here we consider the use (and, at times, the absence) of sets and props. In Chapter 8 we consider costuming, and in Chapter 9 we consider how to obtain props, set items, and costumes. In mainstage productions sets often consist of elaborate carpenter-built constructions such as multiple connected platforms of different heights that might collectively represent the deck of a sailing vessel or the citadel of a fortified city. In contrast, I use "set items" to designate medium-size carry-on/carry-off objects such as a table, chairs, and a small sofa that can collectively comprise a set. Props are smaller, typically hand-held objects, such as table lamps, swords, and whiskey bottles.

No Set, No Props

Some 10-minute plays can be performed effectively on a bare stage or require nothing more than a chair or two. Costuming need be nothing more than the most "neutral" street clothing, by which I mean clothing that evokes very few if any cultural associations. For example, our backyard performance of the "The Spaghetti Crisis" employed nothing in the way of sets or costuming. When Henri faced upstage (away from the audience) to do some cooking, the actor (who was me) pantomimed shaking a skillet over a burner and beating the contents of a bowl with a whisk. Alternatively, we could have placed a sheet of veneer over a folding table to represent the chef's station, and Henri might have used an actual skillet, bowl, and whisk. Furthermore, Henri might have been costumed in a chef's apron and chef's hat. Similarly, "Close Encounters of the Talkative Kind" needs nothing more than three chairs and a coffee mug. However, many 10-minute plays ask for at least a little more in the way of set items and props.

Fidelity and Completeness

Fidelity and completeness are two important concepts in regard to sets and props. In a high-fidelity staging of "Nationalities," the office desk of Sammy D, the head of a Mafia family in the 1930s, might well be heavy, dark toned, and ornate. (His desk chair would be similar.) In a low-fidelity staging, the desk might consist of a folding table with a brown-painted piece of plywood placed on top. Your low-fidelity desk says to the audience: "Please imagine that I am the office desk of the head of a Mafia family circa 1930."

High-fidelity sets, props, and costumes are engaging. Moreover, they communicate a lot of visual information to the audience. The audience sees the characters' day-to-day environment, the implements they work with, and what they wear. A high-fidelity set of an upper-class Victorian parlor might well include period furniture, the appropriate chandelier, elaborate wainscotting on the walls, decorated tea cups on shelves, etc. The high-fidelity set of a warehouse might include stark flat-panel lighting, industrial shelving, and even a forklift. Impressive, if you can do it. Even so, directors often prefer low-fidelity sets. The celebrated Broadway production of *Hamlet*, starring the very famous Richard Burton, that I attended as a teen-ager in 1964 (standing room, at the back of the theater) was certainly not constrained by budget, but nevertheless employed low-fidelity sets and simple street clothing for costuming.

Few theater groups are going to expend the time and expense of high-fidelity set items, props, and costumes for a performance that only lasts 10-minutes. Moreover, theater groups generally perform multiple 10-minute plays in rapid succession, and this requires quick set changes. Therefore, low-fidelity or medium-fidelity sets predominate in 10-minute plays. An exception is the remarkable 12-minute comic riff on Harper Lee's *To Kill a Mockingbird* that was aired as part of Richard Pryor's short-lived, 1977 network television show (www.youtube.com/watch?v=bE1f4awlxVc). This skit-style play features a meticulous high-fidelity set and a cast of more than 20 actors, including Richard Pryor and Robin Williams.

Many community theaters have a collection of wooden boxes in different sizes and shapes that they use in one production after another for low-fidelity sets. The boxes can be arranged and stacked, perhaps along with a few wooden chairs, to represent the counter of a fast-food restaurant, a church altar, the deck of a ship, or what have you. Large corrugated cardboard boxes can also be used if they don't need to bear a heavy load. Because of the predominantly low-fidelity staging, 10-minute plays focus on telling a good story and ask the audience to participate imaginatively in the illusion of theater. Similarly, Shakespeare, through his use of various kinds of narrators, often entreats his audience to imagine what cannot be physically created on the stage.

I like to use one or two high-fidelity props with low-fidelity set items. In the Goat Hill performance of "Nationalities," Sammy D sat at a low-fidelity chair at a low-fidelity desk. However, there was an ornate, 1930s-style cigar box and an old-fashioned cigar-sized ash tray on the desk. Here is an example of how high-fidelity props can communicate in a very specific way to the audience: Later in the play, when Sammy D sits despondently at his desk because he's been forced to authorize a hit on his nephew, there is a whiskey bottle and glass on his desk that was not there during the earlier desk scene. Truth to tell, the bottle and glass never actually appeared on stage due to an oversight, but they were intended to indicate both that time had passed and that Sammy was in despair.

Sometimes a highly creative low-fidelity set solves difficult staging problems. In the early 1970s, I attended a delightful musical, *Chaucer's Canterbury Tales* (Coghill and others, 1968). The play included bawdy episodes from (I believe) "The Miller's Tale" and "The Reeve's Tale," with illicit lovers jumping into bed with one another. How does one do this on stage? Will the audience get a good view of what is happening in a bed? In the performance I saw, the couples stood, embraced, and kissed behind a simple rectangular panel placed vertically just a foot or so in front of the backdrop. The panel was painted to resemble a bed with sheets and a blanket. Actors stepped behind the panel and hugged, kissed, and "rolled over" on each other. This simple but very clever staging concept worked great. For more information about sex on stage, see Chelsea Pace, *Staging Sex: Best Practices, Tools, and Techniques for Theatrical Intimacy* (2020).

Completeness refers to how many objects you have on stage. In a high-fidelity staging of "Nationalities," you might add a side table or cabinet to more fully represent Sammy D's office, and you might add such props as a lamp, a coat rack, an oil painting, etc. In a low-fidelity staging, you might just add more boxes to suggest in a general way that there are more pieces of furniture in Sammy D's office. A set employing both high-fidelity elements and a high level of completeness we would call "realistic." Note that building a realistic set does not mean that you have a realistic play.

Spectacle

Some sets and costuming provide raw visual impact—what Aristotle called "spectacle." When Hollywood movies advertised "a cast of thousands," they were touting spectacle. Many contemporary movies are also rich in spectacle, including fiery explosions, high-speed car chases, and the like. It is easy to be snooty about spectacle. Aristotle himself regarded it as the least important element of tragic theater. But people do take delight in spectacle. Only occasionally, however, do we see anything like spectacle in 10-minute plays or in living room theater. When we see it, it might come from vivid costuming or dramatic lighting effects.

What Is and Isn't Real

When you are planning a high-fidelity or medium-fidelity set, it is actually more important to achieve fidelity to the audience's expectations rather than what is truly real. Unless you announce otherwise, your play is not a documentary. Therefore, your Wild West saloon should look like the saloons we see in Western movies and TV shows. What those saloons actually looked like doesn't much matter. Furthermore, some plays are set in a fantastic or surreal environment that never existed anywhere—for example, a magical forest with trees that listen to and talk to the characters.

Avoiding Dissonance

In my view, what you definitely don't want is dissonance. By this, I mean a set item or prop whose specific characteristics are at odds with what the set and props as a whole are trying to evoke. In other words, the set item or prop is high-fidelity, but in a bad way. It evokes inappropriate associations. If you are staging "Nationalities," and you don't have or don't want a heavy, ornate, dark-toned desk, it is better to use a simple folding table with a plywood board placed on it than a handsome Danish Modern or Queen Anne desk. If your play requires a contemporary handgun, two pieces of wood joined together and painted dark gray (low fidelity) is better than an old-time six-gun revolver that evokes Western movies.

Modern-Day-Equivalent Sets

When performing a play whose setting is some much earlier time period, one option is to provide sets and props that are high-fidelity modern-day equivalents of the actual furnishings and objects that would have been used in that earlier time. I attended a performance of Shakespeare's *Timon of Athens* in which a major set was a contemporary luxury condo instead of a luxurious palace in Ancient Greece (or some kind of Elizabethan/Jacobean equivalent). Not only are contemporary set items easier to obtain than period set items, but they communicate better to the audience. In the production of *Timon*, the audience understood the cultural significance of the set designer's specific choices in flooring, furniture, countertops, etc. In contrast, we are not close enough to past eras for such choices to convey meaning. I will jump ahead a little and say something similar about modern equivalents in costuming. In the Goat Hill performance of "Gawain and the Green Knight," the actors playing royalty and nobility wore upscale modern dress to suggest their characters' high social status. We did not attempt any kind of regal or aristocratic Medieval costuming.

If There Is a Rifle on the Wall . . .

Here is a well-known precept regarding props that originated with Anton Chekhov: If there is a rifle hanging on the wall of a set, it should be discharged (Abbott, 2002, p.56). In other words, the audience will hypothesize about any unusual prop and expect it to have some significance in the play.

Finger Pistols

One very useful low-fidelity option, at least in certain stagings of certain plays, is for an actor to shoot a "finger pistol" instead of any kind of low- or high-fidelity handgun. The Goat Hill performance of "Engagement" employed only a finger pistol for the opening scene in which Roy is shooting at fleeing assassins. If you use a finger pistol, you may also use a very low-fidelity mouth-sound "bam" (either vocalized offstage or even by the onstage shooter) for the firing of bullets. All this works surprisingly well for keeping the audience's attention on the story rather than the prop.

Furthermore, if the character's pistol is some kind of physical prop, it must be drawn from a holster or something similar and probably stowed or set down in some way—actions that may be irrelevant and distracting. However, through the expedient of pantomime a pistol (consisting only of an actor's fingers) can be very quickly and conveniently drawn and stowed. The dagger, rifle, and sword equivalents of the finger pistol may not work as well. I have, however, seen effective battle scenes with virtual (non-existent) broadswords. This is because the two-handed use of the broadsword lends itself well to pantomime. More generally, you might have characters use just their arms and hands to pantomime familiar actions such as eating at a dinner table or hammering a nail.

Door Frames

At times, sets need to indicate two different but adjacent spaces. Perhaps your set is a living room that opens to a hallway or back room. This hallway or back room may be important to the story even if no character in the play ever enters or exits through it. While the act of opening a door can be managed by pantomime in a minimalist or low-fidelity staging of a play, the ongoing presence of a door or a hallway cannot. The audience must see something, perhaps just some painted lines, that at least suggests the door or hallway.

In many productions you will want a door frame with a door that actually swings on a hinge. Theater companies, I have observed, employ door-frame set items, perhaps mounted on rollers for quick set changes. Such a door frame would, for example, enhance a staging of "Luke Meets the Revenue Man."

With my poor carpentry skills, I tried—and failed—to construct a door frame that could be disassembled for storage. The one set item I'd most like to own or have ready access to is a door frame that could be modified for various uses.

Artifacts: Things that Aren't Really There

Stage artifacts (my term) are items that can be seen on stage but which the audience recognizes (or *should* recognize) as not being part of the actual world of the play. An obvious example are the music stands that might be set up strategically on a set so that actors can read conveniently from scripts (Chapter 6). Similarly, if a character needs to pick up a jacket (or other object) in the middle of a scene, and, purely for convenience, the jacket is waiting on a small, nondescript table that is visible to the audience (better if it is not), that table is a stage artifact. If characters engage in a sword fight, the visible rubber tips on the ends of the swords are stage artifacts. Stage artifacts diminish the impact of the play to at least a small extent, but as long as the audience recognizes their status as stage artifacts, they are acceptable.

Safety

Safety is an obvious consideration, but it is not always easy to determine where safety hazards lie. Assess this carefully. Here are some suggestions: Don't use anything but truly harmless foam swords unless you're trained in theatrical sword fighting. Avoid fire, smoke, and anything that produces fumes. Dry ice is hazardous because it is so cold. Avoid anything heavy that might drop on someone and anything that might fly loose with some force. Be careful with anything that someone might slip on or fall from. Another aspect of safety is preventing any kind of sexual abuse or exploitation—especially if young people are involved. With children or even high-school students in your cast or otherwise involved in your production, you should ensure that there is careful monitoring of their entire experience.

Chapter 8

Costumes

Costume choices are much like set and prop choices. The equivalent of the low-fidelity set and prop is "neutral" costuming, costuming that evokes few if any cultural associations. I have attended professional performances in which neutral costuming took this form: For women, a black or dark gray skirt or slacks and a white or off-white blouse. For men, black or dark gray slacks and a white or off-white shirt, probably not a dress shirt. For example, a good way to costume a performance of a Greek tragedy is for the chorus to wear this kind of neutral dress while the protagonists wear something quite different. In keeping with the out-of-your-closet approach of living room theater, it is a good thing that most folks have such an outfit in their wardrobe.

No costuming, of course, is truly free of cultural associations, though the neutral costuming described above comes close. It is at least arguable that given the very informal nature of living room theater, the actors' uncoordinated ("come as you are") street clothes—excluding unusual or culturally specific attire—might function well as neutral costuming. The nature of the script might well affect the director's decision as to what would best constitute neutral costuming for that play. A director, then, intent on neutral costuming could explain what he/she/they has in mind and then leave each cast member to follow through.

High-fidelity costuming is the dress that the people portrayed in the play might actually have worn. If your play has a contemporary setting, your actors' uncoordinated street dress might also be high-fidelity costuming. But if your play is set in the "Roaring Twenties" or King Arthur's Camelot, high-fidelity dress becomes a challenge, and you may well choose not to take the trouble. As with sets, you might choose modern-day equivalents instead of attempting period costuming.

There are some important exceptions to the neutral dress approach. High-fidelity costuming may be necessary for police, soldiers, fire fighters, and others who wear uniforms or workplace-specific attire. "Flames" requires the overcoat portion of a police or military uniform with Eastern European, Cold War vintage styling. On Etsy I found someone from the Ukraine who sold me the exact uniform I needed in near-mint condition for $70, including shipping. Fortunately, because the overcoat in the play does not belong to Elena and because she never quite puts it on, there was no need to get a coat sized to fit the actor playing Elena. Sometimes an appropriate accessory or two are enough to indicate that your character is a police officer, a soldier, etc. For example, a simple "Sam Browne" belt (a wide belt with a diagonal over-the-shoulder strap) plus a solid-color shirt and black slacks might adequately suggest a military or police uniform.

A factor to consider in regard to costuming is that many people really do like to dress-up in a costume. There is a popular recreational activity called "cosplay" in which people dress up in high-fidelity costumes (perhaps from some sci-fi TV series) and don't do much else but enjoy socializing with others wearing such costumes. It may well be that the cast of a particular play wants to go high-fidelity, even if this entails renting elaborate costumes or purchasing key costume elements. Within the limits of what's feasible, decisions regarding neutral or medium- or high-fidelity costuming should be up to the director. As with sets and props, what you probably don't want is discordant costuming, costuming that evokes highly specific associations that don't fit the world of the play you're performing. Also, a director probably won't want the extreme or discordant contrast of high-fidelity and neutral costuming in the same play unless it serves a thematic purpose. Finally, there may be scripts that you choose not to perform because the script makes costume demands that you are not prepared to meet.

Should Characters Change Their Clothes?

If you see me at the grocery store on Tuesday, then again on Friday, and then again on Sunday, my Tuesday clothes will likely be in the hamper, and I will be dressed somewhat differently. So, does a character who appears in scenes that are days, months, or years apart need to wear different clothing? Theater isn't reality. It's storytelling. The invisible fourth wall (the actors, in general, don't seem to notice all those people watching them) proves that we are not truly representing reality. Therefore, I am generally comfortable with characters who appear in the same clothing in a scene set, say, a week after an earlier scene. On the other hand, a costume change does help show a jump in time of at least a full day. For example, "The Spaghetti Crisis" would benefit if the actor playing Simone made a quick, minor costume change in the interval between Scene 1 and Scene 2.

Costuming in Doubled Roles

As noted, when actors "double up" and perform two or more roles in one play, costume change is one way to help ensure that the audience instantly recognizes when the actor is playing each character. If an actor is switching from playing a shy, inhibited office worker to good-time partyer, the addition of just a flamboyant hat and scarf will go far.

Make-up

In performances in large theaters, professionally applied make-up compensates for the large distance between the actors and much of the audience. Living room theater, however, is definitely up-close acting. Therefore, whatever make-up your characters wear in their regular life should suffice for living room theater. As noted, however, there are exceptions. A little white powder in a character's hair can show age. Make-up can also help with doubled roles. Finally, as discussed below, there are special effects you can achieve with make-up.

Costuming and Make-up for Spectacle

Costuming can produce the theatrical element called "spectacle," explained in Chapter 7. In the Goat Hill performance of the original 17-minute version of "Gawain and the Green Knight," the Green Knight, who is green from top to bottom, bursts into King Arthur's court on New Year's Day. Huge, powerful, and only partly human, he issues the extraordinary challenge that kicks off the story. Because I am a large-sized, bearded, big-voiced, boisterous person, I cast myself as the Green Knight and set to work on a costume that might qualify as spectacle. I soaked old clothes in green dye, smeared green stage make-up on my skin and beard, and bought an inexpensive but persuasive cosplay Medieval battle-axe on the Internet. The audience took notice.

Theater Artistry with Sets, Props, and Costuming

I want to briefly revisit the topics of sets, props, and costuming, this time not from a practical standpoint but rather from the standpoint of theater artistry. With reference to the plays summarized in Appendix A (and the full script of "Bitter Cantaloupe"), I will try to envision just a bit of the creative thinking of a trained director.

I suggest that "Bitter Cantaloupe," a snappy, plot-driven comedy, needs nothing more than minimal staging consisting of the two tables, the chairs, and the necessary tableware. In contrast, "The Day of the Deal," a domestic drama that takes place in a graduate-student apartment, calls for at least a medium-fidelity set. The intimacy of the story cautions me against a minimalist production. We need to experience the characters' physical surroundings. On the other hand, "Mordecai in the Time of Plague," which takes place in a single room in Count Leonid's castle, seems perfectly suited for a bare-stage production. The costuming must in some way suggest the Medieval setting and indicate the social positions of the characters, but trying to replicate the interior of the castle seems like overkill. Why? Very likely because "Mordecai" is a conceptual play driven by thematic concerns and because it is set in a remote time and place. Other plays, such as "Regional Distributor" and "Nationalities," don't require anything more than minimal sets and costumes, but, in contrast to "Mordecai," can well accommodate medium- or high-fidelity sets and costuming if that is feasible. Would experienced theater directors agree with these judgments? I don't know. But I've briefly moved my discussion of sets, props, and costuming into the context of theater as an art form.

Chapter 9

Obtaining Set Items, Props, and Costumes

You can purchase, rent, borrow, and make your set items, props, and costumes. Another consideration is whether to keep and store particular items after your performance.

Purchasing

Costumes and props of every description are readily available, new and used, from such Internet vendors as Etsy, Big Cartel, and (of course) Amazon, mostly for very reasonable prices. You can also visit thrift shops for a surprising range of very inexpensive set items (such as sofas and tables), props (such as dishware in all styles), and clothing that will serve as costumes.

Because thrift shops differ significantly in what they stock, I keep notes that remind me, for example, that the Shoreline Goodwill is especially strong in clothing and furniture, but St. Vincent de Paul in Kenmore is better for electronics and electrical items such as an old CRT monitor or a reel-to-reel tape recorder. There are many stores that sell reclaimed building materials which can serve as set items or can be used to make set items. Purchasing used and reclaimed items and materials is not only economical, but satisfying in that you don't add to the world's supply of manufactured goods. So too with rented and borrowed items.

Renting

In many cities there are brick-and-mortar costume shops where you can rent costumes of all kinds (e.g., Robin Hood, Charles Dickens' England). There are also theatrical/film supply houses where you can rent set items, props, painted backdrops (e.g., a forest), stage lights, and special effects equipment. Some companies specialize in costumes and props, others in theater tech equipment and supplies, and some do both. See, for example, www.theatrehouse.com, www.pnta.com, www.mainstage.com, and www.norcostco.com. While you can rent these items via the Internet, it's better to see and touch what you are interested in, while avoiding shipping charges. Some theater companies, especially community theater companies, will rent you items from their storeroom of sets and props.

Borrowing

Most obviously, you can borrow from friends and acquaintances. I now find myself looking at furniture in the homes of friends, noting that this or that item might fit a particular play. Another excellent way to get props is to post a request on your community's Internet message board or other hyperlocal social network platform. I asked to borrow a particular prop on my local Next Door site (www.nextdoor.com) and was rewarded with both the perfect prop and a new friend. Unless the item is very valuable or delicate, most people will be pleased to lend it for a theatrical performance. When I needed a commercial-grade mop and mop bucket, I borrowed one from my gym. As a thank-you, you may want to invite the lender to attend the performance or even thank the lender in the curtain speech or the print program.

Making Stuff

Many items can be fabricated at home depending on your energy level, available tools, and skills. Craft stores such as Michael's and also fabric stores sell all kinds of items that can be turned into props and costumes. Barb Rogers' *Costumes, Accessories, Props, and Stage Illusions* (2001) shows how to create costumes of numerous historical periods from thrift-store clothing and fabric-store remnants.

Sheets of veneer and plywood (preferably SCUFF grade), sanded and perhaps painted, can serve as stage table tops and more. Lumber yards sell veneer and plywood in standard-size sheets that may be too large for your needs, but in my experience they will cut pieces to the dimensions you need for a nominal fee or as a courtesy, and you will likely find uses for the extra pieces.

Papier-mâché costs you nothing beyond the cost of the paint (although spray paint can be expensive) and can be used to make lots of props. Jean Farkas built a realistic 2-foot high rock by covering a corrugated shipping box with irregular contours of papier-mâché and then spray-painting the whole thing with brown and green speckle-style spray paint. Dense foam can be cut more easily than wood and fabricated into various props—for example, a low-fidelity (which is definitely what you want) AR-15 automatic rifle.

As noted, large corrugated boxes, if they don't need to bear much weight, can be used in place of wooden boxes for low-fidelity sets. So, if you have some storage capacity in your home, don't discard the cardboard boxes that large consumer products are shipped in. If necessary, you can purchase unused shipping/storage boxes from U-Haul and similar outlets. Really large "wardrobe" size boxes (24 x 24 x 48 inches) are especially useful. The Uline company (www.uline.com) stocks all kinds of corrugated boxes (1600 different sizes!) as well as cardboard tubes, packing materials, and similar items. You normally have to buy in bulk (often a 25-item minimum order), but you may find yourself paying not that much more for 25 boxes from Uline than what a self-storage warehouse or U-Haul outlet charges for a single box. It shouldn't be too hard to store a few of these (knocked down) boxes and find folks who can make some good use of the rest.

Storing this Stuff

Storage is not an insignificant issue. It's a shame to toss out what you will likely need again, but there's likely a limit to what you can hold on to. It's probably the organizer who will do most of the storing. Jean and I are beginning to fill our house and garage with set items, props, and costumes. Our rule is to borrow as much as possible, and when we purchase from thrift shops, we return, as donations, "commodity" items that we can easily obtain again. For about 5 dollars I can always find an old-fashioned wooden rocking chair, so I would avoid storing something that big. However, I am definitely keeping the two 1960's-style, quasi-psychedelic fiberglass chairs that helped to represent Barry Bright's studio in our performance of "Final Brushstroke." These $6 chairs would be difficult to obtain again at any price. Playwrights might want to hang on to set items and props specific to their play because they might want to assemble an entirely different cast at some later time to perform that play again.

Sounds

Some plays require sound effects. One approach is to use recorded audio files. There are many companies, such as Pond5 (www.pond5.com), from which you can download a great variety of stock sound clips (and music) for a low price. There are also public domain special-effect sound clips.

You may be able to record your own sounds. While preparing for a performance of "Flames," I was pondering how I would get an audio clip approximating the "chukka-chukka" sound of an old-fashioned mimeograph machine. By chance I was in a hardware store where a machine was energetically shaking a gallon of newly purchased paint. The store clerk was puzzled to see me pull out my iPhone and record his machine, but he had no objection. The iPhone' microphone was adequate for this particular sound. Be aware, however, that it is not easy to get a digital device to play back a very brief recorded sound such as a gunshot or the breaking of glass at the exact moment you want it heard. An ongoing sound such as traffic or factory noise is easier to manage.

Often you can create an adequate low-fidelity sound with minimal effort. Consider, for example, the vocalized "bam" for a pistol shot (Chapter 7), special whistles that produce birdsong, and banging two halves of a dried coconut for horses' hooves. Old-fashioned, low-tech methods such as these often require only minimal effort and also provide more control over the timing than playing recorded audio clips.

Chapter 10

Transitions Between and Within Plays

Most 10-minute plays consist of just one scene. Others are divided into two or even more scenes. In most cases, the different scenes are forward jumps in time, whether a few minutes or much longer, and the different scenes may be set in different locations. Sometimes, as in "Echoes of the Professor," the scene transition moves backward. Of course, there are also transitions between the plays comprising the program. Assuming that your living room theater group is performing three 10-minute plays, there will be a transition between the first play and the second play and between the second and the third. There is no transition to the first play because the set is already in place. In both scene and play transitions, actors enter and exit. But the big challenge is dealing with set items and props.

House Lights and Stage Lights

The use of curtains for transitions is now rare. The modern equivalent of closing curtains is the blackout and the dim out. In a well-equipped theater, you can independently control the lighting of the stage and the lighting of the seating area ("the house"). This gives you lots of options for managing transitions. One benefit of a true stage blackout (where the stage hands must use flashlights) is that you can surprise the audience when the stage lights go up.

Very often, however, in any non-theater venue such as someone's living room, not only is it impossible to independently control the lighting of the acting area and the seating area but, because of ambient light, it is impossible to truly darken the room at all. In this situation, you might want to dim the entire venue as much as you can between plays. But it is probably better—and certainly simpler—to keep the venue lit from start to finish and not to rely on lighting for transitions. What you definitely want to avoid is confusing the audience by dimming the room in the same way for *both* play and scene transitions (if there are such). You don't want audience members uncertain as to whether a play has ended.

A simple and effective approach, which I have come to favor for living room theater, is to use freezes (explained below) for most scene transitions and to have someone step on stage to announce each play in the program. But before going further, I need to talk about how both scene transitions and play transitions should be physically executed—which is fast and smooth.

Fast and Smooth

Scene transitions should not exceed 10 or 15 seconds. You don't want the play to lose its momentum. It is OK for the play transitions to take longer—perhaps two or three minutes. For one thing, audience members will feel free to chat about the play they have just seen. If, as discussed in Chapter 14, each upcoming play is not simply announced but is also introduced by the playwright (or director), still more time is available for the play transition. Because all transitions in living room theater are very likely (even with dimming) to be visible to the audience, all transition activity should be handled smoothly and efficiently (which also contributes to speed). It took the Goat Hill folks some time to recognize the importance of transitions, and some of our transitions have been clumsy and much too long. Think of yourself as *choreographing* transitions. For example, the actors leaving the stage can carry off props and set items, while others bring in new props and set items. There are lots of small decisions and a few tricks. For example, decide whether the plates and utensils need to be taken off a table before the table is carried off or whether they can remain on the table. If the set item is a desk with a sheaf of papers, you might tape the sheaf of papers to the desk with a bit of transparent tape. Theater artist and educator Kerry Hishon (2017) offers good advice on planning and rehearsing scene transitions.

Signaling Scene Transitions with Freezes

In the case of a multi-scene play, we can usefully distinguish between two different kinds of freezes. We can call them "cut-off freezes" and "kick-off freezes.

Cut-off freezes

Cut-off freezes signal the audience that the scene has ended. They terminate, or "cut off," the scene by having everyone on stage cease all movement for perhaps 3 seconds. When this freeze is over, the audience knows that the transition period between scenes is underway. Actors may leave the stage, new actors may come onstage, and actors may take new positions for the upcoming scene. Some or all of these actors may well serve as stage hands, along with other folks not in the cast. During the transition period, actors should use their body language to accentuate their role as stage hands. That is, they should walk with the business-like mien of stage hands, not like the character they were playing and not with the walk and manner we associate with actors. You can think of the cut-off freeze as akin to closing the curtains or dimming the lights, except, of course, everything is fully visible to the audience. In the Jumpstart scripts (Appendix C) that consist of multiple scenes, cut-off freezes are the default means of signaling the end of a scene.

There are, however, instances in which a scene will not end with a cut-off freeze. Notably, many scenes end with all the actors exiting. When the stage is empty, there is no one who can freeze, so what we have instead is a 3-second pause before any actors or stage hands appear to effect the scene transition. In the Jumpstart scripts, the transition to Scene 2 in "Echoes of the Professor" does not employ a cut-off freeze because the stage has been cleared at the end of Scene 1.

There are also fluid scene changes in which one group of actors leave the stage and a new group replaces them without any kind of freeze or pause in the action. Theater people sometimes describe this as new actors "chasing the old actors off the stage." Such transitions are especially easy to do on a bare stage. If, however, the first scene employed a set, the new scene can take place far downstage to keep the audience's attention away from the now irrelevant set. In productions of Shakespeare, brief battle scenes or scenes in which characters quickly exchange information are often staged this way.

In the case of a split set (discussed in Chapter 4), the cut-off freeze (or pause) is handled differently. During the freeze, the actors in the upcoming scene move to the set that they will be using when the next scene begins. "Professor Jim the Janitor," which packs 11 scenes into 12 minutes, uses two techniques to move smoothly through the many scene transitions. First, there is a split set consisting of Dan Resnik's campus office and the Resnik kitchen. Second, there are multiple scene transitions in which Dan and Jim move to the periphery of the stage to end a scene and immediately begin the next scene by returning to the main part of the stage. We can think of this as a kind of fluid scene change.

Kick-off freezes

Kick-off freezes are associated with the upcoming scene. Here the actors freeze for about three seconds to signal that the transition period is ending, that the actors are now back in character, and that the action is about to begin.

Because so many different things can happen on a stage, I allow myself considerable flexibility in how I indicate kick-off freezes in my scripts. Sometimes the phrase "Freeze" appears just before the stage direction that explains the new scene. Sometimes it seems better to place the phrase "Freeze" directly after this stage direction. When the stage direction itself implies a freeze, I omit "Freeze" and use "Action" as the kick-off signal. When a scene begins with characters entering an empty stage, there is no kick-off freeze—for example, in the transition to Scene 3 in "Echoes of the Professor." To sum up: A kick-off freeze, however it is indicated in the script, makes clear that the next scene is about to begin.

It is not necessary for the actors to be absolutely motionless during a kick-off freeze. For example, in the kick-off freeze (signaled by "Action") that begins Scene 2 of "The Spaghetti Crisis," we see Chef Henri at his chef station, back to the audience, beating the contents of a bowl with a whisk. If two characters are sitting together in a living room, one of the characters might be scrolling through a tablet.

One technique that can be used in a kick-off freeze is for a stage hand to step quickly onto the stage in the midst of the freeze (which might therefore be extended by a second or two) to conspicuously place a new prop on the set. This will normally be done when the set is largely unchanged and the function of the scene transition is to indicate the passage of time—perhaps a relatively short amount of time. In a staging of "Nationalities," if a stage hand appears specifically to place the whiskey bottle and glass on Sammy D's desk during the scene transition, the audience will recognize the jump in time.

Special Scene Transitions

There are, in fact, all kinds of ways to effect scene transitions, including variations on what we have discussed. Here are some special scene transitions. You can blend the transition with the play. As noted, when actors serve as stage hands in a cut-off freeze, they generally go out of character. However, in some plays, typically comedies, the actors can remain partly in character. For example, if one character has been lusting after another character during the first scene, a little bit of this behavior might be exhibited as they move the set items and props.

Certain scene transitions are fully integrated into the script. Envision a scene in which a couple begins to fight about a badly chosen birthday present. The recipient angrily throws the present offstage, and the two characters storm off the stage in opposite directions. The next scene begins with them hesitantly stepping back onto the stage with thoughts of making up. In Mary Louise Wilson's 10-minute play "Deer Play" (2011), an announcer (essentially a narrator) briefly introduces each of four scene transitions—for example:

> **ANNOUNCER:** End Act Two. Act Three: Madge and Local Man
> stand in garden.

In a whimsical comedy, the scene transition might be indicated by someone who simply walks across the stage carrying a banner: "Scene 2. Ten years later in Tokyo." In the make-believe world of theater, you have many choices.

Costume Changes and Transitions

Perhaps the most challenging transitions are those that require a character to completely change their costume between scenes or even within a scene. Thoughtful playwrights try to avoid this situation or else make sure that such costume changes are manageable. For example, if a character exits a scene mid-way within the scene, that character has time to change costumes for the next scene.

Full costume changes can be executed quickly through careful planning. Do it like a pit stop in an auto race. You may have the added challenge of having to manage costume changes in the confines of a narrow cross-over. Ideally, at least one item of dress, such as trousers, can remain unchanged. A clip-on necktie might well prove useful. Perhaps an actor can wear a garment necessary for the upcoming scene beneath the garment for the present scene. Costume designers in mainstage productions create very special costumes with one-click buckles and other mechanisms that would not be used in any actual street attire.

In certain plays, such as fantasies or highly conceptual plays, an actor can change costumes on the stage in full view of the audience. For example, the stage directions for "Good-bye from SILVE" call for the actor playing Colonel Ingram to transition into George right in the middle of Scene 1. (See the script in Appendix C.) This is not disruptive because the presence of the apparitional dancers has already moved the world of the play away from realism.

Chapter 11

Acting

This chapter provides actors with a simple and straightforward approach to preparing and performing their roles in the context of living room/do-it-yourself theater. I assume folks are going to put some time into preparation. Everyone likes to carry off their role with style. I'm also assuming relatively little rehearsing, and by "rehearsing" I mean true rehearsing with your scene partners under the guidance of a director. I use the term "self-rehearse" to refer to practicing on your own. This chapter divides into three sections. The first is about the process of preparing to perform in a 10-minute play. The second is a quick and dirty conceptual overview of acting that gives you a workable set of ideas to employ while preparing and performing. The third consists of specific techniques for using your voice and body.

Preparation

Preparing to perform consists of the initial orientation, private study, self-rehearsal, and finally rehearsing with others.

Orientation by the director

At the outset, the cast should receive early guidance from the director regarding how the director interprets the play and plans to stage it. This guidance might come in an email, or the director might hold an introductory meeting with the cast. Because living room theater employs small casts, the director might also speak individually with each cast member. Without some early guidance, each actor is less able to prepare his/her/their study script, and so the individual actors may diverge significantly from both the director and from each other in their image of the final performance of the play. This of course, leads to incompatible performances. You often read theater reviews complaining that a particular actor "seemed to be acting in a different play." You need to avoid such divergences from the director's image of the play. Perhaps the director intends a subtly comic or else broadly comic interpretation of the script. Or, for a serious play, the director intends a pensive, understated performance or else an intense, highly emotional performance. Perhaps the director sees the bad guy as innately and thoroughly evil or perhaps just a product of a bad environment or perhaps someone seeking moral redemption. Finally, actors always like to know what their costume will look like. Costume information is especially important in living room theater because the actors are charged with supplying their own costumes.

The study script

You gain insights and plan your performance through a process called "scene analysis" or "script analysis." This entails creating a "study script," which is your own personalized copy of the official script. You can use underlining, colored highlighting, and brief annotations to indicate intonations and pauses and even gestures and movements. You can indicate to whom your primary attention will be directed during each speech—to this character or to that character or to the audience. The Australian theater magazine *Oz emag* offers a detailed discussion of scene analysis and the creation of the study script (2013):

www.ozemag.com/2013/03/26/how-to-analyze-a-script

The study script is an evolving document. Throughout the preparation process, you will likely gain deeper insights into your character, deeper insights into the dynamics of each scene, and a more detailed idea of how you should perform your role. However, as you add detail to your study script, you may also delete from the study script ideas that you have internalized. Eventually, you will create an entirely different script, your digital or print onstage script (Chapter 6), but the onstage script is a descendent of your study script. Because the playwright's original script undergoes so much change, you can see fully now the value of getting the playwright's script as an editable (word processing) file. If I had only a print copy of the playwright's script, I would probably invest an hour or two typing myself an editable copy.

Half-memorizing

At some point in the process you should begin to half-memorize your lines for peek-and-speak performing. Read your study script and, later on, your onstage script. You can also record yourself on your smartphone and then speak or subvocalize your lines as you listen. You should also become familiar with the entire script and, especially, with your cue lines, the lines of the other characters that directly precede your speeches. These are good tasks to get done at the gym or while taking long walks.

Self-rehearsal

Self-rehearsal includes voice intonations, facial expressions, gestures, movements, and actions—such as the exact motion of swinging an axe. It is best if you can approximate the set items and props of the eventual performance. So, for instance, if the script calls for you to be seated at a table, you should self-rehearse at a table of similar dimensions. If the script calls for you to move from one spot to another, you should have a clear mental image of the approximate distance and direction of movement. This might include measuring off reference points and then setting down pieces of tape (on a hard floor) or yarn or string (on carpet or grass). If the scene calls for you to place roses in an ornate vase, you should try to place something akin to roses into some kind of vase—just to make the rehearsal gesture approximate what you will do onstage. Relatively early in the preparation process, you need to think about how you will be holding your onstage script and when to switch hands. When Fran Montano says that audiences barely notice onstage scripts, he is surely assuming the deft use of onstage scripts.

You may want to video yourself with a smartphone (ideally using a tripod). Reviewing videos of my self-rehearsing, I have been appalled at my sloppy enunciation, purposeless gestures, etc. Full-length mirrors also work well for self-rehearsal. Also, you can ask for critiques.

One self-rehearsal technique is to make a recording of your speeches (a sit-down reading is fine for this). Then, while listening to the recording, act out your lines in pantomime, complete with facial expressions, gestures, and movements. Why do it this way? Acting creates a very considerable cognitive load. You are multitasking, trying to attend to many things at once. In the early stages of your private preparation, you halve the cognitive load by learning your facial expressions, gestures, and movements without having to think about your voice. As time goes on, your facial expressions, gestures, and movements become more automated, and so you can better handle the extra cognitive load of delivering your lines.

Perhaps the biggest challenge in self-rehearsal is imagining your interactions with your scene partners. One reason why, as a director, I like to cast co-habiting people in the same play is that their private preparation will very likely include rehearsing their mutual scenes. To a certain extent, however, anyone can serve as a rehearsal proxy for your actual scene partner.

Concepts for Actors

Here is a brief conceptual overview of acting.

We all "act"

In a certain sense, we—meaning most people—act every day. Most people naturally use their voices expressively as they speak and make use of gestures. Those people who do not are noticed. They are often referred to as "low affect." Beyond this, most people present themselves differently, to at least some extent, to different people and in different situations. The kind of acting being discussed in this chapter—theatrical acting—entails drawing upon our natural emotions and habits of self-presentation and applying them to the demands of a script.

Stage acting is exaggerated behavior

Theatrical acting very often exaggerates our natural behavior. The amount and kind of exaggeration varies with the director, the script, and the actor's own personal acting style. We all routinely watch scenes in movies and TV shows in which an actor is engaged in a conversation. If you saw those same facial expressions and gestures in real-life, you would notice the artificiality of the behavior. You would think, "What a theatrical person!" Watch a few movies or TV shows with the sound turned off, and you will see what I'm talking about.

During rehearsals, directors routinely ask actors to "dial it up" or "dial it down." But, very often, the level of the dial they are looking for is higher than what is normal in real life. This is even more the case when plays are performed in large venues, where both the acting style and the make-up need to compensate for the greater distance between the actors and much of the audience. But even in the intimate confines of living room theater, you must learn how to dial up your normal level of emotion. I should also note that in some kinds of theater the actor stylizes or warps their behavior rather than simply moves the dial higher. Slap-stick comedy and dream-sequences with dance-like movements are forms of highly stylized acting.

The presence of the audience: Blocking and managing attention

Acting differs greatly from our everyday behavior in another important way: When you act—even in an intimate scene—there are a bunch of people sitting in chairs looking at you. Moreover, you will sometimes turn to them and even talk to them.

One aspect of having an audience watching you is blocking (Chapter 4). If the audience is seated along the sides of the acting area as well as downstage, you must shift around so that no one in the audience is looking at the side or back of your head for too long a time. Similarly, actors cannot hide other actors from view by standing in front of them for long periods of time, and they cannot get themselves hidden behind tall props and set items. They must even take care that their faces aren't covered by their own gestures at critical moments.

Also of great importance is trying to control where audience members focus their attention at every moment in the play. Audiences will pay more attention to an actor who is:

- Facing the audience

- At center stage

- Downstage of another actor

- Isolated from a group of actors (unless it is intended for the isolated actor to recede from view)

- Moving when other actors are not

- Being reacted to by several actors

- Lit by spotlighting

Because audiences pay special attention to actors who are facing them, there is an acting technique called "opening up to the audience." To draw the audience's attention, an actor who is speaking directly to another actor will nonetheless turn about a quarter turn toward the audience. Note that this is entirely a stage convention. If I am talking to my buddy, I have very little reason to turn partly away from that person.

Scene partners need to coordinate the overall effort to manage the audience's attention. Transferring the audience's attention to another actor is called "giving the scene." A director, then, might say something like this: "After this speech, Omar needs to give the scene to Kim." In professional theater, blocking and managing the audience's attention are worked out scene by scene under the guidance of the director. In living room theater, especially when there is only a walk-through rather than one or more rehearsals, we have what is called an "actor-directed performance." In other words, it is up to you, the actor, to do some of the thinking that might otherwise be done for you by the director.

Reacting

Reacting to the other actors in your scene is an important and challenging aspect of acting. You are definitely not "off duty" while your scene partner or scene partners are speaking. It is especially hard to find meaningful ways to react to a long, relatively uneventful speech. You must also avoid the other extreme of drawing the audience's attention ("taking the scene"), without good reason, from the actor who is speaking. In certain complex scenes, you will be challenged to make clear moment-by-moment which of your scene partners is receiving your primary attention. When there is nothing special you need to react to, you might use the opportunity to peek at your script.

Many plays include scenes in which an actor addresses and reacts to one or more offstage characters and therefore, in reality, is interacting with nobody at all. Offstage characters are especially prevalent in 10-minute plays because authors of 10-minute plays generally try to minimize cast size. In "Final Brushstroke" the actors playing Rafael, Lucy, and Barry have some non-existent scene partners:

> **RAFAEL:** *(Gesturing offstage.)* Barry, this is Simeon. He'll drive us out of the City and get us settled in his country place. It's way out on Route 17, nothing fancy, but it will be fine for now.
>
> **BARRY:** *(Nodding.)* Thank you, Simeon.
>
> **LUCY:** *(Gesturing offstage on the other side.)* This is Helena. That's Tony. They will get your paintings out of here before the video gets posted. They're artists. They know how to take care of big canvases.
>
> BARRY nods in thanks.
>
> **RAFAEL:** You're ready, Barry?
>
> BARRY nods.
>
> **LUCY:** You did it. You're breaking free. It's good to live free. I know.

Asides and soliloquies

An aside is a speech that is directed to the audience. A soliloquy, strictly defined, is a character's self-directed musings, but you can also have partial soliloquies and, less easily, partial asides. In one of Hamlet's famous speeches "What a piece of work is man" (Act 2, Scene 2), Hamlet is to some degree addressing Rosencrantz and Guildenstern, but is primarily speaking to himself. Furthermore, the actor playing Hamlet might choose to, in part, address the audience as well. In Shakespeare's *Richard III* (Act 1, Scene 2), the extremely evil Richard employs his rhetorical ingenuity to half-seduce Lady Anne, even though she knows that Richard has murdered her husband and her husband's father. Then, Richard, alone on stage, gloats, "Was ever woman in this humor wooed? Was ever woman in this humor won?" This speech is sometimes delivered as a soliloquy, but it works much better as an aside in which Richard gleefully shares his success with the audience. Playing Henri in the "The Spaghetti Crisis," I got a bit of a laugh by treating this line, which is clearly directed at Simone, partially as an aside, "It would be Americans who would do this thing—bring a child . . . " The humor is that I'm confronting my American audience with Henri's prejudice toward Americans. The big point here is that actors should consider opportunities provided by the script to employ full and partial soliloquies and asides.

Acting from the inside. Acting from the outside.

Very broadly, you can approach acting from the inside, where you try to "become" or "inhabit" your character, or from the outside, where you focus on eliciting particular thoughts and emotional responses in the minds of the audience. No doubt actors very often—perhaps always—do both.

Modern acting theory, pioneered by Konstantin Stanislavski (1893-1938), emphasizes acting from the inside. Prominent approaches based on Stanislavski are Lee Strasburg's Method Acting and Sanford Meisner's Meisner Technique. In this tradition, your performance emanates naturally from your own memories and your own mental and emotional state. You dig deep for experiences that bring you close to your character. In its extreme form, you actually copy the life experiences of your character. So, for instance, Robert De Niro worked 12-hour shifts as a taxi driver while filming the movie *Taxi Driver* (Maio, 2020).

When you act from the outside, you are thinking less about your character's inner life than about what you want to show the audience. This kind of acting is a set of consciously planned external behaviors—particular facial expressions, voice intonations, gestures, etc.—orchestrated to impact the audience in the ways you intend. Directors who focus on this approach are more apt to make comments such as these: "Emphasize that last idea with a strong gesture . . . Make it just a little stronger." Or, "Perhaps you can get a bit of a sob into your voice." This approach is less natural and less authentic, but it is more direct, more explicitly communicative. If I enter the inner life of my character but fail to speak and gesture persuasively, the inner life I've found achieves nothing. For this reason, the two approaches ultimately complement each other.

Regardless of which approach they favor, actors should consider acting-from-the-inside questions such as these when preparing their roles:

- What does your character feel at this moment?

- Where is your character in their life's journey?

- To whom is your character paying most attention to at this moment?

- What does your character want?

- How truthful is your character at this moment? How fully does the character understand the situation?

- How will the current speech or episode or scene change your character?

In addition, actors should consider these more audience-centric questions and others like them:

- If you could see your character at this moment, what would your character look like? How might the character be standing? What expressions could be read on your character's face? What gestures might your character use?

- What combination of vocal techniques, facial expressions, gestures, stance, and movement will communicate my character's emotional state at this moment in the play?

- Am I over-acting? Am I under-acting? Am I "taking the scene" when I shouldn't be?

- How is my timing? Am I coming in too early so that the audience doesn't have enough time to register the impact of my scene-partner's speech? Am I coming in too late and slowing the scene down?

Quick Tips

Here are quick, practical tips for using your voice, your face, your gestures, the posture of your body, and your physical movements.

Voice

First and foremost, your voice must be audible and clear. You achieve this in various ways. One is the overall volume and timbre of your voice, another is the distinctness of your consonants, and a third is the length of your vowels. When a referee introduces a boxing match in a noisy arena, the referee lengthens his/her/their vowels like this: Lay-dees ahnd gehn-tell-mehn. To make your voice expressive, you can vary the pacing, faster or slower. Also, you can pause for dramatic emphasis, you can stutter and choke on your words to show inner turmoil, you can shout, you can snarl, you can weep.

Facial expressions

Facial expressions are central to acting and are especially important to show how you are reacting to another actor. Many facial expressions naturally accompany the actor's speech. When you growl, your face will naturally produce a growling facial expression. This natural growling expression, however, can be made stronger, be held longer, or something else. Other expressions, such as the comic double-take and rolling one's eyes to show skepticism, may derive more from planning.

Gestures

When you think of your body as an "instrument" for acting, you begin to recognize the variety of gestures that two arms, a neck, and a head can produce. It is worthwhile to experiment with the full range of motion of your stationary body. Take note of all the ways your fingers can move, and the ways your wrist will allow your hands to move, and so on. Many gestures are strongly associated with particular emotions and situations. Some of these associations span different cultures, and some don't. Often these associations change in certain ways over time. Let's consider the old-fashioned theatrical gesture of showing dismay by throwing your head backward and placing your hand, palm outward, on your forehead. These days, this gesture still communicates dismay, but we associate the gesture with the overly dramatic style of acting called melodrama.

If you take an interest in acting, you will pay more attention to the range of facial expressions and gestures trained actors employ and how well they use them. But you should also pay attention to the world around you. These days, if I am waiting at a bus stop, I use the time to observe how passers-by walk and how two people gesture as they talk. One good exercise is to repeatedly watch talk-heavy (not dance-heavy) TikToks until you pretty much know the dialogue. Then watch with the audio muted to see how the speaker uses their face and body to deliver those lines. Then try it yourself. Incidentally, when you take an interest in acting, you will see why actors—back when smoking was commonplace—benefitted from the many ways you can hold and smoke cigarettes, pipes, and cigars.

An important question, which I ask trained actors when I have the opportunity, is how much line-by-line planning they do. I get different answers, but most actors plan certain vocal intonations, facial expressions, and gestures for particular moments, but also let them arise naturally each time they rehearse or perform the part.

Posture

The overall posture of your body is a kind of summative product of the positioning of your limbs and joints. In other words, you can stand ramrod straight or with a slouchy posture, etc. Your posture can project arrogance, determination, timidity, or supplication, just to name a few. As Dean and Cara point out (1989, p. 41) and as I will attest from direct experience, it is helpful to pay attention to the balls of your feet. Because acting is a multitasking activity, you cannot easily pay attention to every joint and limb that contributes to your posture, but when you pay attention to the balls of your feet, you have a general awareness of your posture and the subtle shifts of your body.

Movement

Actors know a great deal about how to walk expressively. You can walk into your boss's office timidly, confidently, angrily, or seductively. Walking can also serve as a kind of prolonged gesture when there is no actual destination. Speaking to an audience of theater fans, the highly acclaimed actor Lisa Wolpe suddenly walked in a quick, tight circle as an expression or a consequence of the intense emotions she was feeling at that moment (Taproot Theater, Seattle, on 2/8/2020). In "First-Rate Man," the stage directions call for Frederick Taylor to step back and forth to show his emotional distress at having to fire the underperforming worker, Mary Johnson.

Chapter 12

Directing and Rehearsing

In this chapter we look closely at directing living room theater.

Limited Authority

A key point is that the authority of the director is limited. It comes in large part from the group members' personal rapport with the director, their confidence that the director can guide the group in an enjoyable way to a successful performance, and their recognition that the director is doing a lot of the work. Whatever notions you have of the imperious Hollywood-style director need to go out the window. If you are a tough manager in your workplace, you need to remind yourself that in the world of living room theater everyone is a volunteer.

One area in which the director's limited authority may become apparent is in regard to costuming. In professional theater, costumes are designed by the play's costume designer or are selected from the theater's costume collection, all under the broad guidance of the director. In living room theater, your actors are providing their own costumes, which gives them much more control of their costuming. This can present problems. Some of your actors will prioritize looking good over the director's preferences.

You Do a Lot of Theater Tech

Think of one of those comical drawings of an upside-down org chart with the boss at the very bottom. Unlike mainstage theater or even community theater, the director in living room theater personally sees to a whole lot of theater tech tasks. This includes measuring the dimensions of an unfamiliar venue and deciding how best to use it—for example, whether or not to set up a backdrop screen. Also, the director will likely decide about the lighting and will obtain set items and props by visiting thrift shops and perhaps getting out the handsaw and spray paint. On the day of the performance, you can recruit folks to help carry and set-up, but in the weeks before the performance, you may be operating on your own.

Choosing Your Cast

A great deal depends on the choice of the cast members. Note the differences in what different roles demand. In "First-Rate Man," Frederick W. Taylor is on stage almost throughout the play and projects a wide range of moods and emotions. Most important, the whole point of the play is to examine this complex man. Therefore, I would not attempt to stage "First-Rate Man" without a good actor playing Taylor.

Keep in mind that non-professional actors tend to have a limited range in the parts that they can do well. Therefore a good strategy is to select actors whose personal style is a natural fit for their part. I attended high school with Ronald F. Maxwell, who later became a professional film director. As a student, he directed numerous plays, and I saw him use this technique to get surprisingly good performances from unskilled actors. Try to imagine the actor in your group who is the best natural fit for each of your roles and let that be a major factor guiding your casting decisions. For the roles to which you can't match the natural style of your actor, look for a strong actor whose broad range will likely encompass that role. Note that this kind of decision-making can be made, with some variation, whether you are casting your actors with the boutique approach or the one-shot approach (as explained in Chapter 5). Fortunately, because this is living room theater, you will never be casting more than a handful of actors, so the process should not be arduous.

The Director as Actor

Especially if you don't have a lot of folks ready and willing to take part in your next performance, the director can take a role. But there is much to be said for having the director focus entirely on directing. Also, there is a risk that a director/actor will see the play through the prism of the role he/she/they has taken on. One compromise is for the director to take one of the smaller roles.

The Director's Interpretation

There is no such thing as "just doing a play." There is always interpretation, a succession of large and small artistic decisions that are made consciously or not. For example, when two individuals commit to a romantic relationship at the end of a play, the interpretation can imply that they will be happy together or can show signs of future discord. Most directors stay within the parameters of meaning established by the script. Others are aggressive, sometimes wildly so. For example, in Shakespeare's *Richard III*, the thoroughly evil king is finally defeated by the Duke of Richmond, the future King Henry VII, the progenitor of the Tudor dynasty, and the grandfather of Queen Elizabeth. I saw a performance in which Richmond was played in the manner of a sleazy politician or perhaps a TV preacher from the American South. This produced laughs, but totally overturns the meaning of the play. Certain scripts are open-ended, leaving the director to decide key questions. Very famously, *Hamlet* leaves open such important questions as why Hamlet is slow in taking revenge on Claudius, the nature of the relationship between Hamlet and Ophelia, and whether Denmark will be well governed by Fortinbras.

Turning from the Shakespearean summits to my humble efforts, "Final Brushstroke" projects a very clear value system and concludes with the implication that all will go well for Barry. Any director of this play, I think, is relatively constrained. There is nothing to stop a director from suggesting that Lucy and Rafael aim to exploit Barry, but I would call this a perverse interpretation of the script. In contrast, "First-Rate Man" and, even more so, "Return from the Dead" are open ended. In "First-Rate Man" much depends on the performance of the actor who plays Frederick W. Taylor. How much empathy should we feel for someone who is altruistic and kindly but also self-deluded, unbending, and destructive? In any staging of "Return from the Dead" a central question is our moral assessment of both Sophie and R, who jointly deceive and ensnare Joel but who, apparently, believe deeply in the social value of what they do. Furthermore, one director might interpret

Sophie as sincere in her hope for a loving relationship with Joel, while another could present this as one more deception.

If the director is the playwright, the director will have a vast storehouse of ideas about how to stage the play. If the director is not the playwright, the director should undertake a serious study of the script and apply lots of theatrical thinking. When at all feasible, the director should consult with the playwright. Furthermore, directors should always listen to and respect the suggestions of the cast, especially in regard to each cast member's interpretation of their own role. Whatever decisions are made, it is important to remember that each production of a play is a one-time thing, a new work of dramatic art. Whatever happens, the script lives on ready to be the armature of a new production of the play.

The Director's Image

The director's image of the performance encompasses the interpretation, but is broader. It includes the sets, props, and costuming; the style or styles of acting the director wishes to bring forth from the cast; the moods that can be created by lighting (to the degree that this is possible); and blocking as an artistic element in theater. Thus far, this book has treated blocking merely as the practical problem of not obstructing the audience's view of the actors. However, at a more ambitious level, blocking encompasses the creation of dynamic visual tableaus, something akin to a painter creating a visual composition on a canvas (Dean & Cara, 1989).

The director's image should be an achievable plan. Directing, like politics, is the art of the possible. For the final scene of "Flames," you can imagine a complex set that vividly represents a building's smoldering ruins. This is what Great Britain's National Theatre can and most likely would do. But in living room theater an achievable goal might be siren sounds and the flashing red and blue of police car lighting.

Rehearsals—Or a Walk-Through

As explained in the preceding chapter, the director needs to provide early guidance to the cast about how the director interprets the play and plans to stage it. This greatly helps each actor with their preparation. At some later point in the process come the rehearsals—or, at least, the last-minute, pre-performance walk-through.

A key issue is how many rehearsals to schedule. The likely answers are one, two, or just the pre-performance walk-through. The director must determine the preferences of the cast members. Some folks may have very busy schedules or reside a significant distance from the rest of the group. Some folks just have a "let's wing it" mentality. On the other hand, there will be cast members who will be truly uncomfortable without a rehearsal, and others who are happy to spend time rehearsing and socializing with friends. With all this in mind, the director needs to decide both how much rehearsing he/she/they wants and how strongly to call for one or more rehearsals. This might be the issue on which you draw down on the limited authority you get as director and declare that the production truly needs a rehearsal. It may not be necessary for everyone in the cast to be present to conduct a good rehearsal. What matters most is assembling the scene partners for the most important and most challenging scenes. While not ideal, someone can stand in for a missing actor, especially in scenes in which that actor's role is secondary.

The rehearsal should not be scheduled too early. The actors should have already done most of their private study and self-rehearsal, and they should certainly be working from a version of their onstage script. I attended a presentation by a well-respected Seattle director who places a high priority on conducting rehearsals in the venue where the performance will ultimately take place. This is clearly advantageous, but may not be feasible. Also, there is something to be said for rehearsing in the comfort of someone's home.

The amount of rehearsing you actually need depends on various factors. High among them is the complexity of the interaction among the characters.

For example, "Close Encounters of the Talkative Kind" and "The Spaghetti Crisis" are largely conversations and present few complications. In contrast, "Return from the Dead" and "Stones and Rope" are more complex plays that call for more rehearsing. (For one thing, a character in "Stones and Rope" throws herself in front of a bus.) Plays with dancing (for example, "Good-bye from SILVE"), plays with challenging technical requirements (for example, "Stripes"), and plays with highly complex staging (for example, "Solo to Tandem") are in an entirely different category in regard to the need for rehearsals.

I conducted a rehearsal of "Engagement," and our final run-through was so rough that we all agreed that a second rehearsal was necessary. A second rehearsal may also be called for if the director/playwright decides to significantly revise the script. This, in fact, is apt to happen if the rehearsal is the first time (or one of the first times) the director/playwright has seen actors perform their play. Director/playwrights, however, must keep in mind that extensive late revisions are hard on the actors, who must keep altering their performance and their onstage scripts.

Conducting the Rehearsal

How do you conduct the rehearsal? As it happens, Shakespeare, in *A Midsummer Night's Dream* (Act I, Scene 2 and Act III, Scene 1), gives us a great picture of a group of very amateur actors, including the very difficult leading man, Nick Bottom, getting together for their rehearsals of a play. Shakespeareans generally laugh at these folks, but Peter Quince proves himself to be a shrewd and tactful director who knows when to give way and when to insist.

I am perhaps too accommodating as a director. I watched my close friend Bob Boiko lead two rehearsals of his play "Black Box" in a more rigorous way than I would have, sometimes asking an actor to deliver a line repeatedly until Bob got just what he was after. The actors responded well to Bob's approach, and he achieved an impressive improvement in the performance.

It is very helpful to have some kind of audience attend your rehearsals. Just one or two audience members make the run-throughs of the play a lot more real. Certain aspects of the performance such as how the actors will manage the audience's attention (Chapter 11) are difficult to rehearse without some kind of audience. And, of course, audience members can and will offer valuable suggestions.

Deena Baron, Bob Boiko, Jean Farkas, and Bill Baron rehearsing Bob Boiko's "Black Box." The box, not yet painted black, and its accompanying baskets are on the coffee table.

Although a rehearsal should be an enjoyable social event, it's easy to spend too much time socializing, especially when you have invited audience members. Much better to serve coffee and cake rather than wine and cheese. The good news is that if you keep things moving, a 10-minute play can be rehearsed with some degree of thoroughness in 2 or 3 hours. One pitfall is to get bogged down with minor problems. In some situations the director should take up an issue privately at a later time with an actor or with scene partners.

What Does the Director Focus On?

Of course, the more rehearsal time you have scheduled, the more aspects of the performance you can work on. Prioritize the aspects of the performance that the actors cannot undertake in their private preparation. First and foremost are the complex interactions among characters. Omar may do a good job preparing his speeches and gestures and imagining how Suzie and Kim will react to him and how he will react to them. Suzie and Kim may have done the same. But only when the three work together as scene partners will the performances truly synch—all the more so if there is quick repartee or physical actions, such as a fight or romantic activity. Also, if at all possible, work on any scene transitions that may be in the play.

Rehearsals may uncover problems that have nothing to do with the actors. In rehearsing "Black Box," Bob Boiko recognized a design flaw with the black box that is the visual and thematic focus of the play. Bob brought a larger and more smoothly functioning black box to the second rehearsal.

If there is more rehearsal time, the director can fine-tune all aspects of the actors' performances—voice, facial expressions, gestures, stance, and movement. From the perspective of acting from the inside, the director may remind the actor, or perhaps ask the actor, what the actor's character is thinking and feeling at a particular moment in the play. From the perspective of acting from the outside, the director will suggest a longer pause, greater or less emphasis, a different gesture, and so forth.

When I discussed self-rehearsing in Chapter 11, I noted that actors, during self-rehearsal, might use masking tape or yarn to represent his/her/their locations on the stage during the eventual performance. Directors may choose to set down tape or yarn reference markers during a rehearsal. These reference markers should certainly indicate the positions of major set items that are not present during the rehearsal. In fact, these markers can be set down on the stage just before the actual performance. Stage hands will benefit if they can see small pieces of tape (possibly color coded) that show where a table and a cabinet need to be placed. Actors will appreciate a few markers that show just where they should be standing at key moments in a scene. If you walk up to and closely examine the stage of a mainstage theater during the intermission, you will often see small pieces of special theatrical "spike tape" (available in many colors) that are used for this purpose. In living room theater, it's OK if audience members spot your markers—though they should be inconspicuous. When your play concludes, be sure to remove your tape or yarn to avoid distracting or confusing the actors who may be performing another of the 10-minute plays in your program of plays.

One issue regarding rehearsals is how often the director should interrupt a run-through of the play in order to offer guidance on a specific issue. Feedback works best when it is timely. On the other hand, it is desirable to keep the momentum so that the director and the actors feel the flow and rhythm of the play. Fortunately, you can do multiple run-throughs of a 10-minute play in one rehearsal. My thought is that the rehearsal should culminate in one full-on, no-interruption run-through, followed, if necessary, with individual conversations.

Taking Notes

Directors typically take notes so that they are clear about what changes have been agreed to. They may choose to email some suggestions and updates to cast members based on these notes. Cast members may want to take their own notes, especially regarding complex stage actions.

Just a Walk-Through

If there is to be just a 10- or 15-minute walk-through of a play immediately before the performance, the director needs to focus on avoiding a train wreck. This means cueing the actors through their entrances and exits and rehearsing complex actions and crucial speeches. Doing nothing more than a walk-through may result in a successful performance, depending on the play, the cast, and just plain luck. In some instances, I've wished we'd done more than a pre-performance walk-through. But, whatever happens, living room theater is a recreational activity by and for family and friends. Nobody has purchased a ticket.

More Information

Vast amounts of guidance on directing, acting, and all other aspects of theater can, of course, be found on the Internet. You can choose between web pages and YouTube/Vimeo videos. Dean and Cara's textbook *Play Directing* (1989) is valuable, even though it focuses on mainstage productions and is fundamentally a very old book, originating in the 1930s. It is clear, practical, and comprehensive. It even includes extensive exercises.

Chapter 13

The Stage Manager

The stage manager, coordinating with the directors and the organizer, supervises and performs a wide range of logistical tasks. With checklist in hand and the ability to multitask, the stage manager makes all the pieces fit together. As noted, one special responsibility of the stage manager is to deal with issues that span the individual plays making up the program. Perhaps one of the directors does not want the backdrop. The stage manager will decide if it is feasible to carry off the backdrop in the transition preceding that director's play.

In professional theater there is very often a "house manager," someone who is in charge of the lobby, the audience seating area, and all aspects of the audience experience other than the actual performance. But in living room theater, the stage manager is also the house manager. Especially if the performance is being held in a church basement or martial arts studio rather than someone's home, the stage manager's duties could well expand to include figuring out what refreshments are permissible and where to set them out. The stage manager might decide whether it's necessary to set up a free-standing sign board or two in the parking lot to direct audience members to the right door.

The stage manager's job becomes more complex as the number of plays in the program increases. So, if you're thinking of performing more than three plays, consider the extra burden on the stage manager. For one performance in which the logistics were more complex than usual, we hired a high-school student to assist the stage manager.

Before the Performance

It is perfectly possible for each director to individually obtain and bring the set items and props for that director's performance, along with any special theater tech equipment such as portable lighting and a Bluetooth speaker for music. But there is much to be said for some coordination. A proactive stage manager can inquire early on what each director, especially new directors, is looking for in regard to sets, props, and equipment and then let them know who has this stuff available.

It may also make sense for directors to share items. There is no reason why the same low-fidelity table used in one play cannot be used in the next. In fact, doing so not only eliminates the duplicate effort in obtaining and transporting two tables, but very likely makes the transition between those two plays go faster. If directors are sharing items, the stage manager should do a last-minute check to find out who is bringing what. The stage manager might also remind the directors to do a quick transportation assessment to ensure that what they are bringing will fit into their vehicle. For one Goat Hill performance it proved necessary to arrange for one of the actors to come by our house with his pick-up truck.

If close-in parking is an issue, the stage manager might ask someone to drive to the venue well before the performance, keep their car in a parking space very close to the venue door, and vacate that parking space just as a vehicle with the heaviest set items arrives to take that space.

If there are a significant number of set items, the stage manager decides where outside of the audience's view the set items should be placed so that the stage hands can quickly and efficiently carry them on and off the stage. When the performance will take place in a small venue, especially in a home, this can be a tricky business—almost a game of set-item Rubik's Cube. If you are sloppy, you may find yourself hurriedly lifting a chair right across your dining room table to get it into the acting area.

As the audience members come in, the stage manager, as house manager, deals with any special issues, such as an audience member with a disability, and ensures that every audience member receives a copy of the printed program.

To better deal with last-minute problems, the stage manager should bring such items as a pair of scissors, duct tape, and an extra extension cord. In addition, the stage manager must have everyone's mobile phone number. In Chapter 5, I noted that because living room theater is performed script-in-hand, it is feasible to recruit a last-minute substitute for an actor who cancels at the last minute. However, to make this possible, there must be a copy of the script to give your bold, last-minute volunteer. It is even possible that one of your actors will forget to bring their own copy of the script. The stage manager, therefore, will do well to have an extra script of each play in the program plus a script for any play, such as a dramatic monologue, that can be added to the program at the last minute. Finally, the stage manager might make plans to have someone take photographs and perhaps make a video recording of the plays. If so, it is necessary for folks to give their assent as to the uses of the photographs and the videos they appear in.

During the Performance

During the performance, the stage manager supervises the transitions between plays. Also, the stage manager will step in to solve any kind of last-minute problem. All kinds of things can go wrong during a performance. In a venue open to the public, someone might wander in thinking this is where they will get help with their income tax. There may be a costume malfunction. A set item might prove surprisingly uncooperative. I attended a mainstage performance of a play in which a central set item was a fake and (as it turned out) surprisingly delicate spinet piano. In a scene-transition mishap, the piano toppled, broke into pieces, and had to be crudely re-assembled with duct tape for use in the remainder of the play. This surely created some interesting moments for the stage manager. I am not suggesting that living room theater performances are full of problems and fraught with tension. Far from it. These are relaxed affairs in which everyone accepts screw-ups good naturedly. Still, it's always good to do the best job you can.

After the Performance

When each play ends, the stage manager may need to signal the audience to applaud. Audience members may be unsure whether they should applaud after each play or hold applause to the end of the show. After the performance, the stage manager supervises the process of getting all the things that were brought to the venue back into the cars that brought them. If there is limited parking near the door, this can take some coordination. Finally the stage manager oversees the task of restoring the venue to its original condition. To conclude, the stage manager's job is complex and demanding. Every stage manager should be deeply appreciated.

Chapter 14

The Meta-Performance

The prefix "meta" means "along with," "more than," or "beyond." This chapter is about information and interactions that surround and supplement the program of plays. The chapter covers these forms of meta-performance: (1) Personal invitations, (2) the printed and PDF program, (3) the curtain speech, (4) the playwrights' introductions, and (5) the talk-back.

Personal Invitations

I recruit folks to take part in the Goat Hill Theater through casual conversations that lead to an invitation. I invite people to choose between attending a performance as an audience member or performing. I address any reservations the person expresses regarding active participation, such as the time commitment or stage fright. It's especially important to tell prospective actors that they are committing only to a script-in-hand performance. In addition, prospective audience members should be told that this is script-in-hand, recreational theater so as to avoid raising unrealistic expectations regarding the show. If someone expresses interest, I include them in the list of folks who get emails inviting them to participate in the next performance. If I don't hear back from them, I eventually remove them from the email list. Loaning someone a copy of this book is one way to fully introduce the idea of living room theater.

Programs

The Goat Hill Theater distributes a printed program to audience members as they walk in the door. We also email a PDF file of the program to everyone on our invitation list soon after we have chosen a date, performance venue, and the program of plays. Often we email a revised PDF program, even if the revision is nothing more than a cast change. Sending a revised program is a useful reminder to folks who might otherwise forget to attend. Folks may not look carefully (or at all) at the revised PDF program, but they will read the body text of the email if it is just a sentence or two. Just the subject line of the email can serve as a reminder: "Updated program for Saturday's performance." Our PDF/printed programs are short and simple. Below is an approximation of one of them.

"Black Box," "Engagement," "Stuck in Camp"

A program of three never-staged 10-minute plays by Bob B. Boiko, David K. Farkas, and Jim Halliday, performed recreationally (script in hand) at the Shoreline Public Library, February X, 202X.

Black Box
By Bob B. Boiko (directing)

There is a black box at the center of the Dataist nation of Harari. Inspired by the book *Homo Deus*, by Noah Harari, this allegorical work pits the new religion of Dataism against the Humanist religion of democracy. The result is not pretty.

Input	Jean Farkas
Output	Bill Baron

Engagement
By David K. Farkas (directing)

In the violent world of espionage, love takes strange forms.

Roy	Dennis Moore
Sara	Jean Reid
Theater-goer 1	Rick Ells
Theater-goer 2	Tyson Greer

Stuck in Camp 1957
A young man grows up quickly working construction north of the Arctic Circle.

By Jim Halliday (directing and performing)

Agenda
Cast walk-throughs:	1:30 (Everyone invited to watch)
Curtain:	2:30
Talk-back:	3:15 to 4:15 (No need to stay for this but the talk-backs are lively.)
Socialize:	4:30 All are invited to Jean and Dave's house for refreshments and hanging out.

Shoreline Library: 123 NE 123th St, Shoreline, WA / **Jean & Dave's house:** 123 NE 123 St. Lake Forest Park, WA (206) 123-1234 – (206) 123-1234 - farkas@xxxx.xxx

---

A program of a Goat Hill performance.

The Curtain Speech

Each program of plays should begin with a curtain speech, perhaps 5 minutes long. It should consist of some welcoming words, a brief explanation of living room theater, and acknowledgments to all the contributors who will not be appearing on the stage. This would include the stage manager, anyone doing theater tech, folks who brought refreshments, and folks who loaned you set items and props. The curtain speech should also include housekeeping information such as the locations of bathrooms. If the plays are being performed in a public space and the social get-together is at someone's home, those in the audience who are not closely acquainted with someone in the group may shy away from attending the social get-together unless the invitation in the curtain speech is emphatic. This invitation should be repeated at the conclusion of the talk-back.

The Playwrights' Introductions

It is very desirable for each playwright to give a 3 or 4 minute introduction to their play. What might the playwright talk about? There are lots of possibilities: How the playwright got the idea for the play, something about the playwright's interpretation of the play, the kind of feedback the playwright is hoping for in the talk-back session. If the playwright is not available to introduce the play, the director is a good candidate to give the introduction. Note that these introductions serve a function similar to the interview with the playwright that is often part of the booklet-style programs distributed at mainstage productions.

You might have a reason to group these introductions together before the first play in the program. But I prefer that each playwright deliver his/her/their introduction just before the start of that playwright's play. This allows more time for the transition from the first play to the second and from the second play to the third and also prevents any confusion on the part of the audience about which play will be performed next. Furthermore, the playwright's introduction sets the mood for the play. For example, if one of the plays on the program is an impassioned political statement, the audience will be more prepared for this kind of play having heard the playwright's introduction.

The Talk-Back

The final element that can be regarded as meta-performance is the talk-back that follows all three plays and precedes the social time. Talk-backs are central to the participatory nature of living room theater. If moderated well—and there should be a moderator—most audience members will contribute their ideas and become more fully engaged in the entire enterprise. And, of course, talk-backs are extremely valuable to the playwright and everyone else involved in putting on each of the plays. George Sapio (2017) provides a good discussion on talk-backs that are focused on improving scripts. As a playwright or director, you should never argue or respond defensively if an audience member finds fault with your play or how it was performed. Such answers will quickly dampen the mood of the talk-back.

Talk-back questions and comments tend to be directed toward the playwright and director, but the moderator should make sure that questions are also addressed to cast members. The moderator does not need to wait for a question or comment from the audience. Rather, the moderator can simply turn to an actor and say "Can you tell us something about your experience acting in this play?" You might want to give the actors advance notice that you will be asking them a question during the talk-back.

As you are reaching the end of the talk-back, the stage manager plus volunteers can begin taking down the set. Conclude the talk-back with a thank-you to the audience and a final invitation for everyone to take part in the socializing. I recommend against letting the social period get started before you do the talk-back. Once the social period gets going, you may not be able to round up your audience for the talk-back.

Chapter 15

Keeping It Going

Much of human activity consists of observing one's present circumstances, evaluating, and then improving on what you have. This process certainly applies to living room theater in matters both small and large.

Post-Mortems

It's very helpful to reflect upon each performance—what's called a post-mortem. There is a natural impulse to unwind after the performance, but it's a good idea to exert some discipline and assess the performance, if not immediately, then within a day or so: "Suzie, Omar—Did we really get the comic timing right in the café scene? I thought we were too slow some of the time." Many years ago, as I left a church-basement performance of an intense play, I peeked through a small window into the basement and saw the entire cast intently engaged in a discussion of their performance. Several of the actors were jotting down notes. Hats off to those folks! Other post-mortems are carried out quite promptly but less intellectually in a bar over beers. There is a natural linkage between your post-mortem and the advance planning for your upcoming productions. Below are issues that will shape the short- and long-term future of a living room theater group.

Future Programs and the Audience

What does the audience's response to each play tell you about what plays to perform in the future and how you might stage them? What are you learning about your audience? Is a ratio of two comedies to one serious play a good formula? If you performed on a bare or nearly bare stage, would higher fidelity and more complete sets have helped—and similarly with costumes? You may well want to change the composition of your audience and the group itself. Perhaps you should find and invite folks with a background in theater and a strong interest in literature. Perhaps you should look for new participants whose age range, professional backgrounds, ethnicities, and gender orientations will add to the diversity of the group.

Assessing the Venue

Is this a venue you would like to use again? Was it too small or too large for the size of your audience? Was it sufficiently comfortable? Are there ways to improve your experience with the venue? For example, if the back room of the tavern was too noisy on the Saturday night you performed there, might a Tuesday work for you? Will the manager agree to keep the volume of the music lower? If you discovered that the community room of your local library has its electrical outlets in inconvenient parts of the room, you might make note of this for the next time you plan a performance there.

Your Audience's Scheduling Preferences

On what days of the week and at what hours should performances be scheduled? Are folks too tired for an evening performance on a work day? What about weekend mornings, especially if you are going to provide bagels and coffee?

Guest Actors and Directors

Might you occasionally cast a professional actor or a student majoring in theater or perhaps bring in a guest director? If so, what is your objective in doing this? Do you want to perform a play that requires a particular background that your acting pool does not have? Are members of the group interested in learning more about theater by working with a professional? How might these decisions affect the dynamics of the group? Might some of your group members feel displaced or intimidated by outside actors?

Expenses

There is nothing wrong if members of the group pitch in to help defray the costs of a particular production or the ongoing costs of running a living room theater group. While a living room theater group can be managed on a very low budget, expenses can become significant if you hire folks to build set items and props, rent storage space for your collection of set items and props, perform in venues that charge a fee, rent fancy costumes or theater tech equipment such as stage lighting, pay some of your actors and directors, hire a professional to videotape your performances, or serve more-than-basic refreshments. If you collect donations from audience members, you have very likely forfeited the exemption in copyright law that allows you to perform copyrighted works without paying a royalty. I recommend that you forget this exemption and pay royalties if any money is changing hands.

No money has changed hands within the Goat Hill Theater. Jean Farkas and I have spent modest sums on set items and such, but our expenses have been sufficiently low that we regard them as normal expenses we expect socializing and enjoying a hobby. Probably, we spend about the same on living room theater as we would if we were members of a bowling league. Surely it's cheaper than golf.

Managing Size

Perhaps the most critical and most complex problem is managing the size of the group. This problem naturally divides into (a) managing the size of the audience and (b) managing the size of your acting pool in relation to the number of available parts.

The size of the audience

In a regular theater, it's great to sell out. Possibly you can extend the run. If you can't, you may regret that you did not choose a larger venue or plan for a longer run, but you're still feeling very good. You were never under any obligation to provide a seat to everyone who wanted to attend. But living room theater is a cross between a theatrical performance and a social event such as a party. In living room theater there is a core group who definitely expect invitations. You don't know how many of these folks will be able to attend each performance, but you don't want to lock them out. When you invite people to a performance, you can ask for RSVPs. Then, if you get more than the expected number of "regrets," you can send out another wave of invitations. You can also count on a certain number of last-minute cancellations and even no-shows.

The problem of audience size disappears if you book a venue large enough to accommodate everyone who might possibly want to attend. The drawbacks here are that such venues may be hard to find, you are losing out on the cozy environment of someone's home, and the negative vibe that develops when a small audience is seated in a really large venue. It's better, therefore, if you can manage the size of the entire group so that the number who are likely to attend each performance is a good fit with the capacity of the venue. Keep in mind that public indoor spaces have occupancy limits posted by the fire marshal, and your friendly, helpful librarian may get nervous and troublesome if you overfill the room.

In the Goat Hill version of living room theater, when we invite a new person (and very likely that person's significant other) to an event, we are implicitly inviting them to join the group. Therefore, we can't be overly free about these invitations. On the other hand, people will definitely drop out: They will lose interest, they will move to another city, etc. Perhaps they will start their own living room theater project so that they can invite their own friends.

There will be folks who attend a performance only because their buddy or family member is acting or directing or has written the play. These folks probably won't have any further interest in attending—very possibly they live too far from the neighborhood your group is centered in. So, if you know that you can accommodate these folks for the single performance they are interested in attending, you can invite them knowing they won't likely expand your pool of attendees.

The acting pool
When you have a certain number of people who want to act and who are on your actors list, you will ideally offer them a role every time the group performs. However, you need to match your actors with the roles you have available, and you definitely want to cast people who have recently joined the group. Fortunately, most folks are understanding and will give you a pass if you tell them you won't be able to cast them in your upcoming program. These folks, however, should get high priority for the program after that. We

have not had this happen, but it might be necessary to gracefully move a really difficult person or a truly impossible actor into the periphery.

As noted in Chapter 5, there are ways to increase the total cast size for a performance. Many scripts of 10-minute plays allow for doubled roles, but you can undouble those roles to increase your cast size—though many of these extra roles will be small ones. You can match your acting pool with your available roles by means of cross-gender casting. Another way to increase the cast size is to add another play, or perhaps two plays, to the program. When our Goat Hill folks performed four 10-minute plays, the audience remained fully attentive. We could have done one more play.

Splitting the Group and Creating New Groups

Because, as I have shown, there is a natural limit to the size of a living room theater group, you might become a victim of your own success and face the prospect of dividing the group. In locales where heavy traffic or limited public transportation is a consideration, you might split a group geographically. Or, aesthetic differences might emerge or differences in how people want to manage a living room theater project. Here I am only speculating because we've never approached conditions where anyone thought to split the group.

Offshoot Theater Models

There are ways to do recreational theater that are related but different from the living room model. The ideas described below were scratched because of Covid-19. When Jean Farkas and I were planning a vacation with her brother and sister-in-law, we had thoughts of performing a few 10-minute plays as an evening activity. Also, a group of about six friends were planning to stay at a rustic lodge for several days of hiking and hanging out. Not only could we perform for ourselves as an evening activity, but in my wilder moments, I envisioned proposing to the proprietor that he invite all their guests to the main lodge building to watch us perform. Most important, our living room theater group had—and still has—plans to take our show on the road as a way to contribute to our community. A troupe of three or four actors, with minimal sets and props, can perform at senior centers and before other groups who would welcome some live theater and some socializing afterward.

Chapter 16

Auditions. Submitting Scripts.
Living Room Theater.

If you start writing 10-minute plays, you are likely to think about getting them performed by theater professionals. Most likely, this means a community theater. Community theater is thriving in small and large cities across the United States. Similarly, if you are amazing your friends with your acting talent, you may seek to perform in more professional productions—again, most likely in community theater. Below are thoughts on both of these options, beginning with auditioning. I will not consider how to reach a more professional level as a director or in any other theater function.

Auditioning

Many community theaters hold open auditions for their upcoming performances. You can typically sign up online both to audition and to receive emailed notices of future open auditions. The theater company's call for auditions will generally describe the requirements—age, height, etc., for particular roles. The call for auditions will also indicate when the call-backs will be scheduled, when rehearsals will take place, and the dates of the production. You show up at the appointed time and perform a monologue that you have prepared. These monologues have a specified time limit and should show your range as an actor and/or should target a particular role that you are especially interested in. Actors prepare these monologues very carefully and bring to the audition a photograph and a theater resume listing their training, credits, and special skills such as singing, dancing, acrobatics, and accents. Those selected for call-backs will audition for specific roles in the play.

Some groups holding auditions set minimum requirements. They may keep a waitlist for actors who don't meet the minimum requirements. Seattle's TPS (Theater Puget Sound) conducts "general auditions" in which hundreds of actors audition before casting directors from approximately 50 theater organizations. You are on the audition waitlist unless you meet requirements such as these: Actors Equity membership, a significant role in a mainstage production, or a college acting degree.

The acting workshops that I attend are intended primarily for experienced actors who seek to fine-tune a monologue for an upcoming audition in local community theater and mainstage productions. These are very talented and very amiable individuals, but they experience high levels of anxiety. It is easy to see that aspiring to a professional acting career is to start on a rough road.

Submitting Your Scripts

Although there are a great many 10-minute play festivals (and similar performance opportunities) in the US and abroad, the world is awash in 10-minute plays—many of which are very good. Some festivals choose their playwrights and plays by invitation and sometimes even commission a new play. When there is an open submission process, the competition is fierce. Obscure community theaters will likely receive over 100 scripts for their seven or eight slots. Well-known theater groups and festivals receive hundreds of scripts. In most cases, there is a $10 to $20 dollar submission fee. Very often, playwrights are asked to submit scripts without their name on the title page so that all submissions are anonymous in the evaluation process.

Many playwrights submit their scripts to one community theater after another, hoping to see their plays chosen. Payment for a chosen play is zero or else very modest, but some festivals offer a significant cash prize for the one or two plays that are judged to be the best. In a parallel process, playwrights submit scripts for their one-act, full-length, and musical plays. In large part because community theaters are overwhelmed with scripts, many impose restrictions on what scripts they will consider. A 10-minute play festival may accept submissions only from Michigan residents. Some festivals have oddball requirements—the script must mention "take-out food." Many festivals will look only at plays that have not been previously performed (or not previously performed in the city where the theater is located). The meaning of "previously performed" is defined by the individual theater. Generally it means a full production and an audience that buys tickets. It is very unlikely that any festival's interpretation of "previously performed" would disqualify a script performed in living room theater.

If you submit to community theaters, you should adhere to the more-or-less standard script format. The key elements of this format are these:

- The character's name appears on a separate line above the character's speech in all upper-case letters with an indent of perhaps 2.5 inches.

- Full-sentence stage directions are significantly indented.

- Short, speech-specific stage directions are embedded within the speeches or appear just below the character name.

Recall that throughout this book all the example speeches and all the full scripts are formatted in a more compact manner.

Because community theaters have very low budgets and very often a small acting area, most festivals specify small casts (often a maximum of four or five actors) and specify scripts that can be staged with minimal sets.

How do you learn about submission opportunities? You can certainly search the web for openings posted on the websites of individual theater companies, but there are more efficient methods. The Playwrights Center (www.pwcenter.org) enables members to view well-categorized calls for script submissions, including those for 10-minute plays. An inexpensive subscription service, Play Submissions Helper (www.playsubmissionshelper.com), also provides a comprehensive list of new (and year-round) submission opportunities, including those for 10-minute plays. You can also join the Official Playwrights of Facebook, through which you can learn about submission opportunities and participate in a large community of playwrights who post and answer queries on all aspects of playwriting.

Beyond this is the process of networking. If you participate actively in your local theater community, you will become known to local directors and theater company managers. After a while, they may read your scripts outside of the public open-submission process. Donna Hoke, a highly successful playwright who is very active in the national playwriting community, offers a look at how she skillfully manages her submissions and networking activities: http://blog.donnahoke.com/my-playwrights-submission-diary-or-one-week-of-it-anyway

Living Room Theater

Living room theater short-circuits the established process of auditioning for roles and for getting your scripts chosen for a production. If you want to perform, you will perform. Furthermore, you will perform regularly and before an encouraging audience. We all improve as we gain experience. Similarly, if you want to write a 10-minute play and know that you'll see it performed, that will happen in living room theater. Recognize that your audience will likely be smaller than a community theater audience and that the community theater performances will almost certainly be better. Fundamentally, these are two different enterprises. Living room theater is a highly participatory, recreational activity carried out by and primarily for friends. I would think that community theaters will be pleased that the many playwrights whose 10-minute plays they are unable to stage will find an alternative means to see their work performed.

Whatever living room theater experiences you have, I invite you to share them with me at farkaswords@gmail.com. I also welcome feedback of all kinds on this book. Because it is published via Kindle, updates are possible. Because you've gotten to the end of this book, let me offer you my appreciation for your interest in living room theater.

Appendix A

Summaries of the Plays Used as Examples

This appendix consists of summaries of the 10-minute plays used as examples in this book. Please revisit the Preface for further explanation. In some cases, I've slightly modified stage directions and speeches to better fit the summarized version of the story. An asterisk after the title indicates that the play is part of the Jumpstart Collection.

Baucis and Philemon

From his throne on Mt. Olympus, Zeus announces to the assembled Olympian gods and goddesses that he plans to exterminate humankind. Their impiety and sinfulness are intolerable. But Athena, goddess of wisdom, protests. Surely there must be at least some human beings for whom such a fate would be an injustice. In a partial concession, Zeus decides that he and Hermes will spend three days on Earth disguised as impoverished, hungry travelers to see who, if anyone, will offer hospitality and thereby provide a reason to withhold the terrible punishment that Zeus intends. Athena reminds Zeus that the Olympian gods themselves have a long history of immorality and hints at the future that awaits them:

> **ATHENA**: Zeus, heed me. There may be powers in the Universe greater than our own. We may yet be held to account for our unruly behavior.

After nearly three full days on Earth, Zeus and Hermes have been turned away harshly at every door and have witnessed nothing but sin and impiety. There is time for just one more test of human behavior. They will beg hospitality at the door of a run-down cottage sitting on rocky, barren ground on the outskirts of Tiana, perhaps the most sinful of the places they have visited. Baucis and Philemon, an elderly, frail couple, welcome them graciously and most willingly share what little they have to eat. They are pious as well as generous. In a dramatic moment, their Olympian guests reveal themselves:

> **HERMES:** This meal has done much to revive us. But I would have more stew.
> **PHILEMON:** I am sorry, but there is no more. I carefully spooned out every bit from the bottom of my cooking pot.
> **HERMES:** Look again.

Baucis and Philemon are surprised by Hermes' peremptory tone, but Philemon complies. She immediately sees that the cooking pot is full. Astonished, she shows it to Baucis. Realizing that something supernatural has occurred, they fall to their knees before their guests. Zeus and Hermes wish to reward the couple. But Baucis and Philemon ask only that they may die together so that neither will face life without the other. Zeus grants the wish. Hermes hints at something greater.

The passage of centuries is indicated by the chanting of the Archetypal Mother and the Archetypal Daughter:

> Mothers, daughters,   Daughters, sons.
> Sons take wives   And time flows on.

Now enter a newly married young couple, Sylvia and Damien, who will make their home in Tiana, a town known throughout Greece for its virtue and piety. As we learn, Sylvia was raised elsewhere, and so Damien is taking her to see the holy shrine dedicated to Zeus and Hermes. The shrine consists of two closely placed trees with their branches intertwined. No one knows that one tree was once Baucis and the other Philemon and that they were transformed into eternal lovers.

Damien tells Sylvia of the ritual she will witness later in the year, and this ritual is mysteriously enacted on stage by a priest of the temple. Sylvia and Damien embrace, and the limbs of the tree become supple and mirror the embrace of the young couple. Sylvia, in a visionary moment, recognizes that the trees were once mortals who in their lives greatly pleased Zeus and Hermes.

Then, surprising the audience, the priest re-appears bearing a wooden cross. He is a secret Christian. The priest foresees the downfall of the Olympian deities, but he cannot help but being deeply moved by what he has just witnessed at the shrine:

> **PRIEST:** Our time will come. But for now, I cannot deny the power of the Old Gods.

Bitter Cantaloupe*

Stevie is a young woman who works as a waitress in a small café in Buffalo, New York. A customer, Mr. Harold Damerst, is seated, with menu, at a table. Another customer, Mr. Johnson, takes a seat at an empty table. Mr. Johnson asks for coffee. He will have breakfast when the person he's waiting for arrives.

When Stevie comes to take Mr. Damerst's order, Damerst takes an interest in her name tag. He finds her lively and fun:

> **DAMERST:** "Stevie"? That's not your real name? *(Laughing)*. Did your parents name you Steven?
> **STEVIE:** No, I'm "Stephanie," but I never cared for it. I've been "Stevie" since 7th grade.
> **DAMERST:** Did your folks like the change?
> **STEVIE:** They got used to it.

Stevie cautions Mr. Damerst not to order the cantaloupe, which are green and bitter today. Intrigued, Mr. Damerst inquires further and learns that Stevie, though it could cost her job, regularly steers customers away from menu items on the days they don't look good to her. He is impressed by her integrity—and also by her unwillingness to gossip about the shortcomings of the cook, "Sir, I wanted to do right by you, but I don't think I should be talking about Sam and the restaurant."

Meanwhile Rose, a young mechanical engineer working for Mr. Johnson, has joined her boss at breakfast. Their conversation grows increasingly acrimonious because Rose does not want to switch from her successful microsensor work to Mr. Johnson's top priority, a "personal project" that entails illegal employee surveillance.

Much to Stevie's surprise, Mr. Damerst asks her about moving to Milwaukee to work at Mr. Damerst's company, Great Lakes Casting. Mr. Damerst, who like Stevie came from a poor family, makes quick decisions and has decided that "my company could use a kid like you." He assures Stevie that he has no sexual agenda. Guessing that Stevie has not attended college, he tells her that she will need to start working part-time toward a college degree, but that the company will cover her tuition. Though somewhat wary, Stevie recognizes this extraordinary opportunity and gratefully accepts the offer.

Then comes a rude surprise: Mr. Damerst demands that Stevie help him out during his stay in Buffalo. She will need to quit the restaurant giving only two days' notice. Reluctantly, Stevie agrees, but now Mr. Damerst upbraids Stevie for her lack of integrity—supposedly one of the reasons Damerst wanted to hire her in the first place. He hasn't changed his mind about the job offer, but he does count this as a strike against her. Stevie explains her thinking:

STEVIE: I did not *like* the idea of quitting without proper notice. But I made my decision. Lots of girls just walk out on Sam. He's used to it. The opportunity you're offering, that's huge. It may be my one shot. But, Mr. Damerst, I don't appreciate what you're making me do. And, I'm wondering how come you need me so badly. Thirty minutes ago you didn't know who I was, and now you can't get through the week without me? To tell the truth, asking me to walk out on my job is a strike against *you*. But it's just one strike, so I'm still ready to leave Buffalo.

Damerst is deeply impressed by Stevie's perspicacity and judgment. His demand was a kind of test, and Stevie has more than passed. Meanwhile the dispute between Rose and Mr. Johnson has reached a climax. He fires her for refusing to work on the surveillance project. But Stevie has overheard this conversation and has an idea. With Rose's permission, she proposes that Mr. Damerst make a second hire—a talented mechanical engineer who, like Stevie, possesses good judgment and integrity. Damerst likes the idea. And, when Mr. Johnson begins to order his breakfast, Stevie heartily recommends the cantaloupe.

Black Box (by Bob B. Boiko)

On a table in a small room deep within an enormous government building in the data-driven nation of Datopia sits a black box. Two technicians, Input and Output, will operate the black box. Input and Output can be played by actors of any gender orientation, but for convenience they are here assigned the pronouns "she" and "he."

This is Input's first day on the job. She enters the building and furtively pulls out a phone: "I'm in!" She stows the phone and enters the work room. Output and Input take their seats, and the day's work begins. Input removes 2x6 inch slips of paper from a small basket and pushes them through an opening on her side of the box. Each slip contains a query and the name of the person who has queried. Output removes these slips from an opening on his side and places them in his basket. When Output removes the slips, they contain the black box's very succinct answer to the query.

The black box controls life in Datopia, making decisions large and small that everyone follows. Disguising her true motives, Input explains that she recently came to Datopia from the Humanist Republic, looking for a change in her life. Output expresses scorn toward the Humanist Republic because they constantly argue among themselves. Their decisions are not made objectively by a data-driven black box. Input, on the other hand, is skeptical that all questions regarding human affairs can be definitively answered by the black box and the data it draws upon. Input reads a query by one Kari Shin: "Who should I marry?" Output intent on working efficiently, takes no interest in the black box's answer to this or any other query.

When Output leaves the room to pee, Input quickly writes and submits a crucial query: "Will Datopia attack the Humanist Republic?" The answer is "Yes." Input queries again: "Can the Humanists defeat Datopia?" "No." Another query: "Why can't the Humanists defeat Datopia?" "Datopia is unified. The Humanist Republic is divided." Output returns, is suspicious, but says nothing to Input.

On the following morning, Output arrives early, submits his own queries, and receives appalling answers from the black box:

> **OUTPUT:** Is the new Input a threat?
> **BOX:** Yes.
> **OUTPUT:** What should I do?
> **BOX:** Strangle her with your tie.

Input arrives, work begins, and very soon Input takes a definite interest in one of the queries she is to feed into the black box: "What's worth dying for?" She moves to Output's side of the box in order to read the answer: "Love and your people." Now Output poses his own question to Input, "What is worth killing for?" Input, responding as a Humanist, gives an open-ended answer, "Some might say 'nothing,' others might say, 'many things.' Still others might say 'Only to save yourself or your people.'" Input and Output clearly have conflicting world views:

OUTPUT: Sheesh, you even argue with yourself. But still you're just like the box. Gather possibilities, calculate probabilities. Only you are dim as a candle. The box is the sun.

INPUT: *(Agitated.)* I may be dim, but I'm free. No black box thinks for me.

OUTPUT: And what gives you the right to think your little thoughts?

INPUT: I embody a unique perspective on the world. Everybody, including you, has something to add, something to say that can only be said from where you stand.

OUTPUT: The box knows everything. It sees the universe from your perspective and from everybody else's too. The collective is the corrective.

Output removes his tie. The debate continues:

INPUT: You are free whether you like it or not. Why not just admit that every time you follow the box it is because *you* have decided to?

Suddenly Output steps behind Input, reaches over her, and begins to strangle her with his tie. As Input struggles, Output exclaims:

OUTPUT: I do decide! I decide to trust the box.

When Input slumps over dead, Output, deeply shaken by the murder he has committed, seeks justification from the black box, but he gets none:

OUTPUT: Did I do the right thing?

We hear Output exclaim, in anger and sorrow, the answer he has received from the box:

OUTPUT: What'a ya mean, "No"!

Bowling with Tape

It is 1969, the era of hippies and Haight-Ashbury, illegal marijuana and LSD, and the Vietnam War. In Chicago, Tim Jenkins has just been hired as a library tech at the Federal Textbook Archive—Midwest Center. The Center archives a copy of every edition of every textbook, grade 7 through 12, starting from 1920. Mr. Robert Collins, an older, traditional librarian, supervises this operation. But there is a competing microfiche operation at the Center, supervised by the young, hard-charging Diana Chalmers, who aims to replace the archiving of printed books with microfiche.

Tim, an English graduate student, was happy to find a summer job at the Center. He's been assigned to the third floor, where many thousands of American history textbooks are stored on row after row of heavy-duty shelving, each row longer than a bowling alley. Conscientious and energetic, Tim has been pulling textbooks out of cartons and scurrying off to shelve them—when he is approached by his fellow library techs, the hippie slackers Rex and Ringo:

> **REX:** Hey man. Like, what are you *doing*?
>
> **TIM:** Well, I'm shelving these books.
>
> **RINGO**: You can't do that, man. We *need* these books. Need them here! These are all the books we're likely to get for the next few months.
>
> **TIM:** If you don't have many textbooks, why did Mr. Collins hire me?
>
> **REX:** Mr. Collins needs to use up his budget. That's all you're here for. At the high levels of bureaucracy, spending your whole budget proves that what you are doing is important.

Tim decides that he will regard this strange job as a kind of fellowship. He will work conscientiously all summer improving his Latin. Rex and Ringo spend their time "bowling" rolls of masking tape down the long rows of bookshelves. Tim is startled by other irregularities, all countenanced by Collins. Rex and Ringo routinely leave the building during the 10:00 break. Then they return for the 2:00 break and mix in with the rest of the staff. Because they've skipped out on four hours of work, they don't clock out for their lunch breaks, and hence get rewarded with 45 minutes of extra pay.

In Scene 2, Tim is surprised to encounter a young woman, Julia, who is on their floor conducting research. Julia shows a surprising interest in Rex and Ringo's tape bowling. Covering for his colleagues, Tim explains that tape bowling loosens muscles that get sore from lifting a lot of heavy books and that Rex and Ringo only bowl on their own time.

In Scene 3, Rex and Ringo are distraught. Julia wasn't a researcher. She was a detective, with a hidden camera, working for Chalmers. Rex and Ringo expect to be laid off. They could get drafted or, even worse, have to take jobs where you are expected to work. Diana Chalmers has won her war against Mr. Collins. In meetings in Washington DC, Chalmers successfully made the case that archiving physical books is unnecessary. Also, using Julia's photographs of Rex and Ringo bowling with tape, Chalmers showed that Collins permitted violations of Federal Law:

> **RINGO:** Chalmers got us, man. We just didn't know. She's so damn smart. Just too smart, man. She's gonna run the whole damn Center. And it's gonna be microfiche. We are so fucked! I wanted to work here forever, but now . . .

Tim makes clear that he protected Rex and Ringo by insisting that they only bowled on their own time. So how could the photographs provide the damning evidence?

> **REX:** Tim, you're not a veteran of the Federal bureaucracy like Ringo and me. She didn't get us for not working. She got us for *misusing* rolls of masking tape paid for by Federal dollars. If we'd just brought in a few rolls of our *own* tape, if we'd bowled with a ball or a can of tomato soup, we'd have probably been OK.

Looking to be positive, Tim suggests that perhaps the Center was not the best place for Rex and Ringo to spend their working lives, "Maybe there's something better in store for you." But the hippie slackers are having none of this, "We're fucked!" They exclaim, ending the play.

Close Encounters of the Talkative Kind*

Christopher and Ferdinand, dressed identically, are seated near each other on two plain metal chairs. Some distance away, David is seated in a more comfortable chair. The set is austere and suggests the inside of an alien spaceship. Christopher and Ferdinand are very polite and a bit formal in speech. They ask after the comfort of their guest:

> **CHRISTOPHER:** Is the coffee to your taste?
> **DAVID:** Yes, it's good. Thank you.
> **FERDINAND:** Did you sleep well, David?
> **DAVID:** Yes. Under the circumstances, very well.
> **FERDINAND:** We are pleased.
> **CHRISTOPHER:** Shall we begin our conversation? We'll take a break for your breakfast.

We soon learn that "Christopher" and "Ferdinand" are space aliens who have come to Earth in order to gain more nuanced information about human civilization than can be obtained from Earth's media transmissions. Week-long interviews are being conducted with a limited number of Earthlings, David among them.

David need not worry about being missed by his wife, Andrea, and his children. Christopher and Ferdinand can pull David out of the Earth's time stream for the duration of his visit. David will return to his family a moment after he was taken on board the spaceship. David also learns that "Christopher" and "Ferdinand" (names they've taken for David's convenience) do not have bodies in the Earthly sense and don't use audible language. All this has been contrived just for the purpose of conducting interviews with humans. David wonders why he, instead of some Nobel Prize winner, was chosen. He is told:

CHRISTOPHER: A key reason is that you are very talkative. From extensive observation, we determined that very few Earth citizens are so willing to talk non-stop all day long—to answer any and all questions, to elaborate on each answer, and then begin talking about other topics. Based on our observations, as long as we keep serving you coffee—plus of, course, periodic meals and necessary sleep—you will keep talking and talking and talking.

FERDINAND: With undiminished enthusiasm.

CHRISTOPHER: Not many Nobel Prize winners can or will do this.

FERDINAND: May I ask if this has caused you difficulty in your social relations with other human beings?

> Christopher silently chastises Ferdinand for the unintended insult. Their week together goes very well. In fact, David would like to stay longer:

DAVID: There is *so* much more I could tell you. So *very* much more. Might we add another week? Maybe a month? More than a month? I cannot fully express how much I enjoy talking with the two of you. I will never be able to replicate this experience once I return to Earth.

FERDINAND: Why won't you be able to engage in satisfying conversations when you return?

DAVID: Nothing in my future can be anything like this. Friends listen, but not for very long. Andrea hasn't listened to me on any serious topic for years.

But the aliens cannot extend the duration of David's visit. The topic turns to the "disengagement process." According to the ethical standards of this highly evolved alien civilization, David has the right to choose among three disengagement alternatives: (A) Forgetting the entire experience. (B) Retaining all memories of the experience. (C) A middle-ground option in which David retains only faint memories and recollections in dreams. David opts determinedly for B, but the aliens warn him that B almost always ends badly. Those who choose B can rarely return to a normal life.

They are laughed at. They experience extreme alienation, mental illness, substance abuse, even suicide.

Finally a compromise is reached. Before leaving the spaceship, David will be permitted to write a 10-minute play detailing his experience. What he writes will be permanently imprinted in his brain. It will be much better for David to share his experience as a work of fiction rather than have his claims regarded as the ravings of a madman. After some improvisational consultation with the audience, David agrees—provided that the aliens promise that at the conclusion of any performance of the play, the house lights will flash on and off as a sign from the aliens to the audience that the play is indeed based on true events. Immediately, the house lights *do* flash, proving that David was indeed abducted by aliens.

Echoes of the Professor*

Sandra and Sam, her husband, are meeting with the attorney who is serving as the executor of the estate of Sandra's mother, Julia. The attorney had a long and cordial relationship with both Julia and her husband, Nick, who died at some earlier time. There is, however, a complication in the will. Julia wrote a codicil whose provisions are disappointing and puzzling. The couple must choose between taking possession of a Marc Chagall lithograph or a cremation urn containing human remains that sat on a shelf in the home of Julia and Nick for as long as Sandra can remember.

If the young couple chooses the lithograph, the urn must be thrown in the trash. If the couple chooses the urn, the lithograph will be sold and the proceeds donated to the United Fund. The dialogue makes clear that the urn always seemed to hold meaning for Sandra's parents, that they referred to it as "The Professor," but that they were unwilling or unable to tell Sandra anything more about it. On one occasion, when Sandra pressed her mother for an explanation of The Professor, Julia had replied, "Some things in life you need to learn on your own." Sandra feels that she has no choice but to keep the urn, both to prevent human remains from being consigned to the trash and because the urn held some special meaning for her parents. Sam, with some reluctance, is willing to follow his wife's lead. After the decision has been made, the attorney expresses relief that the urn will be preserved. Six months earlier, Julia had entrusted the urn to him when she was about to enter a nursing facility. The attorney, who lives a solitary life, has developed a certain rapport with The Professor. He says his own good-bye to the urn and suggests that there is a kind of wisdom in Julia's final directive.

In Scene 2, set back in time to 1968, Julia and Nick are engaged and are about to graduate from college. We see them as they finish a springtime stroll through the large and very historic cemetery that adjoins the University. They spot a quaint gingerbread-style structure with a disproportionately large, industrial-style chimney. The door is half-open, and Nick coaxes Julia to step inside with him. They are greeted by an elderly man, John, who has been employed at the crematorium for 35 years. When Julia notices an urn sitting high on a shelf, John tells them that this is The Professor. He was once a faculty member at the University, but because his ashes were not claimed, he has been in the crematorium for over 50 years. John actually knows very little about The Professor, just the few things he was told by his predecessor. Official records were lost. However, through the long years, John has developed an attachment to The Professor, and he's been looking for younger people to whom he can entrust The Professor. The crematorium is about to be torn down and replaced. At that time, John will retire, and his death is not too far off. Looking especially at Julia, John makes an offer:

> **JOHN:** You look like a nice young couple. That's an engagement ring—am I right? . . . Would you like The Professor? *(Chuckles.)* "To have and to hold." If you're students at the University, you have professors. Maybe you'd like to have this one?
>
> John suggests that good things will come if the couple takes ownership of the urn.

In Scene 3, Julia and Nick are strolling through the cemetery on their way back to campus. An elderly man, Professor Horace Smith, in apparitional form, greets them by name. He relates that long ago, as an English professor, he used great literature to help his students think and feel with greater depth. For many years he helped John grow as a person, and now he hopes to do the same for Julia and Nick. Julia and Nick form a spiritual bond with The Professor, as everyone in the play does. Professor Horace Smith is very pleased, "Living with a young couple like you, there will be new shelves for me to watch from and more that I can do. Today feels like the first day of a new semester."

Engagement

"Engagement" employs a *Groundhog-Day*-type plot with multiple endings. It is both an off-beat romantic comedy and a dramatized discussion about the structure of 10-minute plays. The three endings are unified by a single motif: "I'm afraid you're going to have a lot of time on your hands."

On a dimmed stage, Roy, kneeling behind an overturned piece of furniture, takes two shots at departing gunmen. After a pause, Roy steps cautiously to a floor lamp, turns it on, and then turns to Sara. They were lucky. Their wounds are minor. Roy has a disciplined, professional reaction to what has happened:

ROY: You're not bleeding much. Neither am I. These were low-level guys, not professionals. Could have been much worse.

Sara, unsurprisingly, is deeply upset by the attack, but we learn that she did have an idea that Roy is involved in espionage:

SARA: You never made a secret of your gun. But this? I never expected *this*.

Roy and Sara have been on a vacation—or perhaps it was more than just a vacation—in an Eastern European nation. Sara is not pleased that Roy does not want the nation's regular police and medical responders to come to their hotel. Instead, he contacts people from his own agency and tells them to keep the locals away from the scene. In light of these events, Roy reveals more about his professional activities:

> **ROY:** I work for a government agency that keeps a very low profile. I was a field agent. Eastern Europe, the Baltic, other places. Now I'm a desk officer, so I plan and monitor projects. But I'm in the field a lot too . . . Primarily, my group neutralizes people, people who are in a position to do a lot of harm.

Roy explains that because Sara has gotten a close look at Roy's activities, he will almost certainly be permitted to marry her. Sara declares that she too wants to work for Roy's agency. Roy is confident that they will find a good job for her, but—of course—it won't be in the field. Sara must understand, therefore, that she will have a lot of time on her hands. As the people whom Roy summoned arrive to help them, Roy proposes to Sara.

Sandy and Roger, two audience members, discuss the play as they leave the theater. Roger complains that the play's crisis, the attempted assassination, comes much too early. After those first moments, the plot is just their decision to get married: "No surprises, no nothing." The play, therefore, has no dramatic arc. Sandy responds she enjoyed the play anyway. The situation was interesting and "maybe a little play like this doesn't need a dramatic arc or a surprise ending." Sandy asks if the alternative ending she has in mind might satisfy Roger. This is now enacted on stage.

In the second ending, Sara is an agent for the "other side," and the people who come to the hotel after the attempted killings are *Sara's* agents. Roy will be imprisoned. Furthermore, Sara has her own plans for Roy:

> **SARA:** In a manner of speaking you'll be my . . . husband. I'll visit you whenever I can. I hope we can have a really enjoyable relationship. But, I am afraid you're going to have a lot of time on your hands.

Roger tells Sandy that her new ending, in which Roy becomes a kind of sex slave, is creepy and unpleasant. Sandy tries to accommodate Roger with one more version of the story. This time, Roy, fearing he has highly placed enemies inside his own agency, willingly defects. A deal is struck:

SARA: You know we'll never fully trust you. But there's plenty you can do for us, and we'll keep you well out of sight and safe. Yes, you'll have your personal freedom, and we can marry. Of course, I'll be spending a lot of time in the field, so I'm afraid you're going to have a lot of time on your hands.

Sara and Roy kiss. A mood of whimsy has now enveloped the play.

ROGER: I like that ending. Not entirely plausible, but fun. Will you marry me?

SANDY: Not entirely plausible, but . . . why not?

They embrace and kiss.

Final Brushstroke

The set is the studio of Barry Bright, an elderly "psychedelic" painter who was hugely popular back in the 1960s and 70s. Far downstage, an auctioneer enters and begins hawking Barry Bright paintings to unseen couples who are passengers on a cruise ship:

AUCTIONEER: Barry Bright is known as the "van Gogh of Haight-Ashbury." That was the hippie capital of America back in the 1960s. Barry is one of the most important American artists. His paintings are in private collections and museums worldwide. A-list celebrities are big fans. Barry has been a guest on Oprah. *(Beat.)* And now, you have your chance to acquire your own Barry Bright—a *signed* Barry Bright, signed and dated. These are originals, not prints. No two are exactly the same.

In Scene 2, Barry is having a difficult conversation with his daughter, Deborah, and his son-in-law, Carl. Their business is selling Barry Bright paintings. Greedy, unscrupulous, and harsh in their dealings with Barry, they demand that he sign a new batch of paintings that Barry doubts he ever painted. They tell him he has memory loss. They suggest that he add a few final brushstrokes to each painting to settle the issue of authenticity. But when Barry sees a "Barry Bright" portrait of Melania Trump, he becomes certain that these unfamiliar paintings are counterfeits. Barry angrily ejects the couple from his studio. But Carl has a plan for dealing with the ornery old man.

In Scene 3, Carl is talking to Lucy, a hipster whose boyfriend, Rafael, is an avant-garde painter. Lucy is Barry's new studio assistant, but her real job is to employ her feminine charms to make Barry more cooperative. Within limits, Lucy is willing to do this. Deeply cynical, she tells Carl that she has no respect for his business or for Barry:

> **LUCY:** OK. You *know* what I think of all this. It's all phony capitalist bullshit. Whatever talent Barry Bright once had, he sold out 50 years ago. He should sign each painting Barry Bright—with three dollars signs. If you want to exploit his reputation to rip off *other* rich people, the kind who go on cruises, that's fine with me.

In Scenes 4 and 5, we see Lucy and Barry bonding. Barry shows Lucy a group of his paintings that he cherishes and would never sell. They are gritty street scenes of Haight-Ashbury, totally non-commercial in subject matter and style. Lucy also learns that Barry still grieves deeply for his wife and never felt like painting after her death. These days, when he does paint, it's because he's been bullied by Carl and Deborah. Lucy tells Barry that she lives in a world where people have integrity. If Barry is ready to break free of Carl and Deborah, she will help him do it.

In the final scene, set late at night, Lucy has brought Rafael and several friends into the studio. Simeon has a country home where Barry, Lucy, and Rafael can stay while they make decisions about the future. Helena and Tony will carefully move Barry's cherished paintings safely out of the studio. Rafael films a video, to be posted on YouTube, in which Barry apologizes for the uninspired paintings he did under coercion and warns against bogus Barry Brights that may be in circulation. Barry signs an updated will making Lucy and Rafael heirs to his estate and his artistic executors. Feeling free and strong, Barry prepares for his new life. He relishes the thought that someday he might teach Lucy and Rafael's children how to draw.

First-Rate Man

In 1911, Frederick Taylor is giving one of his famous "Boxwood talks" to an audience of corporate chieftains. Taylor's gospel of scientific management has swept the nation. Not only America's businesses, but America's hospitals, schools, government agencies, and more have embraced his ideas about efficiency and performance measurement. The talks are called "Boxwood talks," because Taylor hosts them at his splendid estate, Boxwood, outside of Philadelphia. Two staffers, concerned about the late-arriving executives from Dupont, give us a hint about Taylor's personality:

> **STAFFER 1:** A limo is coming up the drive. It must be Dupont. Shall we ask Mr. Taylor to wait a few minutes for the Dupont men to take their seats?
> **STAFFER 2:** No. Mr. Taylor never delays—not even a single second.

In his talk, a long monologue, Taylor reminds his audience that he no longer accepts paid consulting contracts. He works solely for the benefit of American industry, the American worker, and ultimately humankind. He reviews some of his data-driven innovations, emphasizing that they are humane as well as highly profitable for employers. Workers, he has shown, are more productive with two 15-minute breaks added to their workday. At Bethlehem Steel, he much improved the design of shovels and implemented careful training in shoveling. The company's shovelers are now much more productive, and no man works beyond—or below—his physical ability.

Taylor will have only "first-rate men" in his factories. Every step, every motion, everything lifted, every screw turned, is measured and timed. Those who are less than first rate are retrained but, then, if they don't meet the mark, are fired. Scientific management, he promises, is the pathway to industrial Utopia. A brief flash-forward to the present-day belies Taylor's promise. A 21st century industrialist bullies his Chinese supplier into pushing his workers still harder, "You will *have* to find a way . . . Do we understand each other, Mr. Hong?"

In Scene 2, Taylor, despite his personal regrets, fires Mary Johnson from her job packaging ball bearings, "Mrs. Johnson, I know how conscientious you are. No one could have worked harder during our re-training sessions. But the science is clear. You simply fall below your peers in manual dexterity." Mary, a widow raising two children, needs to keep her job. She is willing to work through her breaks and even into the next shift in order to make her quota. Taylor tells her this is impossible.

We learn that Congressman William B. Williams, Democrat of Pennsylvania, has opened hearings that will address the human cost of scientific management. Williams began his working life as a coal miner. He too knows a thing or two about shoveling and working almost to the breaking point. One of those who will testify for Williams is Mary Johnson, who suffered greatly after she lost her job. Just outside the hearing room (Scene 3), she and Taylor converse briefly and exhibit mutual respect and some affection.

In Scene 4, we see Williams fully expose the evils of scientific management. Under William's fierce questioning, the poorly prepared guru suffers a nervous breakdown. Williams excuses Taylor from further participation in the hearings. Following the hearings, Taylor and his wife undertake extended travel in Europe. Afterward, Taylor scales back his participation in public life. Four years later, at age 59, he dies a deeply disillusioned man. As the play ends, Taylor re-lives his days of glory as the visionary of Boxwood:

An industrial Utopia lies directly in our future. Men will produce more. Greater production means that goods will sell at lower prices, enabling workers to enjoy material possessions they have never been able to afford. Labor strife will cease . . . employees will love their employers. Employers will care for their employees. This is the promise of scientific management.

But other voices are heard:

MARY JOHNSON: I think I should have kept my job!
WILSON: He truly believes he's a latter-day Moses, but his Promised Land runs short on milk and honey.

Flames

An officer of the security police of a brutal totalitarian state watches as Elena, an insurgent, is forcibly seated in an interrogation room. She is married to Anton, another insurgent, who, with Stefan, has been working hard in a secret printing office turning out anti-government leaflets. The security officer speaks a terrible thing, "The printing office—the whole building—will be gone by morning. Just smoldering ashes." Even worse news follows, "There are some things we want you to tell us—and you will. We have snipers ready to kill both of your children when they leave school this afternoon."

Overwhelmed by the prospect of losing her husband and her children, Elena is willing to betray her cause—but only if she gains permission to bring Anton out of the building before it burns. An agreement is reached:

OFFICER: We can do that. If you tell me everything you know, and if you and Anton stay out of further trouble, you can live your lives as good citizens. You and Anton can make up for your disloyalty by contributing to the security of the state. You see, I am a reasonable person.
ELENA: I will not say what I think you are.
OFFICER: Enough! I have my limits.

In Scene 2, Elena joins Anton and Stefan in the printing office. Elena says that Anton must leave because his mother is ill, but Anton responds that Elena can take care of his mother. He and Stefan must keep working. In desperation, Elena takes Anton aside and reveals the truth. Anton angrily rejects Elena's plan to save him. He will die fighting for freedom, working side by side with Stefan, who need not be told about the imminent firebombing of their building. Furthermore, Anton does not trust the security officer's promise that Elena and the children will be left alone after he and Stefan are dead. The best way to protect their children is for Elena to stay with him in the building:

> **ANTON:** With us dead, what will they care about two children? My mother will care for them. In time, Bojana and Daniel will understand why we were not there to raise them.

But Elena cannot agree to this, and Anton pushes her roughly back into the main area of the printing office. Stefan thinks they have been enjoying a moment of intimacy and offers a comically vulgar suggestion as to how Anton and Elena should exit the building to avoid rousing the suspicion of any security police that may be watching. Elena is horrified by Stefan's unsuspecting joviality at this terrible moment. She leaves the building, knowing she will never again see her husband.

In Scene 3, Elena, in the custody of the security police officer, watches in horror as the building collapses in the flames. In a gesture that asserts his control over her, the officer beckons a subordinate to drape a police overcoat over Elena's shoulders. Then, the officer tells Elena that if she does not continue to inform on the insurgents, her children's fate will be much worse than a quick death. Anton and Stefan now appear in apparitional form. Stefan condemns Elena's betrayal of their cause with savage humor. Alluding to the police overcoat, he jokes, "My goodness, you've already gotten a promotion. You're moving up quickly. Anton and I—now we've been so well toasted, we'll never need coats again!"

But Anton offers forgiveness and enduring love. He also offers desperate plans for moving forward. Perhaps she can save herself and the children. But perhaps she will need to kill them and herself. Elena resolves to carry on, "I will be resolute. From soft iron, I am now flame-forged steel. I will find the best way out of this terrible trap I'm in." In the final words of the play, she tells Anton and Stefan that they will be remembered as martyrs, but that her sad deeds of this day are best forgotten.

Gawain and the Green Knight

A narrator provides introductory exposition by reciting some lines of unrhymed verse adapted from the 14th century narrative poem from which the play derives:

Of all who've reigned   As Britain's King,

Arthur ranks first   As well we know.

So by your leave   I will speak a wonder

That befell in his court   To Gawain his knight.

Renownéd for arms   But for goodness still more

So hark to my story   For just a short while . . .

The half-wild, (entirely green) Green Knight bursts into Arthur's Court in Camelot on New Year's Day and issues an extraordinary challenge that young Sir Gawain accepts. Taking up the Green Knight's huge axe, Gawain strikes a mighty blow upon the Green Knight's bare neck. In the poem, Gawain severs the Green Knight's head, the head bounces on the floor, and the Green Knight retrieves his head and restores it to his neck. The Green Knight then announces that to fulfill the terms of the challenge, Gawain has one full year to find the Green Chapel, there to receive the Green Knight's return blow. Shortly afterward, Gawain sets out to find the Green Chapel, fully expecting to be killed by the Green Knight.

In my original version of the play, which runs 17 minutes, Gawain's axe blow does no injury at all to the Green Knight. This is because I could not imagine any way to stage the beheading. In the 10-minute version of the play, the entire challenge episode is related rather than enacted on stage.

It is now two days short of a year since the Green Knight's visit to Camelot. Gawain has endured the harshest conditions on his long, lonely quest in search of the Green Chapel. In accordance with the Code of Chivalry, Gawain paused in his quest only to right grievous wrongs and join in some just and needful battles. But this evening he has accepted the hospitality of Lord and Lady Bercilak, whose castle is deep in rural England.

After Gawain has told of the Green Knight's intrusion at Camelot, Lord Bercilak conveys astonishing news. The Green Chapel is just a short ride away. Gawain, says Lord Bercilak, should rest at the castle for one day and then keep his New Year's appointment with the Green Knight. Furthermore, Lord Bercilak proposes a little game. Lord Bercilak will spend tomorrow hunting. Whatever he brings home is his gift to Gawain. But whatever Gawain may gain while resting at the castle must be given to Lord Bercilak. Reluctantly, Gawain agrees to his host's proposal.

The next morning, Lady Bercilak slips into Gawain's chamber and gives him three kisses, honorably bestowed in the spirit of friendship and hospitality. Then, Lady Bercilak half-undresses and offers him her body (deleted from a kids' version of the play). The virtuous Gawain declines. Now Lady Bercilak offers a magical green sash, which, she says, will protect Gawain from the Green Knight's impending axe blow. She tells Gawain that if he reveals this gift to Lord Bercilak, her husband will take the sash as part of the bargain he made with Gawain. Better, she says, for the gift to remain a secret between themselves. At dinner, Lord Bercilak presents Gawain with a fine buck. Gawain, however, repays Bercilak with three kisses—nothing more—and declines to say whence he obtained them.

The next morning, in the Green Chapel, the Green Knight simply nick's Gawain's neck. Gawain is overjoyed to have survived the axe blow, but soon learns that he has been egregiously tricked. Lord Bercilak and the castle were illusions. Lady Bercilak was, in fact, the enchantress Morgan Le Fay. Because of Gawain's moment of weakness, his failure to follow the Chivalric Code, the Green Knight and Morgan Le Fay can now proceed in their plan to destroy Camelot through the internecine warfare that will follow from Lady Guinevere's infidelity to Arthur with Lancelot. Gawain asks:

> With what twisted justice is the weakness of one man cause to destroy the best thing Humankind has wrought in all of Britain? Arthur has brought laws and peace, good harvests, and learning to a land that reeled from violence and cruelty. Camelot might serve as the seedbed of civilization. Why do you seek to wipe it out?

The Green Knight responds that Human Beings will ultimately build cities and factories that will poison the forests, water, and skies. If possible, this must be stopped. The battle between Humankind and Nature has begun. Gawain's failure will not be recounted in the stories about Arthur and Camelot that will come down through the ages. However, Gawain must live with the knowledge of what he has precipitated, and he must helplessly watch as a civil war among the Knights of the Round Table pulls the cornerstones from the walls of Camelot.

Good-bye from SILVE*

Colonel Ingram addresses a NASA audience at a luncheon that marks the termination of the decades-old research program through which the SILVE space exploration vehicle conducted groundbreaking planetary fly-bys. SILVE, however, has now reached interstellar space, and her transmissions can no longer be received on Earth. Presumably intact, SILVE will continue her space flight for hundreds or thousands of years.

This event also marks the retirement of Skip Wilson, who helped launch SILVE in 1977, became operations manager seven years afterward, and spent a long career monitoring and caring for SILVE every day at work and thinking about her through many of his non-work hours. When she suffered a system failure, Skip's software patch, a significant technical achievement, brought SILVE back online. As SILVE's transmissions grew weaker and unreliable, Skip recognized that the research program to which he'd devoted his life was concluding. During Ingram's monologue, two dancers, representing Skip and SILVE, enact their history together. The dancers will re-appear at brief intervals throughout the play.

Leaving the event, Skip converses with George, a fellow NASA engineer and his only close friend. The conversation sharpens our sense of Skip's loneliness and spiritual desolation. But George and his wife Martha will continue to be good friends and help Skip find some meaning in his life. The conversation ends with dinner plans at George and Martha's house for the next evening.

Scene 2 finds Martha setting the table on their patio but increasingly concerned because Skip, a very punctual individual, is now 30 minutes late. On the split set we see why. Skip is not planning on attending this or any other social event. He is lying on his shabby old chaise lounge swallowing pills and washing them down with beer. The remainder of the play is essentially a telephone conversation between George and Skip, who is increasingly dulled by the sedatives he's swallowed. The dialogue draws an explicit parallel between Skip and the failing spacecraft. It also points to a spiritual union between Skip and the love of his life—all of which is enacted by the dancers:

GEORGE: Skip, you OK?

SKIP: Yes, I am.

GEORGE: What are you doing?

SKIP: I'm taking a look at the solar system. Well, the part I can see from my backyard, which, right at the moment, is just the sun.

The dancers representing SILVE and Skip resume their interpretive dance. They lock arms tightly and spin together as a single entity sailing through space.

SKIP: But, in my mind, I'm looking at the whole damn cosmos. I'm out there riding with SILVE. Keepin' her company, so to speak.

GEORGE: Skip. What are you saying? Would you repeat some of that?

SKIP: You're not copying too well? Well, I guess my transmission signal is failing a bit. I'm drifting pretty far away from things. I've been on an outbound orbit for a good while now, and this evening I've intersected SILVE's flight path. She's just a thousand meters ahead of me. We're off to see the wizard.

> Skip, by threatening suicide with a pistol, makes George promise not to call the EMTs. Skip helps George recognize that Skip may have made the right decision:

SKIP: George, can you imagine me with a fishing rod and a tackle box? . . . You know, SILVE's still hummin' away, still talking to me. She's a sturdy old girl. Most of her solar panels are OK. Electronics good, just reduced voltage. She's too far away from all of you. But I'm right with her, George.

GEORGE: I know you are.

Martha's final wish for Skip closes the play: "I hope it's a long, sweet ride with SILVE."

Graduation

Graduate students Jenn and Betty are chatting at a coffee shop with Christine, their wild-side friend who left graduate school to work as a cocktail waitress. Jenn and Betty face a serious problem. They had planned to do their doctoral research under the direction of Professor Peter Smith. But Peter has had a nervous breakdown and may leave the university. Jenn thinks she understands Peter's problem:

> **JENN:** He's lonely. No one has ever seen him with a woman. Or a man either. Blacksburg is not a place for a single guy. All the faculty have families. Everything is about families and kids—

picnics, Little League. He just works. He's always in the building on weekends.

Christine has a plan to address the problem which, in Scene 2, Jenn sets in motion with a visit to Peter during his office hours. Peter tells Jenn that he is feeling better but very much regrets not finishing his classes last quarter. He suspects that his academic career is ending. Jenn emphasizes that many students regard Peter as a friend as well as a highly respected professor. Then, in answer to Jenn's direct questions, Peter allows that loneliness may indeed be his problem. He has had relationships with women, but he is very shy and has trouble making a connection. Jenn suggests cryptically that Peter's situation with women may soon change.

In Scene 3 the women are getting ready for a nude photoshoot of themselves. Christine is the ringleader and photographer. She wants the poses to be "sexy, but not vulgar—doctoral-student sexy." In Scene 4, Jenn again visits Peter in his office:

PETER: Jenn, I think you said something about a book you wanted me to see?

JENN: Yes, I have it right here. It's not exactly a book. It's a . . . photo album . . .

Peter looks at the photographs and is startled.

PETER: What? What *is* this?

JENN: *(Mischievously.)* You know what this is, Peter. It's *me*. *(Turning the page.)* And this is also me.

Peter tells Jenn to take her book and leave his office, but Jenn reveals her plan. Exercising great discretion, the three women will arrange sexual interludes with Peter. Jenn and Betty want no special favors with their academic work. Jenn notes that this is the reverse of the typical situation in which male professors take advantage of their female graduate students, "For the record, we're the 'aggressors.' And all we want is for you to keep your job and fulfill your regular duties." To allay Peter's objections,

146

Jenn proposes a compromise. Christine will drop out of their plans. Jenn and Betty will "go slow." Each will spend time with Peter and develop a friendship. Perhaps it will evolve into sex, perhaps not. Peter, half-convinced, asks for time to consider.

In Scene 5, the three women are looking back on the past two years. Jenn and Betty have each enjoyed a caring sexual relationship with Peter. Now they are about to complete their doctoral work and leave Blacksburg. However, Jenn, Betty, and Christine are worried about Peter. They have no evidence that he will be able to meet women on his own. Again, Christine has a plan and her special way of expressing it:

> **CHRISTINE:** When it comes to relationships, Peter is like some animal that's been raised in captivity. Never had to hunt for his dinner. So . . . we teach him to hunt, so we can let him out in the wild!

They will coach Peter in the necessary social skills, just as clueless men are tutored on the TV show "Queer Eye." Christine outlines a curriculum in how to approach likely women. She is confident that Peter is ready to earn one more "advanced degree." In Scene 6, Jenn and Betty are attending a gallery opening, as is Peter. They watch as Peter, after an initial stumble, approaches and makes a connection with a woman:

> **PETER:** *(To unseen woman.)* We can certainly see a major shift in Doisneau's aesthetic after the war years. Don't you think so?
> **JENN:** *(To Betty).* Yes. They are talking. Mr. Smooth! Go Peter. I think the *three* of us are on track for graduation.

Horizons*

Sea–Tac Airport Operations Chief Sander Arneson and Duty Officer Shirley Esposito are at a computer monitor intently tracking the unauthorized flight of a Horizon Embraer 175 that was stolen by Jeff Ruston, a Horizon Airlines ground crew employee. We see Jeff Ruston at the controls of the otherwise empty airplane. There is a chair at the periphery of the stage for another actor, who will play (in different voices) the two McChord Air Force Base pilots designated Red Dog 1 and Red Dog 2. Arneson and Esposito will communicate by radio to both Ruston and the military pilots.

Arneson and Esposito are surprised and appalled that an untrained civilian could take control of an airliner. They make plans to deal with this crisis. This includes establishing radio contact with Ruston and finding someone who knows the Embraer 175 cockpit and can talk Ruston down. The military pilots, who are following Ruston, confirm that they can quickly destroy his plane with their Sidewinder missiles.

Jeff Ruston turns out to be a genial, chatty fellow with a quirky sense of humor. He insists on being addressed as "Sky Commander Ruston." He says he's enjoying his view of Mount Rainier and Mount Saint Helens. Jeff admits that he is a screw-up and is deeply disappointed in how his life has turned out. He does not intend to be talked down from the sky.

Jeff's ex-wife, Val, has been found, and Arneson and Esposito agree to patch her into the radio link so she can help convince Jeff to land the plane. But before they can cut her off, Val (an offstage voice) ridicules Jeff and offers a suggestion, "Crash into the Space Needle. If you can find it. Probably that will be one more of your failures." Jeff tells Arneson and Esposito that he likes the idea. He will crash into the Space Needle—"in honor of Val." in fact, Jeff would not harm innocent people, and so he only buzzes the Space Needle and points his plane toward the horizon:

> **JEFF:** Hey, Sampson, whatever your name is. Tell your pilots not to feel guilty if they have to shoot me down.

Because he has made a terrorist threat, Ruston must be regarded as extremely dangerous. Therefore, Arneson reluctantly orders the pilots to shoot down Ruston's plane if they can do so over an open area. Ruston will soon reach open water on his northward flight path.

Jeff announces that he will take a little stroll on the wing. There, in a fantasy episode, he encounters a child:

148

JEFF: Who are you?

CHILD: I'm the child you might still have. From the happy marriage you might still have. I want you to be my father. I want you to land the plane.

Jeff understands that the child is just a voice in his head, but he is still willing to heed the child. Jeff's rational brain, speaking as the child, grasps that because no one has been hurt, his prison sentence might not be so very long. With a good lawyer, there are ways: He was taking the wrong meds. He can wear an ankle bracelet. Jeff continues to heed the apparitional child:

CHILD: Take my hand. Take me back into the cockpit. After that, I'm gonna disappear. But if you do the right things, I promise to come back to you as your real child. Will you kick a soccer ball with me? Will you love me? Will you love my mother? Maybe I'll have a brother and a sister. Will you do your best to make me happen?

JEFF: I promise. I prom-ise. I know what I want now. Let's go back to the cockpit.

Arneson and Esposito devise a plan. They will take the risk of letting Ruston continue northward to land the plane in the relative isolation of Whidbey Naval Air Station. If Jeff diverges in any way from the plan, he will instantly be destroyed. Gratefully, Jeff agrees and prepares for his new life.

Kalalau Trail

We see Laurie peering down attentively at the far end of a perilous spur trail that extends off the challenging, somewhat dangerous Kalalau Trail on the Nā Pali Coast on the island of Kawaii in Hawaii. She picks up rocks and throws them forcefully at some target below. The target is Sam, her boyfriend, whom she has just tried to kill by pushing him off the edge of the spur trail. Sam, however, grabbed some vegetation as he was sliding down the steep slope. He is now trying to claw his way back up to safety. When another backpacker, Bill, appears along the trail, Laurie becomes a panicked female screaming for help. Her continuous screaming drowns out Sam's calls for help. Displaying courage, Bill helps Laurie back to safety on the main trail, where Laurie leads them somewhat away from the spur trail to ensure that Sam won't be heard. Bill comforts Laurie and listens sympathetically to her grim story: Sam wanted them to kiss at the far end of the spur trail and forced Laurie to step out there with him. As she struggled to get back, Sam slipped and fell. Laurie expresses deep guilt and regret. Bill tries to assuage her guilt:

> **BILL:** I understand. I do. It's terrible what happened, but your boyfriend brought it on himself.

Although Bill does not believe that Sam could have survived his fall, he asks another backpacker who has come by to stop at the ranger station two miles down the trail and ask them to send a helicopter.

As Scene 2 begins, Laurie and Bill are talking comfortably as they await the helicopter. Laurie, a Silicon Valley entrepreneur, originally hired Sam as the company's attorney. However, they became lovers—lovers with a turbulent relationship. Suddenly Laurie sees Sam's bloody fingers grasping the edge of the main trail. She distracts Bill, returns to where Sam's fingers can be seen, and—trying not to draw Bill's attention—kicks at and steps on Sam's fingers. But Bill sees what Laurie is doing, and so Laurie must stop. Sam pulls himself back onto the main trail, fiercely accuses Laurie of trying to kill him, and then tells Bill more about Laurie:

> **SAM:** She's a piece of work. Smooth as silk at a business meeting. One hell of a girlfriend, as long as things are going well. But there's just a bit of the psycho in her, the psycho-murderer, it turns out. She had her own idea about how to end our relationship. Quick and clean, no complications.

Bill cannot evade the fact that he saw Laurie try to kick Sam back off the cliff, but Laurie—improvising—explains that her attempt on Sam's life was justified because "He brutalizes me. He does unspeakable things." Bill,

150

weighing the evidence, reluctantly accepts Sam's version of the truth. Now, Laurie needs to convince both men to tell a story that will keep her from going to prison. She proves to be a resourceful woman.

Laurie's plan is to bribe both men to attest that Sam's fall was just an accident. She wins over Bill by offering him a fabulous, presumably erotic year with her. She will also bankroll the independent film Bill has been hoping to make. Sam will get the luxury condo and the Aston Martin. Moreover, he will be celebrated as a hero. Laurie will report that Sam made a heroic effort to save her when she ventured out on the spur trail and slipped. Laurie makes a good case that all the facts align well with her version of events. If Sam contradicts her, his story will be discounted as a consequence of his injuries. Thoroughly dominated by their female companion, the two men join Laurie in waving off the approaching chopper, no longer needed to search for Sam. They will all tell the same story at the ranger station. Says Laurie, "Looks like we're all friends now."

Luke Meets the Revenue Man (by Hopkins/Farkas) *

This play is my adaptation of "Moonshine," written in 1919 by Arthur Hopkins. At curtain, we see a revenue officer shoved rudely through the doorway into the interior of Luke Hazy's crude Appalachian cabin. Luke, wielding his pistol, greets his guest with laconic courtesy and bids him sit. The commotion and gunshots we soon hear offstage are Luke's men fighting over the firearm they took from "Mister Revenue," as Luke will be calling his guest. This is because Luke cannot pronounce the revenue officer's very difficult foreign name "Diego Oscuro." Diego's father, Luke learns, was a New Yorker, a Spanish importer of wine, and one who always paid his revenue taxes.

Although Luke makes it clear that he is about to kill "Mister Revenue," the revenue officer is surprisingly relaxed about this situation. Luke invites his guest to sit and share some moonshine. Luke expresses disappointment that his captive is not Jim Dunn, a revenuer who has put many moonshiners in prison. In fact, Luke keeps a faded, none-too-clear photograph of Dunn on the wall of the cabin. But, Luke observes, "killing one revenue man is about as good as killing another." Mister Revenue informs Luke that Luke is famous for the number of Crosby men he has killed in a long-running feud between the families. But Luke, who can just barely read, has not seen any newspapers and had no idea that he's famous. Luke also expresses respect and admiration for the entire Crosby clan, "They don't make 'em any braver—they'd be first-rate folks if they wuzn't Crosbys."

Now Luke turns to the business at hand, shooting his guest. But, much to Luke's surprise, Mister Revenue, bored and disgusted with life, is eager to die. In fact, as he explains, he got himself captured specifically because he knew that Luke and his men kill any revenue officers they get hold of. Mister Revenue cannot kill himself because he fears Divine punishment, but he has made several—gallingly unsuccessful—attempts to provoke others into killing him, including insulting and humiliating the local bad guy Two Gun Jake.

Luke tests the veracity of this story by pretending to leave his pistol unattended on the table while stepping outside briefly to investigate a sound. In fact, Luke had surreptitiously removed the cartridges. But Mister Revenue showed no interest in grabbing the pistol. Luke, now alert to the possibility of Divine punishment, and thinking that Mister Revenue must be protected by some kind of supernatural "charm," decides that he will not kill his guest, "I ain't got no call to do your killin' fer you if ye ain't sport enough to do it yerself." Instead, he will lend Mister Revenue his horse so that he can get back to civilization.

Mr. Revenue—"Diego Oscuro"—invites Luke to visit him any time in New York City. He writes his name and address on the back of Luke's crude photograph of Jim Dunn because it's the only piece of paper in the cabin. Luke tells Mister Revenue that he's not likely to get to New York, and he doesn't bother reading what Mister Revenue had written. The two men share a cordial and respectful farewell, and Mister Revenue leaves the cabin.

In a few moments, Luke hears loud laughter echoing its way up the mountainside, followed by "Lu-uke, loook aht the pict-tuure!" Luke turns the picture around a few times and then slowly and painfully reads what was written on the back. Luke discovers that his guest was the much-feared Jim Dunn and that Luke was tricked into releasing him. The audience, but not Luke, will presumably recognize that the name "Diego Oscuro" is a playful Spanish-language pun on "James Dunn." But Luke, as we have seen, is a generous soul who takes a broad-minded look at life. Hence he good-naturedly appreciates Jim's clever escape and contemplates the possibility of some future encounter.

Milton Amid His Enemies

It is 1660. Charles II has assumed the throne of England, ending 20 years of turmoil and civil war. During this time, Oliver Cromwell and his Roundheads, with their unbending Puritan beliefs, defeated the Royalist forces in bloody battles, executed the foolish, Catholic-leaning Charles I, and ruled England harshly and tyrannically. But the second Charles is a generous spirit who loves wine, women, the theater, and poetry. He is surprisingly forbearing in seeking vengeance on those who drove him into exile and would have killed him if they could.

In Scene I, set in the English countryside, a family of fierce Royalist partisans cannot rest easy with this situation. Young Tom sees an opportunity to assassinate John Milton, the poet and Puritan polemicist, who is now living in fear and seclusion in London with his two grown daughters. Tom's cousin, Arthur, is a soldier in the King's Guard charged with keeping watch on Milton. If Tom can meet up with Arthur, he will be able to determine the house in which Milton is lodged.

In Scene 3, Charles is holding court and dealing impatiently with endless issues of governance. A series of courtesans appear at the periphery of the stage inviting Charles to sensual delights, and so Charles seeks to delegate his responsibilities to his advisors. However, when the issue of John Milton is broached, Charles takes an active interest. Charles scorns

Milton as a rebel and regicide, but respects him for his enormous learning and brilliant poetry. Literary men at court have spoken in favor of Milton, and Charles decides that Milton will be left alone and protected from those who would do him harm.

> **CHARLES:** It shall never be said in England that the monarch Charles II caused the death of one of England's greatest poets. I have heard he has partially written a Christian epic that tells of the fall of our First Parents. Those who have seen it say that nothing written in English, or perhaps any other language, scales such heights.
>
> **LORD DUMFRIES:** Be careful, Sire. He is fully capable of defaming you and your father with half-hidden meanings in his poetry.
>
> A courtesan beckons.
>
> **CHARLES:** That may be. But I will let History judge me. Milton will be kept safe . . . I am done with Court for today. I charge thee to arrange our affairs so that I have no more than two hours of these decisions tomorrow—and every other day. Life is short and I mean to enjoy it fully.

Charles has one more reason for sparing Milton. Whimsically, he regards this Puritan poet as a kindred spirit:

> **CHARLES:** I have heard that his Paradise, with its contours and "foliage," is unmistakably the crotch of a woman. His Eve is a temptress indeed. (Gesturing to waiting courtesan.) Like you, My Dear . . . This poet is a Puritan when he is awake—but perhaps not in his dreams. I think that in his heart this pious, pious man is a sinner like me! (Laughs.) I think I love him for his hypocrisy.

In Scene 4, Arthur refuses to help Tom assassinate Milton and, indeed, he demands that Tom leave off his plot and return home. Unlike Tom, Arthur is tired of strife and killing, and if his monarch is willing to let Milton live, Arthur will enforce the law and maintain the peace.

In the final scene, Milton and his daughters are terrified when Arthur demands entry to their lodging. The daughters fear their father will be arrested and taken away. But, no. Arthur has come to ask what provisions Milton and his daughters need. Because there are men who would harm them, they are to stay inside for their safety. Milton, however, cannot believe the King would extend mercy to him. He condemns Charles as a "monarch of villainy and vice."

Arthur, the most forward-thinking person in the play, challenges Milton's outlook. Arthur respects Charles regardless of his personal immorality, and he looks forward to a more enlightened age that is more secular and more tolerant. One of Milton's daughters, Deborah, surprises her father and sister by aligning herself with Arthur. More surprising, she reveals that she has a lover, and he is no Puritan. Milton exits in shock and dismay. Deborah's sister condemns Deborah for burdening their father with such news. Deborah tells her sister—and the audience—that Milton's formidable intellect will expand to encompass what she has just told him along with all the changes he is seeing take place around him. Indeed, these changes, traumatic though they are, may enrich the poetry that lies in his future.

Mordecai in the Time of Plague

Sometime during the Middle Ages, Count Leonid, ruler of the principality of Jurn, now part of Romania, courteously receives Mordecai, an aged Jew and a physician. Mordecai and his daughter, Rebecca, are most welcome to reside in Jurn and have been given quarters in Leonid's castle. Leonid asks why Mordecai left the service of Baron Mihal of Oridea and, with Rebecca, crossed the snow-covered mountains into Jurn. Leonid knows that the deadly plague spreading through the region had infected Oridea. Jewish physicians are known to have the best treatment for the plague. So why, asks Leonid, would Baron Mihal take any step that would cause Mordecai to leave him?

Mordecai explains that when Mihal's son contracted the plague, Mihal, overcome with fear, sought to give Mordecai the strongest possible motivation to save his son: Much gold if the boy survived, death if he did not. Mordecai had answered Mihal, "Your threat is pointless. I exercise the same care with every patient—prince or stable boy." The young prince recovered, but Mordecai, no longer willing to serve Mihal, immediately found a way to slip out of Oridea with his daughter.

Knowing that the plague will soon reach Jurn, Count Leonid is eager for Mordecai's help. But Leonid warns Mordecai that he will not be welcomed by the physicians in Jurn. Mordecai responds that he has dealt with this situation, "When a patient recovers and I am thanked, I explain that it was the patient's Gentile physician and I—our treatments working together— that effected the cure." He continues, "If a Gentile physician wishes to learn what I know, I will share." A more serious problem, says Leonid, is the Church. "If those you have treated recover, certain priests will proclaim loudly that you brought the Devil to our aid. Mordecai responds that this is a problem that Leonid himself must deal with.

Called before Count Leonid, Archdeacon Dorin has no objection to a Jewish physician practicing in Jurn. "Indeed, perhaps on some occasion, perhaps here in the seclusion of the castle, I will be able to meet Doctor Mordecai and converse with him." But Dorin is afraid of Father Grigori. Dorin explains, "Back when there were Jews in Jurn, Grigori's grandfather had trouble with them, and the family lost its land. Father Grigori has long spoken out against Jews. His hatred cannot be blunted, and I have no authority over him."

Count Leonid calls Father Grigori to the castle, but Father Grigori is adamant, "I do not know how you persuaded Dorin, but you will not persuade me. And you cannot stop me. You may govern Jurn, but you don't have jurisdiction over Church affairs. If Mordecai is successful in working his cures, I will attribute his success to Satan. I will say, 'Is it not better to die of plague and rise to Heaven than turn to Satan to keep one's life?'"

Leonid, in an ominous tone, points to the long-standing and close relationship between Father Grigori and Marius, who originally sang in the boys' choir of Father Grigori's church. The role of Head Usher normally rotates among deserving parishioners, but Marius has served as Head Usher for years. "Marius always seems to be by your side. Why is that?" Furious at Leonid's suggestion, Father Grigori responds that there is no evidence whatsoever of any inappropriate behavior between them. But Leonid has a bluff to play: Mordecai, says Leonid, can easily prepare a lethal powder that some parishioner can surreptitiously sprinkle on Marius's garments as he carries out his duties as Head Usher. Leonid will arrange this unless Grigori agrees to accept Mordecai. Believing that Mordecai is capable of such iniquity, Father Grigori is furious, "You are worse than the Jew." Mordecai enters and assuages Grigori's fury, in part by declining to defend the Jews that Grigori believes cheated his grandfather:

> **GRIGORI:** The Jews who loaned money to my grandfather were dishonest schemers. Evil men.
> **MORDECAI:** This may be. I will not defend people I do not know.

Leonid offers to restore the lost property. With no other alternative, Father Grigori agrees to "stony silence" regarding Mordecai. Count Leonid is satisfied, "That will be enough. We will prepare for the plague."

Nationalities

Joe, who has just finished accounting school, is joking around with his baseball pal Dominic on a New York City street in the depths of the Great Depression. Turning serious, Dominic suggests that Joe talk with his uncle Sammy D about a job. Dominic lets Joe know that Sammy D "has several little businesses. You know. Not always legal, but not that much worse than what big corporations do." Joe says that he always figured on working for a Jewish business, but Dominic emphasizes that Italians are

157

comfortable with Jews. In Scene 2, we get a peek at Sammy D's businesses and Joe's job:

> **JOE:** Mr. D, still no payment from Guardino.
> **SAMMY:** Joe, don't worry about it.
> **JOE:** They're way overdue. I sent them two letters already.
> **SAMMY:** Joe, I said don't worry about it. Just clear the books on that account. Mark it "All debts paid."

In Scene 3, we learn that Joe is doing well at his job and has earned Sammy D's respect. Dominic tells Joe that he has "big stuff going on that everyone is going to hear about." In Scene 4, we learn that Sammy D has big trouble, trouble that he hopes Joe will help with. One of Sammy's people has deeply offended Marco Luchese, the volatile head of a larger Mafia family. Sammy, desperate to appease Marco, is willing to give up a lucrative numbers business. Sammy will also give Marco his deed to a large family plot in the new and prestigious Greenwood Cemetery in Brooklyn. "That's offering Marco a lot. That's respectability." To reduce the level of animosity, Sammy would like Joe, who is only an employee, to handle the face-to-face negotiation with Marco. Even so, Joe will still be at some personal risk. Sammy tells Joe he must try very hard not to give Marco the "warehouse on 12th Street," but to do so if that is the only way to prevent a war between the families. The meeting has been scheduled for the eve of Yom Kippur, the holiest religious holiday in Judaism, but Sammy assures Joe that the meeting will conclude in time for Joe to get to shul by sundown.

After Yom Kippur, Joe finds Sammy despondent and can't understand why Sammy is so deeply upset that Marco insisted on getting the warehouse on 12th Street. "I know that street end to end. Not one special building on that street." Sammy reveals that the warehouse was an agreed-upon code name for Dominic's life. It was Dominic who had offended Marco.

> **JOE:** Where's Dominic now?

SAMMY: No one knows just where he is. We don't want to know. He's cut off now. And if you try to help Dom, Marco will likely find out. Don't do it, Joe. Don't join Dominic's brotherhood of young fools.

But Joe is a member of another brotherhood, that of young men and women. He tells Sammy that Dominic has been "seeing" Theresa Luchese, Marco's daughter, and that they are secretly engaged. Joe also tells Sammy that Dominic's offense to Marco was a stupid attempt to impress his prospective father-in-law. Joe draws a new picture, "If Marco has Dominic killed, he'll wish he had the plot in Green Wood Cemetery so he could dig himself a hole, jump in, and escape from his daughter." Joe also tells Sammy that the brotherhood of young people has powerful allies in the mothers and the aunts and the grandmothers who care more about weddings and children than about business and family honor. Sammy realizes that he will now be able to negotiate an entirely new deal with Marco and that the two families are now joining, "My God, one day Dominic could get buried in Green Wood with Theresa." Sammy suggests that Joe may have done some good praying in his shul on Yom Kippur.

Nordstrom Shopping Zombies*

A zombie-like Henry Peck is being dragged through Nordstrom, the upscale department store, by his wife, Priscilla, for a much-disliked shopping trip. Meanwhile, Gerri, a sales trainer, is conducting a training session in the men's clothing department. Two sales associates, Darlene and Suzie, sit attentively.

GERRI: We will begin the afternoon with a discussion of the Male Shopping Zombie—or MSZ. Keep in mind that MSZs have a higher disposable income than the Bargain Hunter, the Hipster, the Dandy, and most other categories of male shoppers. And, as I will explain, they are often big spenders . . . MSZs are easily recognizable.

She points to Henry.

GERRI: Notice the slouch, the glazed eyes, the unkempt hair. The MSZ has been married to the same woman for decades, and no longer pays even the slightest attention to his appearance. Often you will hear the MSZ whining. Like this:

HENRY: *(Addressing Priscilla.)* I have a stomach ache. We need to go home.

GERRI: Or . . .

HENRY: *(Again addressing Priscilla.)* I think I'm having a heart attack. You'd better call 911.

GERRI: Ignore this stuff. That "heart attack" is almost always fake and, anyway, we're here to sell. You will notice that the wife always ignores this whining . . . You will also hear this:

HENRY: Why can't you just order some pants on Amazon?

PRISCILLA: You're between sizes. Also, your butt is too large [or too small]. We need the tailor to make alterations.

HENRY: *(In despair.)* The tailor?!

Gerri asks her trainees how they might approach the MSZ and his wife in order to make a sale. Suzie demonstrates her approach—with little success:

SUZIE: Hello, Sir. I'm Suzie. Great day today! Can I help you?

HENRY: *(Miserable.)* You can't.

SUZIE: Well, what brings you to the Men's Department today?

Henry just points to his wife and pays no further attention to Suzie, who returns to her seat.

Now Darlene shows off what she can do. She approaches Henry with gentle solicitude, finds him a comfortable chair, and assures him that she will help his wife pick out his new clothing very quickly. Gratefully, Henry sinks into the chair. Darlene continues to show great insight into the psychology of the MSZ. Meanwhile, Priscilla continues to address her husband harshly. The training class turns to the topic of "fetish objects." Henry, for example, has been wearing the same old belt, hand-made from elk hide, every day for the past 27 years and intends to die in it. Priscilla, of course, detests the belt. Suzie tries to guide Priscilla and Henry to a rack of fashionable Nordstrom belts, but Henry bares his teeth and growls.

> **GERRI:** Do not call Security in these situations. Unless cornered, the MSZ is not actually dangerous.

Darlene approaches Henry, tells him how much she likes his belt, and tells him that she can quickly pick out some flannel shirts that will go well with it. Henry, ignoring his wife, follows Darlene offstage, and Gerri turns her attention to her class. Soon, Henry and Darlene re-enter, with Henry showing heretofore unseen energy and zest for life:

> **HENRY:** Darlene, do you like working here?
> **DARLENE:** Not really.
> **HENRY:** You do know that us Male Shopping Zombies generally have high disposable incomes?
> **DARLENE:** Yes, I learned that in training.
> **HENRY:** Well, I have a *very* high income.

Gerri, Suzie, and Priscilla are amazed when Henry invites Darlene to leave with him. As they exit, Priscilla shouts that she will sue Nordstrom's. Gerri responds, "It's your own damn fault." Henry concurs:

> That's right, Gerri. Definitely nothing to blame on Nordstrom's!

Professor Jim the Janitor

In a split-set arrangement, we see both Dan Resnik's faculty office at a large university and the Resnik family kitchen. Jim is the quirky, rough-edged, and potentially violent janitor in Dan's building. In those scenes in which Dan encounters Jim mopping the corridor, they stand downstage of both Dan's office and the kitchen. Also, the characters playing Jim, Dan, and Ruth (Dan's wife) withdraw to the periphery of the stage, rather than exit, between the play's twelve brief scenes.

At curtain, an elderly Dan Resnik appears briefly to frame the story that is to follow. Resnik says he'd like to know what happened to Jim. He then picks up a briefcase, changes his demeanor, and becomes Assistant Professor Dan Resnik.

Opening his office door for an evening of work, Dan discovers Jim sitting on Dan's chair with his legs up on Dan's desk. Moreover, Jim is wearing a "professorial" sport jacket. He likes to spend his break time imagining he is enjoying the easy life of a professor. Dan strikes up a friendship with Jim. Each man addresses the other as "professor." Jim is amazed and jealous when Dan explains such perks of faculty life as tenure. Jim never stops causing trouble for himself. He is banned from the city bus system for threatening a "business shit" who took a window seat on a crowded bus and thought he'd keep the aisle seat free by putting his attaché case on it. One evening, Dan sees Jim wearing an extremely offensive T-shirt. It appears to show a woman being raped:

> **DAN:** Hi Professor Jim. *(Looks closely.)* What's on that T-shirt? That's horrible. You can't wear that. Where did you get it? Who sells a thing like that?
> **JIM:** I made it myself. I'm something of an artist. I silkscreen my own T-shirts. Would you like one?
> **DAN:** Thanks, but definitely no.
> **JIM:** I've been written up. I may get fired. I'm the best janitor on campus. I work twice as hard as a lot of the dufus janitors they have here. Look at these arms. *(Flexes his biceps.)* And the Union won't support me. They're supposed to be on my side.

Soon afterward, Jim, who is very protective of his building, interrupts a computer thief. While Jim is holding him by force for the police, he's beaten up by the thief's accomplices.

Ruth takes a dim view of her husband's friendship with Jim:

RUTH: I'm tired of your stories about Jim the Janitor. He's not Robin Hood. He's no working man's hero. He's a misfit. He's probably dangerous. And you're going to get in trouble befriending him.

Dan responds that Jim is misunderstood and unappreciated. If any woman in the building were actually being raped, Jim, whatever the risk, would stop it. Jim tells Dan that he's probably going to be fired. If so, Jim will bring his crossbow to work and put an arrow right through his supervisor's right kneecap. Now Ruth is really angry with Dan because Dan refuses to report Jim. Dan is reasonably confident that Jim won't actually commit this threatened act of violence. Also, notes Dan, Jim was specific about what he'd do with his crossbow:

DAN: If he'd said "right through his heart," I'd report him. I'd have to. But he just said "kneecap," and he's in enough trouble already.
RUTH: *(Angry.)* That's right. Who cares about a little ol' kneecap, a little ol' knee? Especially when it's not *your* kneecap. What you're doing—not doing—is irresponsible, probably criminal.

Days later, Dan is at home with Ruth when he's called to campus by Campus Security. Dan and Ruth fear the worst. However, Dan learns that the emergency is something very different. The large air conditioner that cools their high-performance computing lab has failed. Dan now needs to shut down these complex machines. Moreover, Jim saved the lab by jerry-rigging multiple electric fans to draw out the heat. To his astonishment and dismay, Dan learns that Campus Security failed to respond to Jim's emergency phone call but that Jim has been fired for removing the fans from faculty offices. The Security Chief denies that the computers were ever in any danger. Dan is disgusted by this dishonesty.

Soon afterward, Dan finds Jim's "professorial" sport jacket on his desk—a farewell gift. Deeply moved, Dan tells Ruth that, in homage to Jim, he is going to wear the jacket to class. Dan is unconcerned that the jacket will be far too small for him. Ruth remains unsympathetic:

163

RUTH: OK. OK. Put on his damn sport jacket and teach a class. I really don't care. Thank God, he didn't leave you with his obscene T-shirt. You'd wear *that* to class—then what?

But Jim, appearing as an apparition, has some choice words for Ruth.

Regional Distributor

It is 1936, one of the worst years of the Great Depression, Al Farkas is a young, energetic traveling salesman. He represents the Colony Furniture Company and sells their inexpensive bedroom sets to furniture stores all across New York State. Many of these stores are struggling to stay in business. Today Al is paying a sales call on Abe Goldberg, who owns a small, shabby furniture store in Utica, a town in rural Oneida County. Al likes Abe, but is irritated by Abe's sloppy, inept way of doing business. Throughout the play, the physical Al Farkas is accompanied by a doppelgänger (an apparitional double of himself) whose sardonic comments about Abe Goldberg and his poorly managed furniture store function as a long series of soliloquies. The actor who plays Al pivots his body to become the doppelgänger and then pivots back to pick up Al's part of the dialogue:

AL: Hiya, Abe.
ABE: Come on in, Al.
DOPPELGÄNGER: Gee, this place looks awful. I wonder if Abe will hang on much longer.
ABE: Well, take a load off.
DOPPELGÄNGER: My God, he sits there with his lit cigar in a chair he's trying to sell to customers.
AL: Good to see you. Ya sellin' any furniture these days? *(Chuckles.)* No one else is.

Al notices a Frigidaire in a corner of the store. Refrigerators are a new and expensive consumer appliance that are just starting to replace the icebox. Al cannot imagine why Abe would have a Frigidaire in his store. Abe relates that a Frigidaire executive, Mr. Walter Atkinson, had visited his store. The Frigidaire Company needs to have a regional distributor in each county, and Atkinson had determined that Abe owned the only store in Oneida County selling consumer durables.

Mr. Atkinson, appearing in a flashback, explains that, as Regional Distributor, Abe will receive a commission on every Frigidaire that is sold in Oneida County. All Abe needs to do is purchase one unit for his store. Abe has no interest in selling refrigerators and is not going to spend the 35 dollars. Eager to finish up this piece of business, Mr. Atkinson offers Abe a deal. Frigidaire will front the 35 dollars and the shipping cost. Abe will pay for the refrigerator out of his commissions. Abe agrees only after Mr. Atkinson helps Abe understand that there is no way he can lose on this deal.

Al visits Abe a year later. Abe is barely selling any furniture. However, a newer model refrigerator is in the store, and Abe has this one plugged in. People are beginning to visit his store to buy refrigerators. Furthermore, as Regional Distributor, Abe gets a cut on every Frigidaire sold in the entire county. He's starting to make money.

It is 1947. Al, back from World War II, is getting off the road. He now has a wife and a new baby. Times are good, and Al can sell lots of furniture in Northern Jersey and New York City and come home every evening. He is paying one final visit to Abe—but it is not a sales call. The store, now managed by Abe's younger son, is a thriving appliance store:

> **AL:** Well, this place is hoppin'.
> **ABE:** It is. We got customers in here all day. But a lot of our money comes from new construction. People order their refrigerators through the builder when they're planning out the kitchen. We never even see those folks. We're just the "regional distributor." . . . I was lucky. Mr. Atkinson just *walked* in here. But I *did* know how to seize an opportunity.
> **DOPPELGÄNGER:** *(Looking at Abe.)* I think Opportunity seized *you.*
> **AL:** I guess you did, Abe.

DOPPELGÄNGER: *(Addressing Al.)* One of the worst businessmen you ever sold to! Sometimes lucky is better than smart.

Al and Abe discuss the enduring sadness in Abe's life. Abe and his wife lost their older son in the war, just a few weeks before Japan surrendered. The men say a fond farewell.

Return from the Dead

Late at night in a hospital visitors' room, Sophie approaches Joel, who is deep in grief as his father's life is ending. Sophie tells Joel how much she is comforted by happy memories of her life with her own deceased father. Then Sophie's statement about her father becomes extreme and cryptic:

SOPHIE: I have more than memories, more than photos, more than videos. I talk to my dad regularly. We talk about all the good times we had as a family . . . I'm speaking of something very unusual. A new technology. Are you interested in technology?

Sophie opens her laptop and initiates a conversation with an avatar of her deceased father that persuasively carries out detailed and realistic dialogue. Sophie reminisces with her father and introduces her father to Joel, "her new friend." When Sophie asks her father a question about the impeachment of Donald Trump, her father responds that he doesn't like Donald Trump as a president but has no knowledge of Trump's impeachment. Sophie now explains that, through a remarkable new technology, a technology kept hidden from the public, her father's memories, knowledge of the world, and personality have been recorded and preserved and can be accessed in interactive dialogues. Joel is incredulous and even hostile, but he's also drawn to the idea of maintaining such close contact—even though it is ultimately unreal—with his own father. Sophie emphasizes that Joel must decide quickly—before his father dies. She takes Joel to the hospital's cafeteria to meet her colleague "R."

In Scene 2, R presents the business side of what Sophie is offering. Sophie approached Joel in part because he is wealthy. If Joel agrees to the preservation of his father's memories and then finds that he greatly values his ability to engage in interactive dialogues with his father, he will need to pay $100,000 in a crypto currency. Explains R, "The money keeps the system running and funds enhancements and further research. The project would be shut down if it went public." With Sophie urging Joel to experience the same solace and companionship that she feels, Joel agrees to take R to his father's bedside so that R can record his father's memories and personality before he dies.

In Scene 3, Joel, Sophie, and R are conversing some months after the death of Joel's father. R reveals that Joel must now pay a substantial monthly "subscription fee" if he wants continued access to his father, "Remember, everything is on our server. You stop paying, and your father will disappear, perhaps irrevocably." Joel is disgusted by R's dishonesty, but admits he loves "visiting" his dad. Sophie allows that these experiences are a kind of addiction. But Sophie thinks that her father's avatar will always have an important place in her life—and perhaps beyond her life:

> **SOPHIE:** Eventually, I'll let my father's memory and his avatar recede into the background. I know I have to re-start my life. People need real lives, real relationships. I do. But his avatar will always have a place in my life. I'll be able to share my dad with the *children* I hope to have some day. And perhaps their children will know my dad.

Joel realizes that while Sophie may well be sincere when she attests to the value of this extraordinary technology, she has had a hidden monetary agenda from the moment she approached him. R now astonishes Joel with one final piece of dishonesty. As a further requirement, Joel must agree to recruit new "research partners"—one a quarter, four a year—just as Sophie has done with Joel. Joel reacts with shock and still greater anger. R apologizes once more and urges the larger social value of this technology:

R: We will all be able to converse with living people—political leaders, celebrities, and sages. You won't need to listen to speeches or interviews. You will be able to ask your own questions, learn directly from those who matter most in our world.

R says that Joel and Sophie are a natural recruiting team and, he suggests, may develop a romantic relationship. Joel is silent, overwhelmed by everything that has happened during this conversation. R leaves. Sophie places her hands on Joel's and speaks tenderly, "We share the grief of losing parents, we share the knowledge of something very new and powerful. I think we can share still more."

Solo to Tandem

Franz is enjoying a sunny day paddling down a calm river with the members of the canoe club he has just joined. Amy, another solo paddler, comes up alongside Franz and compliments him on his paddling style and on his physique, "You must be getting a lot of power from those broad shoulders." Franz notices that club members exhibit an unusual interest in romance and sex. Betty and Bob appear paddling their solo boats alongside each other. They are talking about their recent break-ups and seem to be getting along real well. Gary and Garth, also paddling solo, and swigging from beer cans, clearly see the Club as their ticket to friendly females. Ida has intriguing thoughts about the curves on Franz's expensive and finely sculpted canoe, "I just love that tumblehome with those *soft* chines." When Trip Leader Eric calls for everyone to beach their boats for the lunch break at a riverside park, Franz gets some answers from Eric:

ERIC: Married? Monogamously married? Well, I can see why you feel out-of-place. You're perfectly welcome to paddle with us. But you'll have to understand that we have a very definite agenda besides paddling canoes.

Franz is puzzled. Eric explains that Franz missed the hint in the Club's meet-up description:

ERIC: We're the "Solo to Tandem Canoe Club." Get it? When you join, you're going through life solo. But soon, you're tandem!

When it's time to get back into the boats, Pam appears hurriedly zipping up her PFD while carrying her T-shirt and bra. Rhonda, a well-dressed woman who was walking her dog in the park, is persuaded to join Ralph in his tandem boat. Fluffy will sit in Rhonda's lap. Now Franz learns more about the Club's appeal from Suzie:

SUZIE: There's something so invigorating about paddling. Maybe it's the special breeze off the water. Maybe it's the combined sexual energy of all the other "hungry hearts" paddling together. I am never so . . . romantic . . . as when I'm on one these trips. And the moonlight paddles. They are amazing.

Amy checks in with Franz and hints at the evening's festivities:

AMY: I'm gonna save you a spot at my table. But I don't expect you to be flirting with any other woman . . . *(Adding speed to her stroke.)* Catch you later. And I do mean "catch."

When the group reaches the take-out, Franz tells Eric that he's surprised that, after 24 miles on the river, everyone is gearing up for a night of fun. He expects to have dinner with his wife and toddle off to bed. Replies Eric, "Married life will do to that to you."

Scene 2 shows us Franz and Tessa seated on a sofa in their living room. Franz has learned something from his day with the Solo to Tandem folks, and he is about to put this knowledge to good use:

FRANZ: I think I have the answer to the problem we've been having. My . . . lack of interest problem.

Franz holds up a brand new PDF in a female-friendly color.

TESSA: All right . . . You think I look sexy in this?

FRANZ: Not exactly. What I mean is . . . I think it's time you started paddling with me. There's something so invigorating about paddling with the one you love. Tandem paddling generates a special kind of . . . energy. Tonight will be clear with a full moon. The water will be smooth as glass. It will be amazing.
TESSA: A romantic moonlight paddle? Yes, I can see that.
FRANZ: Yes, romantic, at the very least.

Stones and Rope

To set the mood for this romantic comedy about suicide, we hear two verses of the tragically comic song "Willow, Tit-willow" from Gilbert and Sullivan's light opera *The Mikado*. The song tells how a little bird "plunges himself into the billowy wave." Then, very late at night in a wooded area on the north shore of Lake Washington, near Seattle, we see Greg trying, without much success, to throw a noose over the branch of a tree. Terri approaches and teases Greg, "You're not doing very well with this. Lack of experience, I guess." Greg is confused by Terri's odd behavior. When Terri offers some practical advice on how to hang oneself, Greg is angered by Terri's callousness:

> **GREG:** What kind of person says they are going to help someone commit suicide?
> **TERRI:** Well, you know your circumstances. I don't. I figure you must have your reasons.

Terri and Greg are both in their 30s. Terri walks with difficulty. She tells Greg that this spot is very special to her. In explanation, she offers a story, which is enacted on stage: The Despondent Woman is filling her pockets with stones so that she can wade into the lake and drown herself. Terri's father, another lost soul who wanders in the late hours, intervenes. He will not let this happen. He tells his own story, and from this grim conversation comes a plan for the rest of their lives:

> **TERRI'S FATHER:** You don't need to do this.

DESPONDENT WOMAN: What do you know? I *do* need to do this. My life is nothing except pain and misery. I'm best out of this world.

TERRI'S FATHER: OK, your life is worth nothing. Nothing to you anyway. But you are still a human being. You can *do* things. You can help people. *(Pauses.)* You could even help me.

DESPONDENT WOMAN: Help *you*?

TERRI'S FATHER: Yes, I'm raising my young daughter—alone. Her mother is dead. The girl is crippled. I was driving. *I'd* like to end *my* life. But I can't. I'm needed. And it's more than I can do by myself. If your life is worth nothing to you, give it to me, to my girl. Whatever happens can't be worse than what you're trying to do now. Come back with me. Try it. If it doesn't work out, you can always finish what you started tonight.

Terri explains that she was raised by her father and this woman. She tells Greg that there is always something useful to be done with one's life. Terri hints that she is lonely and wouldn't mind putting Greg to use as a romantic partner. Terri observes that organ donors give away their bodies *after* death. But Greg, Terri suggests, can think of himself as an organ donor who will donate his body—for Terri's use—while the organs are still inside him and functioning.

Terri leads Greg to a bench and they talk about their lives. Greg, an introverted software developer, chose suicide because he never succeeded in forming close ties with anyone. Worse yet, he alludes to a series of small "betrayals." Terri explains that, apart from low-level jobs from which she is always fired, she is employed by the Cosmos as a preventer of suicides. She gives an example, enacted on stage, in which she persuades a woman, who had attempted to throw herself under a bus, to recognize a better alternative. The two women are now friends.

It is unclear to Greg and to the audience whether Terri is sane. Furthermore, Terri unmistakably took note of the fact that Greg is a well-paid professional. Baffled but charmed by Terri, Greg allows Terri to guide him toward a romantic relationship. A closing verse, sung to the melody of "Willow, Tit-willow," hints that Terri is indeed some kind of Cosmic agent tasked with persuading desperate people to put their lives to some good purpose rather than squandering them in suicide.

Stripes

On a set that suggests a lecture hall, a comical professor addresses his class. His laptop will project to a screen. He holds a remote that will advance the slides:

> **PROF:** We are here today to learn why zebras have stripes. Actually, I already know why zebras have stripes, but you don't . . . So, why do zebras have stripes? . . . I am waiting.

One student guesses that the reason might be camouflage. The Zebra suddenly enters, takes the remote, shows a few slides making clear that black and white stripes cannot be good camouflage on the savannah. The Zebra is then attacked and eaten by the Lion.

> **PROF:** The answer to the question of why zebras have stripes . . . is not camouflage.
> **ZEBRA:** *(Lying lifeless on the stage.)* I agree.
> **LION:** I agree.
> **PROF:** This is called "survey research." So . . . Why do zebras have stripes?
>
>   The Lion drags the dead Zebra offstage.

A student suggests that stripes enable zebras to align their life forces with "the natural balance of the Universe." The Professor is enthusiastic. This is called "theory." What's really good about theory is that the hypothesis can never be tested. Therefore, we can assume it's true until it's proven false—which will never happen.

The Fly offers first-hand information as to why zebras have stripes. Zebras have thin hides, and stripes protect Zebras by confusing a fly's visual system. The Professor follows the Fly's reasoning:

> **PROF:** This makes perfect sense. We call this "formal logic."
> Clearly it is much better to be eaten by a lion than bitten by a fly.

Eager to advance his career by securing funded research, the Professor plans an experiment and demands that his graduate student quickly obtain a standard zebra and an identical zebra without stripes: This, he explains to the audience, is called "mentoring your graduate students." Unfortunately, there are no stripeless zebras, but the graduate student devises an alternative experiment. A striped cloth is fitted over the rear half of the Horse, who is being bitten by aggressive flies. Encountering the striped cloth, the Fly becomes visually confused and only bounces off the Horse, who is very pleased. However, the Fly soon turns his attention to the uncovered front half of the horse and bites fiercely. The Professor indulges in a reverie of being introduced as the keynote speaker at a conference. However, in the modern university, new knowledge—even with funding—doesn't cut it. You need to *commercialize* your research. The graduate student has an idea:

> **GRADUATE STUDENT:** How about zebra-striped clothing as a healthier alternative to DEET and those other nasty insect repellents?
> **PROF:** *(Completely surprised.)* Yes! Yes! Yes! Very good. Here's our start-up! One moment. Before we go any further, I need you to sign this.
>
> The Graduate Student signs. And then:
>
> **PROF:** Your idea now belongs to me. *(To the audience.)* This is called "informed consent"—very important.

A student wearing a zebra-striped T-shirt enters and stands next to a bottle labeled "Nasty bug repellent (You don't want this)." The Professor explains, "This is called 'unbiased research.'" Now comes the big moment: Research Participant 1 enters and appears to prefer the T-shirt over the bottle. However, when Research Participant 1 approaches the T-shirt, he/she/they becomes visually disoriented and nauseous. Research Participant 2 also responds negatively, "Arrh! My *aesthetic system is* confused—and grossed out. I'm sick. Who would wear such a thing! Give me my DEET!" The Professor declares these research participants to be outliers. There is still value to his idea. The Horse and the Lion contradict the Professor. And the Horse has a request:

> **HORSE:** *(To Student.)* If no human being is going to walk around in a zebra-stripe T-shirt, may I have it?
>
> The Student removes the T-shirt and puts it on the front half of the Horse so that the Horse is more or less covered in zebra stripes:
>
> **STUDENT:** This is called "ethical research."
> **HORSE:** *(Pointing to himself.)* This is called "a happy horse."
> **PROF:** Our lecture is finished.

In an epilogue, the Horse credits biologist Tim Caro and recommends his book, *Zebra Stripes.*

The Day of the Deal

The set is a student-style apartment that includes cinder block bookshelves and an inexpensive desk on which there is a manual typewriter, numerous scholarly books, and sheaves of paper. No one is on stage.

A brother and sister, as voice-overs, discuss their deceased parents, Ruth and Walter. We infer that Ruth and Walter had happy lives together. We also learn that Ruth and Walter occasionally referred to—but would never explain to their two children—what was apparently a defining event in their lives: "The Day of the Deal." Then, in further voice-overs, we hear Ruth and Walter, as an elderly couple, refer to this deal as they reminisce about the first years of their lives together. The brother and sister

174

complain about their parents' refusal to explain. But Ruth and Walter have a response for them:

> **RUTH AS OLD WOMAN (V.O.):** *(Sharply to Son.)* Get over it! There's no rule that says parents need to share everything with their kids.
>
> **WALTER AS OLD MAN (V.O.):** That's right! We were loving parents. This was always a happy family. But there were good reasons why we never explained "The Day of the Deal."

Now Ruth, as a young woman, enters and begins looking at her papers and typing. She is working on her doctoral dissertation. Walter, handsome and well dressed, enters carrying a package that he begins to open eagerly. When Ruth shows a marked lack of enthusiasm, Walter complains, and Ruth's deep resentment comes to the surface. With lots of family money, Walter has purchased from a private party the only surviving manuscript of a never-published Arthurian romance, *Gawain's Vision*. Possessing this manuscript, Walter will be able to publish an edited edition and interpretive essays. These will ensure his success in a grim academic job market. Ruth may be the better scholar, but she'll be lucky to land a position in Enid, Oklahoma—while Walter is destined to teach graduate seminars at someplace like Princeton. Walter acknowledges that he has enjoyed privilege all his life, and reminds Ruth that they began their relationship knowing that it would almost certainly have to end when they finished their doctoral programs.

In Scene 2, Walter and Ruth stand facing each other in their apartment. Walter demands to know what went wrong at the Medieval Studies Conference. She confesses. An acquisitions editor for the Medieval Studies series at the University of Indiana Press approached her. He was familiar with the book proposal she had submitted. Her dissertation, he tells her, is entirely suitable for publication—but so are two others. An hour in his room would tip the balance in her favor. "I did it, Walter. One hour, just one hour. I wanted a chance to get what you always get, what you get without any trouble at all." But the "acquisitions editor" was a skillful fraud who had somehow gotten access to Ruth's book proposal and set his trap. When Ruth followed up with the Indiana University Press, they told her they knew nothing of such a man. Ruth is doubly humiliated: "I sold myself. And I sold myself like a fool."

> **WALTER:** So, you were a kind of prostitute.
> **RUTH:** I needed to plan for my future—a future without you.
> **WALTER:** A fine job you made of it.

Walter leaves the apartment. He needs to think, to consider their relationship. In Scene 3, Walter returns to a fearful Ruth. He has a deal for her: He forgives her infidelity. They marry, as they always hoped to do. He gives her *Gawain's Vision,* through which she will enjoy a high-profile academic career. Walter will switch to law, "Deep down, you're more the scholar than I am. My mind is tuned just as well for law as for scholarship. And with my family connections, I'll have good opportunities in law."

Ruth is grateful and deeply happy. Then Walter turns to what *he* wants from the deal. Now that Ruth is a beneficiary of his privilege, she needs to give up her resentment. Also, they are done with cinder block bookshelves. They will live the life of wealth and luxury that is natural to Walter—regardless of the awkwardness that Ruth may experience with her English department colleagues. Ruth knows his offer is more than fair, and it's a path to their future together. It was "The Day of the Deal."

The Expulsion from Eden*

Adam and Eve, now fallen, discover that they are ashamed to stand before each other naked. Their minds are flooded with new knowledge—much of it appalling. They now understand discord, toil, illness, pain, death, and murder. Adam blames Eve for eating the apple. In one of her glorious moments (John Milton's idea, not mine), Eve asks to take the full weight of God's punishment upon herself:

EVE: I would . . . die. I would see you still in Paradise with another woman—a second Eve, a better Eve. I would have you take her to bed. You would say, "Once I had a woman named Eve, but she was evil."

However, the angel Raphael leads Adam to take equal responsibility for the Fall, and Adam begins to grow as a husband and as a man. Raphael teaches Adam and Eve the most important lesson in human life: The need to forgive. Eve grasps this lesson sooner and more deeply than Adam:

EVE: My daughters will forgive their babes, even as they lie bleeding to death on the bed of childbirth. The woman, in her last moments, will ask her husband to forgive the child for the loss of his wife. In their last moments together, the woman will instruct her husband to love the babe and teach it well. And men shall heed.

Many years later, Adam and Eve confront their son Cain, who has slain his brother Abel and is unable to quell thoughts of further evil. Cain becomes a lonely wanderer in the desert, but departs with his parents' love and forgiveness. Adam also teaches Cain the core of Jewish ethics:

ADAM: You are evil only if you carry out your evil desires. Subduing the evil within you is virtue.

With many more years gone by, Adam and Eve, now aged and frail, receive the messenger Meraltic, Cain's trusted friend and advisor. After years in the desert, Cain was able to forgive himself and to find his goodness and strength. He is now the beloved governor of Nod, a populous city that has established many trade routes. Because of his great responsibilities, Cain cannot leave Nod, and Adam and Eve are too old to travel. But Adam and Eve rejoice in the news Meraltic has brought them. They look back on their lives. Adam wonders if perhaps experiencing the human adventure, with all of its hardships, was better than to have lived always innocent in Paradise. In the final scene, Cain is speaking to his son Enoch shortly after their successful war against the Cimmerian invaders. Enoch reports that people in Nod believe that Cain, in his merciful treatment of the Cimmerians, has shown the softness of a woman, not acceptable in one who governs a city and leads an army. But Cain has learned well the lesson of Raphael and his parents:

> **CAIN:** Our people must learn otherwise. We must forgive the Cimmerians their foolish attempt to conquer Nod. We must teach them to live in peace with us, to join our trading caravans.

In a final revelation, Cain tells Enoch one more reason why he practices forgiveness, "As Abel died from the blow I struck, he forgave me. So, how can I not extend mercy and forgiveness to others? How can I not teach these things?"

The Horse and the Sparrow

Ben Stepnik, a talkative fellow in his 40s, opens a conversation with Sandra Williams, who is about the same age, in the checkout line of a garden store. In Sandra's rolling cart is a large shrub wrapped in burlap. Ben, who wears an eye-patch, holds a much smaller plant, a Peace Lily. Ben notes the size of Sandra's shrub and wonders out loud whether she plans to carry it into her yard and plant it herself. Sandra responds with a bit of irritation, but the conversation continues—and becomes interesting:

> **SANDRA:** You're volunteering?
> **BEN:** Well, I hadn't thought that far ahead. I was just commenting.
> **SANDRA:** Do you really think I'd invite a total stranger back to my house?
> **BEN:** We're not exactly strangers. We've spent some time together.

Sandra, a local magistrate, looks closely and remembers that Ben was the crazy guy whose license she suspended because he rode his motorcycle with a ladder across it and cans of house paint hanging off the ladder. Ben is right. They are not strangers. Laughing a bit, they step out of the checkout line to continue their conversation.

Sandra asks about Ben's eye patch, which Ben was not wearing during his court appearance. Ben admits he's careless about safety. He also reminds Sandra about the circumstances of his arrest, still maintaining that he was driving safely enough with the ladder across his bike:

> **BEN:** I had a job painting a house. Interior, I do interior painting. But my car broke down, and I figured I'd just use my motorcycle. I needed the work. The truth is it was safe enough. Everything was balanced right across the fuel tank, and on curves I steadied the ladder with my hands. There was no need for the cop to have stopped me.

Sandra chooses not to argue the point. Because they are getting along well, Sandra, although normally wary of strangers, agrees to let Ben follow her to her home and help her plant the shrub. Afterward, they share iced tea on Sandra's patio and begin to tell more about themselves. Ben admits to being a life-long "fuck-up." Things have never worked out for him. He worked for weeks on a construction project, but never signed a contract and was ripped off. He insists he was a loving husband and father, but his wife finally divorced him because she was bringing in almost all the money. As much as he's struggled financially through the years, he's always paid his child support.

Sandra tells her story and, like Ben, surprises herself by how much she is willing to reveal:

> **SANDRA:** Well, I've been "sensible," all my life, too sensible. I've never been married. I would have liked raising a child. Sometimes I think my life never got started. My career did, but not my life . . . I'm sorry. I didn't mean to talk quite this way with you.

Ben then tells a story that metaphorically describes his inability to manage his life and suggests what he would have different. Years ago, when he was driving down a lonely road late at night, a panicked horse with a torn rope around its neck appeared right before Ben's headlights. Ben slowly won the horse's trust and was finally able to tether him safely to a strong fence, "Sometimes I envy that horse and how he felt when I tied him up. He knew he was done wandering around half-crazy in the dark. He knew someone would get him in the morning. Does this make sense to you?" To prove that she understands Ben, Sandra tells a story about a sparrow that got into her house and stunned itself banging against the windows. In its bewilderment, the sparrow finally allowed Sandra to take it in her hands, and she released it safely outside. Then Sandra impulsively connects her story to Ben's: "*You're* the sparrow in my story, aren't you? Banging around and a little stunned. Except you're not ready for the sky." They recognize that Ben can fulfill Sandra's need for a loving relationship and that Sandra can provide for Ben both love and the ability to navigate life's complications:

> **BEN:** I think I could be that horse. Tied safely. I'm ready for that . . . Maybe I'm that sparrow. But I don't need to be set loose, just stay here. Be yours.
> **SANDRA:** There's a path here for us. Isn't there?

Ben suggests planting his Peace Lily next to Sandra's shrub. Peace Lilies will grow outdoors. Sandra suggests otherwise, "Maybe . . . but maybe not. It's still a houseplant and a bit . . . delicate. We'll keep it inside, where it will be more . . . protected."

The Robin

> **Note:** With Jean Farkas and I as the audience, Hazel and Jonah, our grandchildren, played themselves in a backyard performance. Hazel also played the robin. Our daughter, Eva, played Alexa. Our son-in-law, Adam, served as the narrator.

Hazel and Jonah, in their backyard, notice a robin who appears to be injured:

JONAH: He looks hurt. Otherwise he wouldn't let us get so close.

HAZEL: What should we do?

Jonah remembers that there is an old bird cage in their garage. Hazel goes inside to get their parents' permission and returns with the bird cage. They ease the robin into the cage:

HAZEL: Hello, Mr. Robin. You're going to live with us for a little while. Until you're feeling better. We'll get worms for you. If you want, you can even have some quesadilla.

ROBIN: Tweet. Tweet.

The children discover that, after some initial confusion, Alexa is able to translate the robin's language into English. Alexa can also translate what the children say into the robin's language. They sort out the issue of the robin's dietary preferences. He does not want quesadilla. The robin explains his injury, which fortunately is not serious:

ALEXA: The robin says, "Thank you for taking me inside. I crash-landed into a big branch, and I'm not ready to fly. I was afraid a raccoon was going to eat me, but now I feel safe."

A few days later, the robin is looking healthy and makes clear that he is ready to be released:

ALEXA: Mr. Robin says, "I feel very good this morning. Hazel, Jonah—thank you so much for taking care of me." Mr. Robin says he can't be your pet robin and live in the cage because he's a wild bird. But he is going to make his home in your backyard so that you can see him and say hello. He says he will always be your friend.

The Spaghetti Crisis*

Simone is the Maître d' at a small gourmet restaurant in Paris, owned by Chef Henri. Henri has an imperious attitude, old-school values, a rigid personality, and more than a little disdain toward Americans. One evening, Simone reports that she has seated an American couple with a young child. Henri is immediately suspicious and unhappy:

> **HENRI:** This is not good . . . But, is the child causing trouble? How old is this child?
>
> **SIMONE:** She is a little girl. Very pretty. Maybe seven years old. She is quiet.
>
> **HENRI:** And the parents? They must be Americans. They are OK?
>
> **SIMONE:** They seem OK. Yes . . . Americans.
>
> **HENRI:** It would be Americans who would do this thing—bring a child. They want a fine dinner—good. But they should have arranged with their hotel for someone to look after the child. But, we will get through this. *(With sardonic laughter.)* They think we have a children's menu here?

But the worst is yet to come: Simone reports that the child has ordered a plate of plain spaghetti. No butter sauce, no olive oil, absolutely plain from the pot to the plate. With great reluctance, Henri relaxes his standards and agrees to serve the child absolutely plain spaghetti, "I hope my Father is not looking down on me tonight from Heaven."

In Scene 2, which takes place the following evening, both Simone and Henri are surprised to find that the Americans have returned:

> **HENRI:** How could this be? All the fine restaurants in this city. So many memorable dining experiences! And they are *back here* a second time?
>
> **SIMONE:** They said last night's meal was delicious, so they wanted to come back.
>
> **HENRI:** And the girl? She wants plain spaghetti?
>
> **SIMONE:** Yes, she wants plain spaghetti. That is what she wants— nothing else. I told the Americans I would ask if you will do this. The man said, "You did it *last* night. What's the problem?"

HENRI: Mon Dieu! He thinks he is back at home. At a Denny's! I do not serve plain spaghetti—not twice—not for *anyone!* They should have known better. You tell them that. If they want to eat here, I will put some oil, some butter, some tomato sauce—something!—on the girl's spaghetti. Or they must leave.

Simone does not want trouble in the restaurant, and she objects—futilely—to Henri's decree:

SIMONE: No. We must serve them . . . You own the back of the house. I own the front of the house. If I tell them to leave, there may be a ruckus. If not the little girl, then the father. Maybe the mother too.

HENRI: I own the back of the house. I also own the entire restaurant. Remember that, Simone. They leave!

Simone resolves the problem by outsmarting her boss. She asks the sous-chef, Hisham, to surreptitiously prepare a plate of plain spaghetti. The plan is good, but almost fails when Henri notices that he has two dinner orders very much like what the American couple ordered the previous night. Henri suspects that the Americans may not have left the restaurant. He threatens to step into the dining room to see for himself who his customers are. Simone is forced to bluff:

SIMONE: No, no, Chef. No little girl, no Americans. They are gone. This couple is from New Zealand. It is just a coincidence.

HENRI: A couple from New Zealand. OK.

Although Simone has resolved the problem, the experience has been stressful, and she does not want to think about a repeat. Initially, she tells the Americans an untruth:

SIMONE: Yes, your order is in. Chef Henri is happy to prepare plain spaghetti for the little girl.

Then, abandoning her professional persona, she reveals the truth:

SIMONE: You do not know, but we had quite a "spaghetti crisis" in the kitchen tonight. If you are in Paree tomorrow night, please . . . please . . . do not come back to this restaurant!

Walkers

The set and costuming suggest a small town in an Eastern European nation. An elderly couple, Sasha and Nikol, dressed for autumn weather, walk slowly and talk in elegiac tones:

NIKOL: I'm glad you took out the photographs last night.

SASHA: Yes, that was good.

They encounter a roadblock guarded by three armed paramilitaries. The paramilitaries tell Sasha and Nikol to turn back. The Resistance has been very active, and so no one can leave town until further orders are received. However, Paramilitary 1 is the couple's next door neighbor and jokes that Sasha and Nikol need to get rid of the smelly stuff rotting in their garden. Nikol responds that Sasha has been ill. This the first time in three weeks that they have taken a walk. They are headed to the old church to pick berries. Paramilitary 1 gestures to his colleagues to let them pass through the roadblock.

Sasha and Nikol are soon stopped at a second roadblock. Nikol explains once more that they want to pick berries by the old church. They are ordered to return to town by Paramilitary 4. However, Paramilitary 5 holds warm feelings toward Sasha. He overrules Paramilitary 4 and waives them through:

PARAMILITARY 4: We have orders. Go back to town.

PARAMILITARY 5: Regius, stick your orders up your butt. Sasha was my teacher in grade school. And, my daughter's teacher too. Sasha, you remember.

SASHA: Of course, I remember, Josef. *(Laughing.)* You were a big dummy. But Maria, she was smart—and so pretty—and the best dancer in all our little shows. The new teacher is not so good, I think.

PARAMILITARY 5 Get your berries. Don't take too long about it. And come back this way so we know you've returned to town.

Three insurgents, Genov, Gregor, and Ivan, are waiting very nervously outside town.

IVAN: Gregor, this was a bad plan. A terrible plan. We have 20 partisans ready to prove that the Resistance is strong. Already some of our people have been arrested, some shot, making these preparations. And everything depends on two old, sick people bringing us the detonators?

GREGOR: What, you think we had a choice? We put a notice in the newspaper? "Wanted, residents of this town who can get past guard stations to deliver a package to the Resistance. Wanted, people who don't mind what the security police will do to them when buildings explode all across the country."

Sasha and Nikol arrive and approach the insurgents:

NIKOL: Good day, gentlemen. What do you think the weather is going to be tomorrow?
GREGOR: It's going to rain granite.
NIKOL: Here are your detonators.

Nikol then asks for the poison pills that were promised them. Knowing that the government will quickly figure out who supplied the detonators, Nikol and Sasha fear they may give up names under torture. However, due to an error, the insurgents do not have the poison pills. Sasha tells them that they must shoot both she and Nikol. After a moment, the insurgents recognize the necessity:

GREGOR: You are asking too much. These are brutal times, but there are limits. There's a level below which we should not go.
IVAN: Gregor, they are right. *(To Sasha.)* I can do it.
Draws a pistol.

SASHA: *(To Insurgents.)* We will lie down, right here on the grass. Give us a moment. We will think back to when we were young, when we fell in love.

NIKOL: I'll take the second bullet. But for God's sake, don't hesitate.

They lie down face up. Sasha places her shawl over her head and Nikol's. They hold hands. Genov and Gregor withdraw to the periphery of the stage. Ivan steps back, then in a fluid motion he quickly puts two bullets into the heads of Sasha and Nikol.

Appendix B

Finding 10-Minute Plays in the Public Domain

This appendix lists some special resources for finding 10-minute plays in the public domain and briefly describes some plays that are promising candidates for your productions.

Librivox.org, a vast archive of public domain audio recordings, includes twelve collections of one act plays: for example: https://librivox.org/one-act-play-collection-008

On their website, search for "one-act play collections." Many of these plays are considerably longer than 10 minutes. But the running time of each play is listed. Often you can find the scripts of these plays somewhere on the Internet. If not, transcribing an audio recording of a 10-minute play is not too arduous a task.

Gutenberg.org is a vast archive of public domain texts. You can search on "one act plays" and then look for plays that run 10 minutes. You can also search on the titles of specific plays. It appears that Gutenberg has done a good job individually indexing in their search facility the titles of plays included in volumes of an author's collected work, but you may choose to examine the tables of contents of certain collections. In Gutenberg, files are provided in numerous file formats. If you download one of their files and open it in MS Word or any other word processing application that provides a word count, you can equate a word count of about 3000 to an approximate running time of 10 minutes. There is significant overlap between the Librivox titles and the Gutenberg titles, so you can often listen to a play on Librivox and obtain the script from Gutenberg.

Also notable are these volumes:

Pierre Loving (Ed.). (1923). *Ten Minute Plays*. New York: Brentano's.
This is historically the first collection of plays that are identified as "10-minute plays." It is not currently in Gutenberg, but it is available in various digital libraries, including the Hathi Trust Digital Library:
https://catalog.hathitrust.org/Record/001372396

Floyd Dell (Ed.). (1922). *King Arthur's Socks and Other Village Plays*. New York: Alfred A. Knopf. This volume consists of plays (almost all 10 minutes or shorter) whose authors were associated with the New York Liberal Club and/or the Provincetown Players. Together this was a remarkable avant-garde literary and cultural movement, notable for progressive ideas regarding politics and gender:
www.gutenberg.org/ebooks/6587
www.provincetownplayhouse.com/history.html

Helen Louise Cohen (Ed.). (1921). *One-Act Plays by Modern Authors*. New York: Harcourt, Brace, and Company. This impressively edited volume consists largely of 10-minute plays. Cohen's introductory essay and introduction to each play are interesting and valuable:
www.gutenberg.org/ebooks/33907

Horace Holley. (1916). *Read-Aloud Plays*. New York: Mitchell Kennerley. This collection of 10-minute closet dramas, written by a prominent member of the Bahá'í faith, are philosophical in nature and scant on dramatic structure. But Holley can be both vivid and eloquent:
www.gutenberg.org/ebooks/15983

Arthur Waley (Ed.). (1922). *The Nō Plays of Japan*. New York: Alfred A. Knopf. This richly explained collection of Nō plays, which run about 10 minutes, makes it possible to experience a highly stylized, much-respected tradition in Japanese theater, very different from the major theatrical traditions of the West:
www.gutenberg.org/ebooks/43304

Individual theater-goers and theater groups vary widely in their taste in plays. However, I will mention that many public domain plays are not obvious candidates for a well-received production. Many were minor theatrical works even in their time. Others are significant literary achievements, but because of the 100 years that have elapsed, are not easy to relate to. Keep in mind that you can update or completely re-write these plays, as I did in the case of "Luke Meets the Revenue Man," adapted from "Moonshine," written by Arthur Hopkins in 1919. Below is a short list, with brief summaries, of some promising 10-minute public domain plays. In this list, I stretch my working definition of "10-minute play" to include plays running up to 20 minutes. Keep in mind that any statement of a play's running time is specific to the individual performance.

F. Anstey, "At a Garden Party."
This 12-minute drawing room comedy makes fun of a society woman's urge to meet a literary celebrity:
www.gutenberg.org/ebooks/37597
https://librivox.org/one-act-play-collection-008

Anton Chekhov, "The Swan Song."
This 15-minute play is very nearly a dramatic monologue. An aged comedic actor speaks to the theater's elderly prompter about his life in the theater:
www.gutenberg.org/files/1753/1753-h/1753-h.htm
https://librivox.org/one-act-play-collection-001/

Colin Campbell Clements, "Yesterday."
This very pleasant 14-minute comedy shows us two older people jointly rejecting modern mores but making a romantic connection with each other:
www.one-act-plays.com/comedies/yesterday.html
https://catalog.hathitrust.org/Record/001372396 (Pierre Loving collection)
www.youtube.com/watch?v=nWzAvKpfjss

Marjorie Benton Cooke, "When Shades Assemble."
This is a witty 6-minute mash-up in which Lady Macbeth, Portia, Ophelia, and Juliet discuss their present and former lives:
www.archive.org/stream/modernmonologues00cook#page/70/mode/2up
https://librivox.org/one-act-play-collection-005-by-various

Floyd Dell, "The Angel Intrudes." In Floyd Dell (Ed.). (1922). *King Arthur's Socks and Other Village Plays.* New York: Alfred A. Knopf.
This is a stylish, witty, and cynical romantic comedy, 17 minutes long, in which lovers and an angel comprise a love triangle:
www.gutenberg.org/ebooks/6587
www.youtube.com/watch?v=-pwXHClovwl

F. Scott Fitzgerald, "Porcelain and Pink." In F. Scott Fitzgerald. (1922). *Tales of the Jazz Age.* New York: Charles Scribner's Sons.
This is a 20-minute jeu d'esprit in which a young woman's bath becomes less private than she expected. It is audacious of me to say this about a literary work by F. Scott Fitzgerald, but in my opinion "Porcelain and Pink" can be productively trimmed to something like 10 or 15 minutes:
www.gutenberg.org/ebooks/6695

John Galsworthy, "The Sun."
This is a disquieting 11-minute vignette in which a soldier returning from World War I cheerfully accepts the fact that his "best girl" is now with another:
www.gutenberg.org/ebooks/2920
https://librivox.org/one-act-play-collection-003-by-various

Ferenc Molnar, "A Matter of Husbands" (Trans. Benjamin Glazer). In Pierre Loving (Ed.). *Ten Minute Plays.* (1923). New York: Brentano's.
This is a sharp-edged comedy with a surprise ending. An anxious wife confronts a famous actress with whom she suspects her husband is having an affair:
www.one-act-plays.com/comedies/matter_of_husbands.html
https://catalog.hathitrust.org/Record/001372396

Appendix C

Nine Complete Scripts You Can Use

To help promote living room theater, I have placed nine of my 10-minute plays in the public domain. I call these nine plays the Jumpstart Collection because they enable any reader of this book and anyone else for that matter to immediately get started performing some contemporary 10-minute plays. Furthermore, I waive the Dramatists Bill of Rights in regard to these plays, so you are free to modify the scripts. Purely as a courtesy, I'd very much like to hear about what you do. The Jumpstart Collection is downloadable as a DOCX file at www.pwcenter.org and as a PDF file at www.newplayexchange.org. Search for "Farkas" or "David K. Farkas."

The nine Jumpstart plays are listed below, each with a brief description. The list also functions as a table of contents for this appendix. In the digital version of this book, the titles of the plays are hyperlinked to the individual scripts. Moreover, the "The End" stage direction that concludes each script is a hyperlink back to the beginning of this appendix.

This is a cheerful drama about making important choices in one's life. Long ago, working as a restaurant server, Jean Farkas warned customers against ordering the cantaloupe on days when they were bitter.

This is an off-beat comedy about a man who is temporarily abducted by two inquisitive aliens. This play is very easy to stage and provides opportunities for improvisation.

This is a cheerful drama with humanistic and spiritual themes. The professor in the play appears primarily as a funeral urn. Long ago,

Jean and I paid a visit to the crematorium in the play and were offered The Professor.

Good-bye from SILVE

This is an intense, spiritual drama that incorporates dance. The protagonist commits suicide with pills, but the mood and message are ultimately hopeful and positive.

Horizons

This is an intense, suspenseful drama based on Richard Russell's tragic theft and unauthorized flight of a commercial airliner in 2017. The play, however, is about love and redemption and has a happy ending. Unless an adult performs the role of the child, the child's grown-up(s) must be comfortable with the play's adult situation and occasional bad language.

Luke Meets the Revenue Man

This is my adaptation of a 1919 comedy, by Arthur Hopkins. The play depicts an encounter between Luke, a North Carolina moonshiner, and an educated revenue officer from New York City. The play makes fun of Luke's lack of education and backward ways, but it does portray Luke as an affable and decent man who adheres staunchly to his own code of ethics. My revision trims down the original script, changes the ending, and eliminates the casual but ugly racism that was acceptable in Hopkins' time.

Nordstrom Shopping Zombies

This is an adult, sometimes harsh comedy about the dissolution of an unhappy marriage during a shopping trip. The belt is real. I deny everything else.

The Expulsion from Eden

This, my favorite of all the plays I've written, revisits Milton's *Paradise Lost*, and carries the story forward to include Cain and Abel. The play is about the primacy of forgiveness in human life.

This is a cheerful comedy about a rigid French chef who cannot adapt to the American family (the Farkas family) that chose to dine at his restaurant. The other character is the resourceful Maître d' (female or male) who resolves the conflict.

Note that when I indicate genders in descriptions of these plays, I refer only to how the actor is choosing to perform the role, not the actor's personal gender-presentation preferences.

"Beat" is a standard stage direction meaning a long pause. I use ellipses to indicate brief pauses.

From my 50-plus 10-minute plays, I chose these because they vary greatly in genre, setting, theme, and mood; and because they are in most cases very easy to stage. Furthermore, for those groups who want to match the ages of the actors to the roles, these plays offer roles with a very wide range of ages.

Because I favor freezes as a quick and easy way to effect scene transitions, you will find this approach used in the Jumpstart Collection. A "Freeze" stage direction indicates that the characters should freeze briefly before leaving the stage and/or that the characters should freeze briefly before the action begins in the next scene. You can, however, employ any kind of scene transition you wish.

Bitter Cantaloupe

A 10-minute play by David K. Farkas

Version 12-31-20

I place this play in the public domain. Anyone is welcome to distribute, perform , modify, or expand upon the script of this play. – David K. Farkas, 2020.

Characters:

Mr. Harold Damerst: A business owner from Milwaukee, in his 60s.
Mr. Johnson: A business owner from Buffalo, in his 50s.
Stevie: A server ("waitress"), in her early 20s.
Rose (or Ross): A mechanical engineer, in her (or his) mid-20s.

[Scene 1]

Mr. HAROLD DAMERST, a middle-aged business owner, is seated for breakfast in a café in Buffalo, New York. A menu is on the table, but he is looking at a newspaper or his smartphone. MR. JOHNSON, also middle aged, enters and takes a seat at an empty table. STEVIE, a waitress in her early 20s, approaches MR. JOHNSON with a carafe of coffee.

STEVIE: Do you know what you'd like for breakfast?

JOHNSON: I'm waiting for someone. Just black coffee for now.

STEVIE: (*Pouring coffee.*) OK.

STEVIE now returns to MR. DAMERST'S table.

STEVIE: Are you ready to order now?

DAMERST looks closely at STEVIE and then at the name tag on her blouse.

DAMERST: "Stevie"? That's not your real name? (*Laughing.*) Did your parents name you Steven?

STEVIE: No, I'm "Stephanie," but I never cared for it. I've been "Stevie" since 7th grade.

194

DAMERST: Did your folks like the change?

STEVIE: They got used to it.

MR. DAMERST laughs.

DAMERST: I'll have scrambled eggs with the sausage. I'll start with the cantaloupe.

STEVIE: Maybe you don't want the cantaloupe. Orange juice?

DAMERST: What's wrong with the cantaloupe?

STEVIE: They're looking pretty green. Might taste bitter.

DAMERST: OK, how about a banana?

STEVIE: They didn't look ripe either. It's good to have fruit with your breakfast, but I'd stick to the orange juice.

MR. DAMERST: What does the kitchen think of you telling people not to order stuff?

STEVIE smiles.

DAMERST: They must have a lot of cantaloupe left over. Bananas too.

STEVIE: Maybe they do. If they look better tomorrow, I'll sell them.

DAMERST: What if they never look better?

STEVIE: Then I won't sell them. This place is no Hilton, and I'm no gourmet. But if I wouldn't want to eat it, I'm not gonna sell it.

MR. DAMERST: Are there a lot of days when you do this?

STEVIE: *(Coyly.)* Some.

ROSE enters the restaurant, spots MR. JOHNSON, and takes a place at his table.

DAMERST: What if a customer has been really rude to you. *Then* would you sell them a bitter cantaloupe?

STEVIE: Never thought about that. *(Laughing.)* It's something to consider.

DAMERST: *(In a serious tone of voice.)* Are you gonna keep your job if you keep steering customers away from the food that doesn't look good to you?

STEVIE: I'll work till they fire me.

DAMERST: And, the cook keeps stocking lousy food day after day? What's that all about? Maybe the cook should re-think how things are done here.

STEVIE: Sir, I wanted to do right by you, but I don't think I should be talking about Sam and the restaurant.

DAMERST: OK, fair enough.

STEVIE: I have another table I need to take care of. I'll check back with you in a bit.

DAMERST: You do that, Stevie. It's always important to take care of your customers.

Approaching MR. JOHNSON'S table, STEVIE overhears the conversation between MR. JOHNSON and ROSE.

ROSE: *(Speaking defensively.)* Everybody knows you're a demanding boss, but you've been more than pleased with my work. My microsensors have significantly improved quality control, and I thought we agreed that the sensor-based inventory system is coming along well. I want to stay with inventory. I don't want to switch projects.

JOHNSON: No. Employee surveillance is my top priority. I'll find someone else to take over the inventory project.

STEVIE: Excuse me. Are we ready to think about breakfast?

JOHNSON: *(Brusquely to STEVIE.)* Come back later. We're in the middle of something.

STEVIE: Sure. You can order whenever you're ready.

STEVIE exits to the kitchen.

Freeze.

[Scene 2]

Twenty minutes later, MR. DAMERST has finished his breakfast.

Action.

STEVIE enters.

STEVIE: How was breakfast? More coffee? Care for anything else?

DAMERST: No, nothing else. The eggs were OK. Sausage too. Stevie, let's talk for a minute. I own a company. Great Lakes Casting. In Milwaukee. We make flow control valves. We ship them all over the world. I think my company could use a kid like you. You have anything special keeping you in Buffalo?

> MR. JOHNSON and ROSE are now talking intensely in pantomime. MR. JOHNSON is impatient and aggressive. ROSE exhibits resistance.

STEVIE: Um . . . No. I grew up here, but . . . I could leave. *(She casts her eyes around the restaurant, and in doing so takes note of MR. JOHNSON'S table.)* There isn't much of a future for me here . . . But . . . isn't this a little . . . sudden? And, shouldn't I know your name?

DAMERST: Damerst. Harold Damerst. Here's my business card.

> STEVIE looks at the card and pockets it.

DAMERST: I built the company. I'm used to doing things my way—and moving quickly. And, by the way, there was no money in my family. I got through college with a scholarship and working 20 hours a week in the dining hall.

STEVIE: If you have any "personal" ideas here, that's not going to work. You know what I'm saying.

DAMERST: That's not at all what I was thinking. You'd be younger than my daughter—if I'd had a daughter, if I'd had children. I am married. When I tell my wife that I hired my waitress—well, I'm *trying* to hire my waitress— she won't be all that surprised. She knows me. About 5 years ago, I gave a talk at the Milwaukee School of Engineering. A kid asked good questions. I told him I'd like to hire him when he finished school. Tom is doing great in the company.

JOHNSON: *(Raising his voice.)* I have no patience with your idealistic bullshit. That's part of engineering education these days?

STEVIE: OK. This whole idea is . . . overwhelming . . . I don't mind working here. *(Gestures faintly at the restaurant.)* But I don't like thinking that waitressing, or simple office work, is all I'll ever do. I can take a chance on Milwaukee. If it doesn't work out, I can get back here easily enough.

197

DAMERST: OK. You move quickly, just like I do. I liked your honest answer about the cantaloupe. You risked your job to do what's right. That's integrity. Then, you wouldn't gossip about your boss. That's discretion. The way I add things up, that's two big points. I'm asking you to work for me. I don't know what you'll do, but they'll be something. A real job. A career. You don't have a college degree. Am I right?

STEVIE: No. I don't.

DAMERST: I don't care. That's one of the good things about owning the company. HR has its rules, but I can make exceptions. So, if you're willing to come to Milwaukee, I'll put you in a job you can grow into. Probably everyone you'll be working with will be a college grad. Lots of engineers. People with business degrees. They'll figure out soon enough that you didn't go to college. Can you handle that?

STEVIE: Yes.

DAMERST: You will eventually need more education. Are you willing to go back to school? To college or . . . community college? What about that other table, Stevie? I can wait until you wait on them.

STEVIE: No, I keep glancing over there, and judging from the tone of the conversation, they don't need me interrupting to ask about breakfast.

DAMERST: So, are you willing to go back to school?

STEVIE: Yes, definitely. More school is . . . in my plans. But there were medical bills after my mother died, and you save money slowly when you're working as a waitress. Car breaks down and your plans get pushed back. Trouble with a landlord, and your plans get pushed back. It's like that.

DAMERST: I know that side of life. But, *we'll* cover your tuition. Go as fast or slow as you want. I don't want you buried in school assignments. You'll be on a hell of a learning curve at work.

STEVIE: Sir. Mr. Damerst, this is more than I ever hoped for.

JOHNSON: Loyalty to me! To me personally! This is my own little project. Not the company's. To me! You just don't seem to get it, Rose.

DAMERST: OK. OK. You'd better bring my check. I have meetings starting at 9:30. We may be acquiring a competitor. *(Long pause.)* Stevie, just one thing. I need you to quit your job today. Today or tomorrow. I'll want you in Milwaukee in two weeks. But there are things I *need* you to do for me here in Buffalo on Thursday and Friday, so you'll need to get free, in two days. That's OK? It's a condition for your new job.

STEVIE: *(After deliberating.)* I'll tell Sam now, and I'll give him today and tomorrow. I'm trusting you, Mr. Damerst.

DAMERST: *(In a surprisingly sharp voice.)* Tell me why you agreed to walk out on your boss? From everything else I've seen, that's not you. We sort of agreed that you have integrity. Is this your integrity? I think this is a strike *against* you.

STEVIE: I will tell you, Mr. Damerst. I did not *like* the idea of quitting without proper notice. But I made my decision. Lots of girls just walk out on Sam. He's used to it. The opportunity you're offering, that's huge. It may be my one shot. But, Mr. Damerst, I don't appreciate what you're making me do. And, I'm wondering what you could need me for so badly. Thirty minutes ago you didn't know who I was, and now you can't get through the week without me? To tell the truth, asking me to walk out on my job is a strike against *you*. But it's just one strike, so I'm still ready to leave Buffalo.

DAMERST: *(Smiling expansively.)* OK, Stevie. That was an . . . experiment. No, a test. I wanted to learn a little more about my new employee—my "protégée" perhaps. You have integrity but you also have judgment. You weighed what you had at stake against what Sam had at stake. And I don't mind that you had doubts—and said so—when I told you that I needed you this week. You're quick . . . You can give your two-weeks' notice. It will take me some time to figure out what we're going to do with you. But, one way or another, my company can damn sure use what you'll be bringing us.

STEVIE: Thank you, Mr. Damerst. Thank you for everything.

JOHNSON: I built my company by doing things my way. I don't let petty rules stop me. You're a damn good engineer, or I wouldn't be wasting my time with this conversation. But I've had about enough of this.

DAMERST: Stevie, hand me back my business card. I'm gonna put my cell phone number on it.

> She does so.

DAMERST: Well, I *do* need to go. *(Pulls out a bill.)* I'm sure this will cover breakfast. See you in Milwaukee, Stevie. I'm glad you steered me away from that cantaloupe.

> MR. DAMERST exits. STEVIE moves toward MR. JOHNSON'S table but, hearing an argument, draws back.

JOHNSON: I'm *assigning* you, not *asking* you, to work with Argus Associates on surveillance.

ROSE: I won't do it. It's unethical, and long term it's bad for the business. To be honest with you, sir. I don't want to go through my career with this surveillance thing as part of my work history.

JOHNSON: I think our breakfast meeting is finished, and I'm finished with you. You're fired. I want your personal belongings out of the building by the end of the day. And by the time you get to work, you'll be locked out of the server.

ROSE: Dismissing me for refusing to violate a law is illegal.

JOHNSON: Listen, Rose. You *don't* want to mess with me. If I were you, I'd be worrying about your HR file and my letter of reference. Now get outta here!

> ROSE leaves angrily. STEVIE follows her just outside the restaurant.

STEVIE: Hey, I heard some of that conversation. Give me your cell number.

ROSE: *(Surprised.)* What? Why?

STEVIE: Trust me. I respect what you said to that guy. I can't promise, but I might be able to make something good happen.

ROSE: OK.

STEVIE: Here, add your name and number to my contacts.

STEVIE hands over her phone and ROSE enters her name and cell number. ROSE exits. STEVIE returns to MR. JOHNSON.

STEVIE: Are you ready to order now, sir?

JOHNSON: I saw you follow Rose out the door. What was that about? I need to know.

STEVIE: She had really cool shoes on. I just want to know what brand they are, and where she bought them.

JOHNSON: *(Placated.)* OK. I guess that's waitressing these days. I'm ready for breakfast.

STEVIE: Let me suggest you start with the cantaloupe. They are really good today.

Freeze.

[Scene 3]

STEVIE is talking on her cell phone to MR. DAMERST.

Action.

STEVIE: I don't mean to overstep. But you said you had a lot of confidence in my judgment. *(She nods as though mentally responding to something MR. DAMERST has said.)* Well, I think I have another new employee for you. A young woman, a mechanical engineer. She knows microsensors. She has real engineering talent, good judgment, and integrity. And you'll *like* her. Her name is Rose Estavez.

STEVIE listens for a few moments, then smiles broadly.

The End

Close Encounters of the Talkative Kind

A 10-minute play by David K. Farkas

Version 12-31-20

I place this play in the public domain. Anyone is welcome to distribute, perform, modify, or expand upon the script of this play. – David K. Farkas, 2020.

Characters:

Christopher: Any age, any gender.
Ferdinand: Any age, any gender.
David: A married man with children.

[Scene 1]

CHRISTOPHER and FERDINAND are seated together on plain metal chairs. They are dressed identically, perhaps oddly. Some distance away, DAVID is seated on a more elaborate, more comfortable chair. DAVID is drinking heartily from a mug of coffee. It's his first cup of the day.

CHRISTOPHER: Is the coffee to your taste?

DAVID: Yes, it's good. Thank you.

He continues to drink heartily, like someone trying to wake up in the morning.

FERDINAND: Did you sleep well, David?

DAVID: Yes. Under the circumstances, very well.

FERDINAND: We are pleased.

CHRISTOPHER: Shall we begin our conversation? We'll take a break for your breakfast.

DAVID: *(Drinking down more coffee.)* I'm just a little groggy, not quite functioning.

CHRISTOPHER and FERDINAND show worried looks.

DAVID: Oh, don't be concerned. That's how it always is before I've downed my first cup of coffee. Anyway, it's all coming back now. My God! It's all coming back! You said there was no issue with Andrea, my children, or anyone else. From their point of view, I haven't left, haven't disappeared. They won't worry about my absence.

CHRISTOPHER: No issue whatsoever. When your visit is done, we will return you to the exact moment of time at which you left. You will be sitting, as before, with Andrea, at your dining room table. She will have noticed nothing.

DAVID: No matter how long I stay here?

CHRISTOPHER: That's right. We would not cause distress to those who are close to you. This entire project will not cause harm to you or anyone on Earth. Morally, we are a highly evolved species. Ultimately, we will use our knowledge of your world to guide you to higher levels of consciousness and far better social and political organization. But we will only guide, only teach. We will not coerce, colonize, exploit, or brutalize. That stage in our civilization belongs to the distant past.

FERDINAND: Our moral evolution came slowly, but it came. As we say in our world, "The arc of history is long, but it is just."

DAVID: The arc of history on Earth seems to wobble quite a bit, but I trust you are right. *(Pausing to change the topic.)* Perhaps we covered this last night, but I don't think so. Why was I chosen?

FERDINAND: David, would you like a refill on the coffee?

DAVID: Absolutely.

> FERDINAND glances directly at the mug. DAVID looks down, and the mug is somehow full again. DAVID shows surprise, then picks up the mug. Because it is full to the brim, he merely takes a delicate sip. He will take several of these sips before drinking more heartily.

DAVID: Good trick, that.

CHRISTOPHER: That "trick" was the very least of the things we are doing to make this project possible.

DAVID: I suppose so. Now why was I chosen?

FERDINAND: You met all the criteria.

DAVID: There are 7 billion people on Earth, and you chose me?

FERDINAND: You are not the only one we will talk with.

CHRISTOPHER: The process is, however, very selective. These week-long interviews require a great expenditure of resources. Just keeping you alive and healthy is very resource intensive, so we can only interview a small number of individuals.

DAVID: So why me? I'm highly educated. I read widely. But I'm hardly a Nobel Prize winner.

CHRISTOPHER: A key reason is that you are very talkative. From extensive observation, we determined that very few Earth citizens are so willing to talk non-stop all day long—to answer any and all questions, to elaborate on each answer, and then begin talking about other topics. We recognize that there is much we need to know that we don't even have questions for, so someone who spontaneously branches off into new topics . . .

FERDINAND: . . . provided that person is well informed and articulate . . .

CHRISTOPHER: . . . is even more valuable to us than someone who just answers our questions. Based on our observations, as long as we keep serving you coffee—plus, of course, periodic meals and necessary sleep— you will keep talking and talking and talking.

FERDINAND: With undiminished enthusiasm.

CHRISTOPHER: Not many Nobel Prize winners and other experts can or will do this.

FERDINAND: Your ability to talk by the hour is very impressive. May I ask if this has caused you difficulty in your social relations with other human beings?

> CHRISTOPHER glances sharply at FERDINAND, who, chastised, looks away. DAVID chooses to ignore the question.

DAVID: I don't know your names. Perhaps it's time for you to introduce yourselves.

CHRISTOPHER: We don't actually have names. We don't actually have language—not any kind of language that you would understand. Why don't you choose names for us? Names you'll be comfortable with.

DAVID: OK. Well, since you've traveled a long way to explore an unfamiliar world, I'll name you after explorers. *You* are "Christopher," after Christopher Columbus. *You* are "Ferdinand," after Ferdinand Magellan. I assume you know Columbus and Magellan.

CHRISTOPHER: Of course. We have detailed factual knowledge of your civilization and its history. But we need to complement this factual knowledge with experiential knowledge, personal experiences that add deeper context and nuance to the factual information. And so we are getting that knowledge directly from Earth citizens—"face to face," so to speak.

FERDINAND: We don't exactly have "faces." Not normally.

CHRISTOPHER: So, let's begin at the beginning. Shall we? Why don't you start with your family background, what you know about your parents' lives before you were born. Then, we can proceed to your earliest memories, then your childhood—along with any topics that come to mind.

DAVID: Yes! I can do that.

FERDINAND: Would you like more coffee?

Freeze.

[Scene 2]

CHRISTOPHER, FERDINAND, and DAVID are still seated. Again, DAVID has his mug full of coffee, which he continues to sip from until the mug is refilled one more time.

Action.

CHRISTOPHER: How are you this morning, David. It's all going well, is it not?

DAVID: I'm somewhat unhappy by your unwillingness to satisfy my curiosity about *your* world. Other than that, I've greatly enjoyed these last five—has it been five?—days.

CHRISTOPHER: Yes, it has been five days. And, I'm sorry about that restriction.

DAVID: My time with you is the apex of my life. As you know, my entire career has been teaching. One way or another, I am always explaining. And what greater explaining could anyone ever do than this? My voice has held up well, hasn't it.

CHRISTOPHER and FERDINAND nod in assent.

DAVID: Now, you *are* certain that no one is missing me, worrying about me, back on Earth? That's what you said.

FERDINAND: Yes. For us, manipulating your time stream is one of the *easier* parts of this project . . . More coffee?

DAVID nods and looks down to see his mug refilled to the brim. He takes a sip.

DAVID: Christopher, Ferdinand. I am very pleased with our daily conversations. I truly believe I am doing something important— contributing to Intergalactic cultural understanding.

CHRISTOPHER: We believe likewise.

DAVID: Moreover, I am not eager to complete these interviews. There is so much more I could tell you. So *very* much more. Might we add another week? Maybe a month? More than a month? I cannot fully express how much I enjoy talking with the two of you. I will never be able to replicate this experience once I return to Earth.

FERDINAND: Why can't you engage in satisfying conversations when you return?

DAVID: Nothing in my future can be anything like this. Friends listen, but not for very long. Andrea hasn't listened to me on any serious topic for years.

CHRISTOPHER: We are sorry, David, that you do not enjoy fully satisfactory social relationships with those around you. However, there is no way to extend the duration of your visit. As we explained, each of these week-long interviews requires an enormous expenditure of resources.

DAVID: I understand. And I'm grateful for this week. I and those few others you selected are having an extraordinary experience, an experience beyond any comparison. I believe I have been transformed.

CHRISTOPHER: Yes, we well understand this. David, I am now going to raise a topic that was scheduled for your final day with us. But, we seem to have gotten close to it now. It's about the "disengagement process," what happens when you leave us.

DAVID: OK. I am ready.

CHRISTOPHER: The key issue is what you will or will not remember when you return to your previous life. First, I must inform you that as a sentient being with a high level of self-awareness, you have definite rights. We can make recommendations, but we cannot choose for you. So, let me explain your options.

DAVID: OK.

CHRISTOPHER: Option A is that we erase all your memories of this past week. You will never know you visited with us. Option B is that you retain all your memories. Option C is the middle ground. We can leave you with a few faint memories and recollections in dreams. That would be all.

DAVID: I want Option B. Why would I want my memories erased or even weakened?

FERDINAND: We understand how you are looking at this, but we counsel very strongly against Option B. Our experience with Earth citizens is limited. But we have extensive experience with other civilizations, and Option B almost always works out badly—tragically.

CHRISTOPHER: Remember, David. You will have absolutely no evidence that any of this ever happened. Anything you say will be disbelieved. But the experience will be so vivid in your mind, such an important part of your total life experience, that almost certainly you will be unable to let it go and resume anything like a normal life. You will be unable to refrain from making claims you cannot support. You will be laughed at, derided. Furthermore, the rest of your life will seem trivial and meaningless.

FERDINAND: With very good evidence, we anticipate extreme social alienation, mental illness, substance abuse, even suicide.

DAVID: I will take my chances with Option B.

CHRISTOPHER: David, we understand very well how reluctant you are to relinquish these memories, but we *urge* you to waive your right to Option B.

DAVID: I will not.

CHRISTOPHER: Then, let us look closely at Option C.

DAVID: Just a few faint memories and dreams? No!

CHRISTOPHER: We can do a little better for you with Option C.

DAVID: What do you mean?

[While CHRISTOPHER should deliver this speech seriously, the actor playing DAVID can, at moments, break out of character and join the audience in appreciating the joke—the playwright is claiming to have been abducted by aliens.]

CHRISTOPHER: Before you leave us, you will be allowed to record your experiences in a play, with a maximum duration of *(CHRISTOPHER ponders briefly.)* 10-minutes. We promise that every word you write will be imprinted in your brain. It will be much better if you share your experience as a work of fiction rather than have your claims regarded as the ravings of a madman. This is truly your best option.

DAVID: I don't know that I can give up my memory of this experience for nothing more than a 10-minute play.

CHRISTOPHER: Trust us, David. For your own sake, Choose the play!

DAVID turns to the audience for help in deciding. Any kind of clowning and improvisation is appropriate.

DAVID: Should I keep my memory of this visit, even at the cost of social alienation, mental illness, substance abuse, and suicide?

Through gestures to the audience, CHRISTOPHER and FERDINAND urge a "no" answer. But DAVID can't make up his mind and looks for guidance from the audience. Finally, regardless of how the audience members have actually responded, DAVID heeds or seems to heed a "no" answer. He turns to CHRISTOPHER and FERDINAND.

DAVID: Well . . . well . . . I will choose the play. *(Beat.)* Providing that any time it is performed, you will give the audience a visual sign that everything in the play is true.

CHRISTOPHER and FERDINAND: This is not feasible.

DAVID: I believe it *is* feasible. Your civilization monitors all electro-magnetic transmissions from planet Earth—do you not? Then you will be able to determine when the play is scheduled to be performed. So, you can indeed do this.

CHRISTOPHER and FERDINAND tacitly acknowledge the truth of what DAVID has said.

CHRISTOPHER: We have never before agreed to an arrangement of this kind. But, David, we will consider it. What sign do you require? Do not be unreasonable!

DAVID: Anywhere and any time, at the end of a performance of this play, you will cause the house lights to flash on and off to verify that every word that has been spoken is the truth.

CHRISTOPHER and FERDINAND turn toward each other. The house lights flash on and off repeatedly.

The End

Echoes of the Professor

A 10-minute play by David K. Farkas

Version 12-31-20

I place this play in the public domain. Anyone is welcome to distribute, perform, modify, or expand upon the script of this play. – David K. Farkas, 2020.

Characters:

Attorney: An older man.

John: Crematorium employee, an older man.

Horace: The long-deceased professor, an elderly man.

Sandra: A woman in her 30s. She is the daughter of Julia, who has recently died.

Sam: Sandra's husband, also in his 30s.

Julia: We know of her initially as the recently deceased mother of Sandra and the widow of Nick. In Scenes 2 and 3, which are set in 1968, she appears as a college senior, about to graduate and marry Nick.

Nick: College senior about to graduate and marry Julia.

Suggested minimum casting:

Attorney/John/Horace

Sandra/Julia

Sam/Nick

Production note:

If necessary for clarity, one of the characters can briefly function as a narrator, offstage or onstage, to announce that Scene 2 takes place in 1968. In addition, proper names and other details can be changed to fit the locale where the play is being staged. Factually, Mt. Hope Cemetery adjoins the University of Rochester in New York State.

[Scene 1]

> SAM and SANDRA, a married couple, professional in manner, have visited the law offices of the ATTORNEY, who is executor of the estate of JULIA, SANDRA'S MOTHER. On the table or desk at which they are seated is a large, buff-colored ceramic urn.

SANDRA: *(Pointing to the urn.)* So there it is. I'd sort of forgotten about the urn.

ATTORNEY: Well, about six months ago, when Julia knew she'd be moving into the nursing facility, she entrusted it to me. I could have kept the urn securely stored here in the office. That's the usual thing we do. But . . . I took it home and put it on a shelf in my living room. It certainly didn't fit the décor, but I don't entertain much anyway—so that didn't matter. Actually, "The Professor" *(Gestures toward urn.)* and I have become friends, so to speak.

SAM: Can you review the codicil for us, before we settle this issue. It's definitely puzzling.

ATTORNEY: Yes, of course. From a legal standpoint, it's entirely straightforward—and binding. And there was no question about Julia's mental competence. But Julia was disinclined to explain her reasons. *(Beat.)* Quite simply, the two of you, as a single legal agent, must choose to receive either the urn or the Chagall lithograph. If you choose the urn, I am directed to arrange for the sale of the Chagall, with the proceeds going to the United Fund. If you choose the Chagall, the urn *(Looks down at notes.)* "must be immediately disposed of as trash." This is disturbing but entirely legal in New York State. Julia was pleasant, as she always was, but very definite. I wish I could tell you more. Speaking only from a personal perspective, and especially as I've been keeping the urn myself, I'd be much happier if you chose The Professor. But, of course, giving up the Chagall would not be an entirely rational course of action. Sandra, you say that Julia . . . that Nick . . . neither one ever explained anything about the urn, even how they came by it?

SANDRA: It was just *there*—"The Professor"—on a shelf in the living room. It seemed *important*, but, no, they never explained it. Perhaps it's the ashes of a distant relative, someone they didn't know by name, but they knew he'd been a professor of something somewhere. Just once, I really pressed Mom about this. All she said was "Some things in life you need to learn on your own." . . . But, how can we learn something like this?

SAM: You can see how unfortunate this situation is. We are reluctant to give up the Chagall, but it's . . . well . . . creepy to . . . you know . . . *(Gestures a tossing motion.)* with the urn. Of course, I'll follow Sandra's lead on this.

SANDRA: I think we need to choose the urn. It seems disrespectful to put *any* human remains "in the trash." And, there was clearly some kind of relationship between "The Professor" and my parents.

SAM: Yes, I guess we'll keep the urn—on a shelf in our living room, just as Julia and Nick did. But, obviously, it would be a lot nicer to display the Chagall lithograph.

SANDRA: I know, Sam. But, somehow The Professor just seems to belong to us. Maybe he *is* a distant relative, maybe not. But, I know he is ours.

SAM: Maybe Marc Chagall is a distant relative. That would be a reason to pass on The Professor and keep the Chagall in our living room . . . Just joking, Sandy.

ATTORNEY: Speaking, again, as a friend rather than as your attorney, I can't help but think that there's some kind of wisdom behind your mother's final directive. Julia was always an insightful woman.

SAM: And she and Nick raised an "insightful" daughter. So, I'm good with this.

ATTORNEY: OK, we've reached a decision. So, first I'll ask Sandra to sign and initial the codicil.

> He hands SANDRA the codicil and points successively to places on the sheet of paper. She signs and initials.

ATTORNEY: And now you, Sam.

> He hands SAM the codicil and points successively to places on the sheet of paper. He too signs and initials.

ATTORNEY: Fortunately, even without the Chagall, the estate is substantial. I think that the codicil was Julia's way to make clear that there is something special about that urn. Giving up the Chagall was perhaps a kind of test—which you've passed. *(Turning to the urn.)* I guess I need my own little good-bye moment with The Professor. . . You know, sitting alone with him in my condo, we used to chat once in a while.

> Hands SANDRA the urn.

ATTORNEY: Well, The Professor is yours now.

> SANDRA takes the urn from the ATTORNEY with an air of gravity and will exit the stage looking closely at it.

SANDRA: Thank you for everything. Especially, how you handled my mother's affairs after Dad died. You've been a good friend of this family for a long time.

ATTORNEY: Thank you, Sandra. And you've been a loving daughter to Julia. *(Turning to include SAM.)* And you too, Sam. You've both given Julia great happiness.

> They all stand. SANDRA and SAM exit. Then ATTORNEY exits from the opposite direction.

[Scene 2]

> Action.

> JULIA and NICK, holding hands, stroll on stage. They are dressed for spring weather. Their clothing suggests college students in the year 1968. They are not "counter-culture." NICK may be wearing a university-branded jersey or sweatshirt with short sleeves. JULIA may be wearing a casual top. This scene can be staged on a bare set, except that the urn must appear on some kind of shelf inside the crematorium.

NICK: I had no idea we'd come out on Mt. Hope Avenue.

JULIA: Me either.

NICK: It's a *big* cemetery.

JULIA: And, Nick. So old and beautiful! And historical. It's sort of amazing that we're finishing up four years of college, with the cemetery right next to the campus, and we never walked through it.

NICK: Well, everyone knows it's here. But it's not like "Hey, yeh gotta go to the cemetery!" Everyone has lots to do and think about.

JULIA: We never did find Frederick Douglass' grave. He's buried somewhere in there.

As they turn a corner, NICK points to a building.

NICK: Hey, Julia. What's that?

JULIA: Sort of a little gingerbread house. Like, out of Hansel and Gretel. Think it's part of the cemetery?

NICK: I don't know. I guess so. That chimney is pretty damn tall for a little gingerbread house. The witch in *that* cottage must cook up a lot of children! Let's take a closer look.

JULIA: I could just leave it be and head back to campus. It's been a long walk.

NICK: Oh, come on!

He leads her forward.

NICK: The door is open. Well, half-open. I take that as an invitation to go in.

JULIA: That does not qualify as an invitation, and this does not look anything like a public place.

NICK: Oh, let's do it! You only live once.

He leads her forward and pushes through the (imagined) door. From deep inside the main room of the building, they hear the voice of JOHN, the elderly crematorium employee.

JOHN: Well, you came through the door. You might as well come *all* the way in.

NICK guides JULIA inside. JOHN is seated on a chair with a small table next to it. He sets down a thick book with a serious-looking cover. He steps forward.

JOHN: Do you know what kind of building you're in?

NICK: I think that smokestack kind of gives it away. This must be a crematorium.

JOHN: That's right. It belongs to Mt. Hope Cemetery. I've been here for 35 years. *(Pointing.)* See that? What do you suppose it is?

NICK: The oven? Far out!

JOHN: That's right. I did a burn this morning. You might have smelled a little smoke as you walked down the path.

NICK: Wow. "A burn." Too bad we missed *that.*

JOHN: No. If a burn had been in progress, I wouldn't have admitted you. I keep the door open for a little cool air, but out of respect for the deceased, I would not have allowed strangers to just wander in. You understand?

JULIA: Yes. Of course we do. *(Beat.)* This is a very . . . picturesque building. Beautiful tiles embedded in the brickwork. Sort of European, Swiss, or something like that.

JOHN: This crematorium is over 100 years old. It was built during the Civil War. A lot of young men were incinerated right here. The bodies were brought here from Gettysburg, Shiloh, Chancellorsville. All those places. Lot of grief when a young man dies. *(Beat.)* We have one of the very last coal-fired ovens. Now they're all gas-fired. Much cheaper and cleaner. We'll be shutting down in about nine months. There will be a new modern crematorium opening offsite. Much bigger than this place. So, if you wanted to see it, you're lucky you didn't wait too much longer.

JULIA points to an urn on a high shelf.

JULIA: That's an urn. Is that where you put the ashes of the person you burned this morning?

JOHN: Oh, no. That's "The Professor." No one even makes urns like that one any more. Long ago, The Professor was a faculty member at the University. His will specified cremation, but he wasn't married. And no family. No one ever claimed the body, so he's been here—waiting you might say. He was here when I was hired. We don't even know his name.

All I know about The Professor was what my predecessor at this job told me—and that wasn't much. The County keeps records of every death, but this particular urn sort of got separated from the death certificate and the Cemetery's records. So, he's "The Professor." He's kept watch on that shelf for at least 50 years, and I'm his only friend. After all these years, I am probably the only living soul who knows he ever lived.

> JOHN looks long at NICK and, especially, at JULIA.

JOHN: You seem like a nice young couple. From the University. And that's an engagement ring—am I right? . . . Would you like to have The Professor?

NICK: What?

JOHN: That's right. The Professor would be yours . . . "To have and to hold." If you're students at the University, then you have professors. Maybe you'd like to have this one?

NICK: You mean, you'd just give us the urn? The Professor, I mean.

JOHN: Under the circumstances, I believe I would. I will retire when we close down, and I *could* take The Professor with me. But I don't have many years left myself, and so I'd still be facing the problem of seeing to his "future," so to speak. After all these years, I'd hate to see someone just throw him into the trash. Someone cleaning out this building when it closes, or someone cleaning out my apartment after I'm gone. Someone who just sees a clay jar and has no interest in what it might be. I don't think The Professor should go into the trash. You're young. You're from the University. Take The Professor. Please.

NICK: Yes! Absolutely. An urn full of human ashes. What could be cooler than that?

> JOHN looks displeased.

JOHN: He's a person. Not a conversation piece! Young lady, do you understand what I'm talking about? If you take The Professor, it's a commitment. You keep him. Wherever you go, he stays with you. You can't just decide to get rid of him—unless, of course, you find someone else who will show him proper respect.

JULIA: I think I understand you. This is a very significant decision.

NICK: Julia, maybe this isn't such a good idea. We're going to be moving around a lot in these next few years. Traveling too. Maybe this thing is too much of a burden.

JOHN: In a sense, he will be a "burden." But you'd be showing respect for a man's life. Not a person you knew, but a person nonetheless. You are truly all he has. At least, that's how it will be after I'm gone.

JULIA: Nick. Burden or not. I think we need to take The Professor. I *want* The Professor, sir. I will take good care of the urn.

JOHN: The name's "John." I'm very pleased.

> JOHN reaches for the urn on the shelf and hands it to JULIA. Then turns toward NICK.

JOHN: Young man. I have spent most of my life with The Professor looking down at me from that shelf. Trust me. Give The Professor a chance, and he will be more than a burden.

JULIA: John, Nick and I will look after The Professor, just as you have done.

> Freeze.

[Scene 3]

> JULIA and NICK, in a dreamy mood, are strolling through the cemetery back to campus. NICK holds the urn. At some distance, an elderly man wearing a black sport coat, tie, and hat, is watching them. He seems to know that JULIA and NICK are headed toward him.

HORACE: Hello, Julia. Hello, Nick.

JULIA: Hello. *(With a knowing smile.)* Good morning. It is very good to meet you.

NICK: Hello . . . You addressed us by name. Do we know you?

HORACE: Well, yes. In a manner of speaking. Also, you are holding my ashes. My name is Horace Smith. I was a professor in the English Department for many years. That was a long time ago. I taught Shakespeare to thousands of young men and women. Also John Milton. I

217

was respected too. Students heeded my words carefully. *(Beat.)* Back in my day, we didn't just do "literary analysis." We used great literature to help students think and feel with greater depth, expand their humanity. Julia, you showed depth of understanding in the crematorium. Nick, you are a little behind Julia in that regard. You will need to learn from her— and from me. I will bring something to your marriage, to your lives. Perhaps to your children. I can still enlarge the human spirit.

JULIA: Thank you, Professor.

HORACE: Julia. Nick. I'm very pleased that my ashes have been entrusted to you. I've been on that same crematorium shelf for 59 years. I did everything I could for John—kept him from getting too lonely, lifted his spirits, gave him a broader outlook on life. He didn't have much of an upbringing, and he didn't have a reflective mind until he began taking long, slow looks at me. I started him reading and thinking, which is the job of a professor. Living with a young couple like you, there will be new shelves for me to watch from and more that I can do. Will you heed me?

JULIA AND NICK: Yes.

HORACE: Very good. Today feels like the first day of a new semester.

The End

Good-bye from SILVE

A 10-minute play by David K. Farkas

Version 12-31-20

I place this play in the public domain. Anyone is welcome to distribute, perform, modify, or expand upon the script of this play. – David K. Farkas, 2020.

Setting:

A large room at NASA's Jet Propulsion Laboratory in Pasadena, California, that is used for special occasions.

Characters:

Skip Wilson: A NASA engineer.
George: A NASA engineer.
Martha: George's wife, a homemaker.
Colonel Ingram: High-level NASA official. (Any gender or sexual orientation.)
Skip Wilson: As dancer.
SILVE: As dancer.

Suggested minimum casting:

Colonel Ingram/George Bedford
Skip Wilson as actor
SILVE as dancer
Skip Wilson as dancer
Martha

[Scene 1]

COLONEL INGRAM stands at a podium, enjoying the limelight. He speaks in a folksy Southern or Texas accent.

COLONEL INGRAM: This is surely the day to recognize Henry "Skip" Wilson *(Gestures to SKIP in the audience.)* Skip joined NASA in 1975, directly out of graduate school, and he was assigned to the Surface-Intensive Luminosity VLBI Exploration, known to us all as Project SILVE.

> Young SKIP, as dancer, enters. The SILVE spacecraft, as dancer, enters. To some kind of ethereal soundscape, they perform an interpretive pas de deux based on COLONEL INGRAM'S monologue. SILVE orbits around SKIP, but SKIP can join her at special moments, including the mention of the software patch that saves her. They pause whenever the audience's attention should be entirely on COLONEL INGRAM. SILVE'S dance style changes as she leaves the solar system for interstellar space. Gradually, SILVE appears more infirm, and SKIP shows concern and then grief. Later, SILVE appears to glide lifelessly into the void.

COLONEL INGRAM: Skip was part of the SILVE launch team in 1977, and he worked on telemetry for the Jupiter and Saturn fly-bys. In 1984, as Operations Manager, Skip managed the extension of SILVE's initial mission to conduct the Uranus and Neptune fly-bys, using the velocity assist from Saturn's gravitational field. *(Beat.)* We all thought SILVE was done for in 1987 when her Articulation Control System failed. But Skip engineered one of the largest and most complex software patches in the history of space exploration, and he brought SILVE back online. *(Beat.)* In 2013, SILVE's flight path took her through the heliosphere and into interstellar space, where she continued to send back data on electron density and solar wind. As new engineers replaced those who rolled off the project or retired, Skip stood out as the only original member of the project team. *(Beat.)* Two years ago, SILVE's data stream became unreliable, and no further experiments could be conducted. But Skip continued to monitor SILVE's voyage and transmit routine system commands. *(Beat.)* We had our last measurable signals from SILVE on May 13. We can still transmit, but we don't know if she is listening, and we're not likely to find out. So, the decision was made to formally close down the project, and Skip decided to coordinate the end of the project with his own retirement from NASA. *(Beat.)* SILVE has been in space for 43 years, longer than any other artifact from Earth. Skip and SILVE have been true partners all this time. *(Chuckling.)* I think Skip hears SILVE murmuring to him in his sleep.

SILVE, as dancer, and SKIP, as dancer, exit.

COLONEL INGRAM: SILVE is expected to reach the Oort Cloud in about 300 years. If there is any intelligent life out there, and if they recover SILVE, they will find a special golden data disk that includes greetings in 86 languages, the works of William Shakespeare, and the music of Chuck Berry.

SILVE dances across the stage to Chuck Berry-like rock and roll chords.

COLONEL INGRAM: We'd be happy to assign Skip to a current project, but he said no. He's been with SILVE his entire career. I guess this old dog *(Gestures again to SKIP.)* is just not in the mood to learn new tricks. I asked Skip if he'd care to come up to the podium to make a few remarks, but he declined. You all know, Skip's a quiet guy, not into speechifying, like yours truly. Now that he's retired, Skip plans to spend his well-earned leisure time fishing on the Gulf Coast. *(Beat.)* So, this luncheon marks the official termination of the Surface-Intensive Luminosity VLBI Project—and Skip Wilson's retirement. *(Raises a glass.)* You all know we can't serve alcohol on the JPL campus. But, join with me in toasting Skip Wilson and SILVE—"To a job well done!"

COLONEL INGRAM solicits applause from the luncheon [theater] audience. Then he backs upstage left or right, still clapping and facing the audience. INGRAM can become GEORGE by changing his costume in full view of the audience. Carrying a sport jacket and his briefcase, SKIP joins GEORGE, who will now speak with a more neutral accent. They walk slowly across the stage.

GEORGE: Well, it was a great event. You must admit the Colonel did a good job up at the podium.

SKIP: Yes, he did.

GEORGE: I didn't know you had ideas about fishing. I don't remember you mentioning that. I don't remember you ever *going* fishing.

SKIP: No, Ingram said he needed to put something about my retirement in his speech, so I said "fishing." No one is going to notice or care if I go fishing or not.

GEORGE: Well, you're going to have to figure out something.

SKIP: I guess so.

GEORGE: OK, tomorrow 6:30. We'll have happy hour and then dinner. It won't be too hot, so we'll do dinner on the patio. Martha is eager to see you.

SKIP: Yes, tomorrow. 6:30. See you then, George.

GEORGE: Yessiree.

SKIP: And, George. Thanks for being my really good friend all these years. Thanks for your support with SILVE. You know, especially in these last few years. And just thanks, in general.

GEORGE: Sure, Skip.

They exit.

[Scene 2]

The set is split. On one side GEORGE is seated at his patio dining set. On the other side, SKIP is stretched out on a shabby old chaise lounge with a big bottle of beer and an open bottle of large white pills.

Action.

GEORGE is idly scrolling on a tablet. SKIP tips the pill bottle and swallows a large handful of pills. He washes them down with his beer.

MARTHA: It's 7:00.

GEORGE: So.

MARTHA: Well, it's not like Skip to be late. He lives on his watch.

GEORGE: Well, maybe not any more, now that he's retired.

MARTHA: Well, you can text him.

GEORGE: OK.

GEORGE pulls out his smartphone and types out a text. Again, SKIP tips the pill bottle, swallows a large handful of pills, and washes them down with his beer. His smartphone beeps. He looks at it, types a return text, and stares off into the distance.

GEORGE: He says he's running late. He'll be here in 20 minutes.

MARTHA: OK.

MARTHA exits. Then she returns and puts something else on the table and exits again. After a short while (which represents 30 minutes), MARTHA returns.

MARTHA: It's after 7:30. Give Skip a call. Let's find out what's keeping him.

GEORGE makes the call. SKIP'S smartphone signals an incoming call.

SKIP: Hello, George.

GEORGE: Skip, you OK?

SKIP: Yes, I am.

GEORGE: What are you doing?

SILVE, as dancer, and SKIP, as dancer, enter together and observe SKIP, who is unaware of them. As SKIP delivers this next speech, we begin to see the effects of the sedatives. His voice is still loud enough, but his speech has become slurred.

SKIP: I'm taking a look at the solar system. Well, the part I can see from my backyard, which, right at the moment, is just the sun.

SILVE, as dancer, and SKIP, as dancer, again to ethereal music, resume their interpretive dance, mostly on SKIP'S portion of the stage or on the periphery of the entire stage. This might include locking arms tightly and spinning together as a single entity sailing through space. The dialogue can be paused to allow adequate time for the dance episode.

SKIP: But, in my *mind*, I'm looking at the whole damn cosmos. I'm out there riding with SILVE. Keepin' her company, so to speak.

GEORGE: Skip. What are you saying? Would you repeat some of that?

SKIP: You're not copying too well? Well, I guess my transmissions are starting to fail. I'm drifting pretty far away from things. I've been on an outbound orbit for a good while now, and this evening I've intersected SILVE'S flight path. She's just a thousand meters ahead of me. We're off to see the wizard.

MARTHA: What's with Skip?

> The dancing may be paused here because the audience is attending to down-to-earth events rather than to SKIP'S imaginings of outer space.

GEORGE: You're drunk. You could have done that over here with Martha and me.

SKIP: No, I'm not drunk. What I've consumed—"ingested" as they say—I couldn't have done at your house.

MARTHA: Drunk?

GEORGE: Fuck! You can't do that, Skip! I'm coming over. No, I'm calling the EMTs.

SKIP: *(With his speech slurred.)* Don't do that, George. Please. You're my friend. You understand. I know you do.

MARTHA: For God's sake, George. What is happening?

GEORGE: Martha's gonna make the call. Then, I'm sticking with you on the phone.

SKIP: Sorry, Houston Control. EMTs—not an option. George, I have a Glock right here. I don't want to do it that way. That's a terrible way to leave things. I need you to promise me—no EMTs. Unless I can trust you, I'm gonna have to use the Glock. Let's just finish our little chat—OK, George?

GEORGE: You have no right to put this on me, Skip.

> MARTHA grows continuously more agitated.

SKIP: Maybe I do. This one thing—so many years, George. Promise me. Make up some story when you need to.

GEORGE: *(Choking up.)* I . . . promise. But . . . Did you really need to do this?

SILVE, as dancer, and SKIP, as dancer, resume their interpretive dance. They gradually become deeply intimate, ecstatic, and triumphant.

SKIP: George, can you imagine me with a fishing rod and a tackle box? . . . You know, SILVE's still hummin' away, still talking to me. She's a sturdy old girl. Most of her solar panels are OK. Electronics good, just reduced voltage. She's too far away from all of you. But I'm right with her, George.

GEORGE is now aware of SILVE and SKIP, as dancers. MARTHA is not.

GEORGE: I know you are.

MARTHA: We should have guessed.

GEORGE stands, full of grief, and gives MARTHA a strong, fervent hug. MARTHA understands. GEORGE and MARTHA now gaze together at the ecstatic dance. SKIP becomes unconscious, perhaps dead. The dancing continues for perhaps 15 seconds to allow the audience to register SKIP'S unconscious state.

GEORGE: Martha, maybe it was the right thing. At least he went out the way he wanted to.

SKIP comes to life, stands, and joyfully watches the dancers, who are aware of him. Everyone on stage is fully aware of one another. The mood is exuberant.

MARTHA: Yes, I hope it's a long, sweet ride with SILVE.

SILVE and SKIP, as dancers, dance themselves offstage as though seeking something new and exciting. MARTHA and GEORGE watch them and then embrace again.

The End

Horizons

A 10-minute play by David K. Farkas

Version 12-31-20

I place this play in the public domain. Anyone is welcome to distribute, perform, modify, or expand upon the script of this play. – David K. Farkas, 2020.

Dedicated to Richard Russell, RIP.

Characters:

>Major roles are indicated in boldface.
>
>**Jeff Ruston:** A Horizon Airlines ground crew employee who has stolen an airliner.
>
>**Sander Arneson:** FAA Operations Chief for Sea–Tac Airport.
>
>**Shirley Esposito:** Sea–Tac Airport Duty Officer.
>
>Valerie: Jeff's former wife (voice only).
>
>**Red Dog 1 Pilot:** Male, distinctive voice.
>
>**Red Dog 2 Pilot:** Male, distinctive voice.
>
>**Apparitional Child:** Girl or boy.
>
>People in Space Needle.

Suggested minimal casting:

>Jeff Ruston
>Sea–Tac Chief/Man in Space Needle
>Sea–Tac Officer/Woman in Space Needle
>Valerie/Child
>Red Dog 1/Red Dog 2/Man in Space Needle

JEFF RUSTON, upstage, sits in a chair that represents the cockpit of an airliner. At a table or large desk Sea–Tac OPERATIONS CHIEF (Sander Arneson) and the Sea–Tac DUTY OFFICER (Shirley Esposito) are looking at the same computer monitor with a keyboard and mouse. On the desk is a mic on a stand, but it's not initially being used. The OFFICER has a headphone that covers one ear and also has a small microphone. The OFFICER periodically receives information through the headphone and speaks softly or in pantomime into the mic. There is a chair at the periphery of the stage for the actor who plays the two McChord Field pilots, designated RED DOG 1 and RED DOG 2. As this actor switches roles, he not only changes voices but shifts in his chair to emphasize that two pilots are being depicted.

CHIEF: What happened?

OFFICER: A guy stole an airliner. He's up there right now. It's a Horizon Embraer 175. He's all alone in the plane. No crew. No passengers.

The OFFICER points to the screen. We see JEFF flying the plane in a carefree manner and looking out of his windshield on both sides.

CHIEF: What!? Fuck! Who? How did he do it? Why did he do it? Is he some kind of terrorist? Does he want money? Just a lunatic?

OFFICER: His name is Jeffrey Ruston. He's a fueler for Horizon. Somehow he learned enough to fly the plane and waited for his moment.

CHIEF: A fueler? How could something like this happen?

OFFICER: He was occasionally assigned to the turn-around team, so he had access to the cockpit.

The OFFICER attends to her headphones and says a few words, probably in pantomime. Then she turns back to the CHIEF.

OFFICER: Colonel Prescott scrambled two F-15s from McChord. Won't take them long to get up here. And we're trying to establish radio contact with Ruston.

CHIEF: We need to know why he's up there and what he wants. *(Directs the OFFICER'S attention to the monitor.)* He's just doing a wide circle around Puget Sound.

OFFICER: Maybe he knows how to land an aircraft. Maybe he's planning to land it.

CHIEF: It's for sure he's never landed one of *these* before. We need to find someone who's talked civilians down. Or has some training. At least we can direct him so he crashes on a runway not over a bunch of houses.

OFFICER: If he listens to us. I'll ask the Tower to get to work on that. There's probably someone in the Tower with that kind of training right now. But we also need someone who knows the Embraer 175 cockpit.

CHIEF: Be good if we could find out how much fuel is in that plane.

> The OFFICER focuses for a while on what she hears through her headphones and perhaps says a phrase or two into the mic.

OFFICER: We're getting our radio link to Ruston. We also have a radio link with the pilots.

RED DOG 1: This is Red Dog 1, out of McChord. Come in Sea–Tac Control. You have operational authority, so tell us what you want. We're National Guard, but we know what we're doing.

OFFICER: OK, Red Dog 1. Do you have a visual?

RED DOG: 1: Affirmative.

RED DOG 2: This is Red Dog 2. Also affirmative.

OFFICER: You are armed?

RED DOG 1: We have sidewinder missiles. We can bring him down quickly if we need to.

OFFICER: Roger that. Can you see Jeff Ruston, the guy inside? Try to get a good look at him. Don't spook him, but maneuver for a good look.

RED DOG 2: I can see him. He's just flying that plane. He's certainly conscious and alert. If there's anyone else in the cockpit, I can't see them.

OFFICER: *(To CHIEF.)* We have a radio link to Ruston. Want to talk to him?

CHIEF: Yes, and patch Ruston to the McChord pilots. But they only get to listen. *(Touches the switch on the table mic and begins to speak.)* Hello, Jeff. This is Sea–Tac Control. How you doin' up there?

JEFF: Please do not address me as "Jeff." Or, Jeffrey Ruston. I am "Sky Commander Ruston."

> The CHIEF and OFFICER look at each other and do a double-take.

JEFF: And this is Horizon Air Flight 0000. The four zeros are sort of the numerical equivalent of infinity. Got it? I work for Horizon Airlines, so . . . *(Chuckling.)* this is a Horizon flight—although I admit it's not on any schedule.

CHIEF: OK. OK, Commander Ruston.

JEFF: You left something out.

CHIEF: OK, Sky Commander Ruston.

JEFF: That's right. Thank you.

The CHIEF mutes the table mic and turns to the OFFICER.

CHIEF: Tell the F-15s to stay close but out of the way. Tell them to report anything that they can see happening in that cockpit.

CHIEF: *(Now addressing JEFF.)* Sky Commander Ruston, may I ask why you stole . . . I mean . . . took command of . . . the plane?

JEFF: Beautiful day today. Great morning to be in the air. Usually I'm looking out the window—I always get a window seat—and just *hope* the pilot brings the plane around so that I can see Rainier or Mount Saint Helens. Today, it's all up to me. I'm looking right out the front, and I can turn the plane any way I want. Hey, Sea–Tac Control, what's your name?

CHIEF: I'm Sander Arneson. I'm FAA Operations Chief for Sea–Tac. I also have Shirley Esposito with me. She's Duty Officer. We have operational jurisdiction from the NORAD Western Defense Sector in Portland. Colonel Adam Prescott is Commander of the 142nd Air National Guard Fighter Wing at McChord. He and his staff are monitoring everything we say.

JEFF: Are you pilots?

CHIEF: Yes, I was military. Transports. Shirley does stunt flying in her spare time—at airshows and stuff.

JEFF: Very cool.

CHIEF: Sky Commander Ruston, can you tell me why you did this? There are easier ways to get a good look at Rainier.

JEFF: To tell you the truth, I can't really tell you. I do a lot of things where I can't say why. I'm a bit of a screw-up. A lot of a screw up. That's why I'm 32 years old and working on the ground crew.

CHIEF: Nothing wrong with working as a fueler.

JEFF: I'd hoped for better. I went to college. I expected to do better than working my butt off for minimum wage, half the time in the rain. There were other things I expected and didn't get. Well, I guess my ground crew days are over. I certainly achieved that much today.

CHIEF: We'd like to talk you down. I bet you're good enough to land that airliner. We're getting someone right now who knows all the controls on that Embraer. You know, thus far, nobody has been hurt. No one needs to get hurt. I won't say you're not in trouble, but you're not in big trouble. Let's keep it that way—OK?

JEFF: That's not exactly my plan.

OFFICER: *(Mutes the table mic and talks to CHIEF.)* We have his ex-wife patched in from Maple Valley. She says she can help talk him into landing the plane.

CHIEF: OK, let's try it.

The OFFICER presses some keys on the keyboard.

CHIEF: *(To JEFF.)* We have . . . Valerie, your ex, on the line. She wants to talk to you.

JEFF: She does? Well, OK.

VALERIE: Hey Jeff, why don't you drop that plane into the ocean? Or burn yourself up in the mouth of a volcano?

The OFFICER and CHIEF are slow to grasp what is happening, and, when they do, they look at each other with dismay.

JEFF: You always were a dumb one. There's no volcano like that for thousands of miles.

VALERIE: OK. Maybe just crash into the Space Needle. If you can find it. Probably that will be one more of your failures.

CHIEF: Cut her! Cut her off, for God's sake!

The OFFICER hurriedly presses keys on the keyboard.

JEFF: OK, Babe, maybe I'll do just that. This will be in honor of you, Val. In honor of our five years together.

CHIEF: What the fuck?

OFFICER: *(Pointing to the screen.)* He's turning.

CHIEF: Jeff, Sky Commander Ruston, what are you doing?

JEFF: Oh, I don't know . . . I just might topple the Space Needle. For the record, this was Val's idea. Quite a woman!

CHIEF: We can't permit that. We'll shoot you out of the sky.

JEFF: Oh, yeah? You need to think twice about that. Twelve tons of wreckage and aviation fuel falling over Seattle? I don't think so. Space Needle, here I come!

OFFICER: Sander, I don't think he really means it. He was pretty friendly until he heard from that woman.

CHIEF: *(Muting the table mic.)* Ruston has issued a terrorist threat. This is an order I need to give. *(Now flicking a switch on the table mic so as to address the pilots.)* McChord pilots, this is Sander Arneson, FAA Operations Chief for Sea–Tac with direct authorization from NORAD Western Defense Sector and Colonel Prescott. Your orders are to shoot down the Embraer 175 you are tracking if you can get him over water or any kind of clear area.

RED DOG 1: We copy. We understand. If we get our chance, we'll do it.

RED DOG 2: But it doesn't seem likely that he'll pass over any open area. He's headed straight for the Space Needle.

JEFF: Well those folks in the restaurant are gonna see something really special today. Way more exciting than the Blue Angels.

The CHIEF and OFFICER watch their monitor in helpless fear as they track the flight of the plane toward the Space Needle. The actor who is providing the voices of RED DOG 1 and RED DOG 2 quickly takes up a waiter's tray and perhaps an apron and moves from the periphery of the stage to join the CHIEF and OFFICER, who have become patrons at the Space Needle restaurant. The CHILD may join them. Everyone is fixed in horror as they see the airliner approach and, finally, they scream all in terror, with the waiter dropping his tray. As the airline suddenly gains altitude and passes over them, they gradually regain some degree of composure.

JEFF: *(Laughing.)* Ha! Ha! Why would I want to kill a bunch of innocent people? Just to make Val happy? Ridiculous. No way. I'm heading off into the horizon. This is a Horizon airplane, so I'm taking it to the horizon. To my destiny. My fucked up destiny. Hey, Sampson, whatever your name is. Tell your pilots not to feel guilty if they have to shoot me down. They follow orders, I understand that. *I* shoulda been better at following orders.

CHIEF: No need for things to get that dire, Jeff. Just keep cool.

JEFF: *(Chuckling.)* Sampson, if I get shot down, I won't even blame *you.*

CHIEF: *(To OFFICER.)* He's still a clear and present danger to hundreds or thousands of people. *(To PILOTS.)* When you get him over open water, take your shot.

OFFICER: He's heading due north. If he holds steady, you can get him off Mukilteo.

RED DOG 1: Roger that. We'll follow him north.

RED DOG 2: Damn, I never expected to do anything like this.

   (Beat.)

JEFF: Hey, Sampson. I have a great view of Mt. Baker.

CHIEF: I bet you have.

JEFF: It's just a great morning, I think I'm gonna take a little stroll out on the wing.

CHIEF: Sky Commander Ruston, with all due respect, that's impossible.

JEFF: You have no idea what's possible in the last half hour of your life.

   JEFF steps out of the chair that has represented the cockpit and walks gingerly downstage, peering downward from the forward and trailing edge of the imaginary wing.

JEFF: Just amazing. I feel so free. I'm gonna do a little jig right on the wing.

JEFF dances but is careful about the edges.

OFFICER: McChord interceptors, do you have a visual? What do you see?

RED DOG 2: Nothing. The plane is still heading north on a steady course.

OFFICER: Roger that, Red Dog 2. (To CHIEF.) Well, he's definitely nuts. But he's not acting hostile.

CHIEF: He issued a terrorist threat and nearly carried it out.

Suddenly the CHILD appears on the wing with JEFF.

JEFF: Who are you?

CHILD: I'm the child you might still have. From the happy marriage you might still have. I want you to be my father. I want you to land the plane.

JEFF: What kind of marriage am I gonna have? How you planning to be born? If I land the plane—that is, if they let me land the plane—there are two F-15s tracking me—I'm going to jail, probably forever.

CHILD: No. It might not be a long sentence. At the trial, you get an expert witness to say you were taking the wrong meds. After you've served some time, a psychiatrist certifies that your mental health issues are resolved. Agree to wear an ankle bracelet and stay 10 miles away from any airport.

JEFF: You're a child. How can you be talking like this?

CHILD: I'm not a real child. I'm coming out of your brain. So I don't have to talk like a real child.

JEFF: I suppose not.

RED DOG 1: He's northeast of Paine Field, about to reach open water. We'll have our shot in about 90 seconds. We await further orders.

CHILD: Part of you really wants to live. Part of you knows you're not really standing on the wing of an airliner flying 400 miles per hour. Part of you—maybe a big part—thinks there's hope, even after a jail sentence. That part of you created me, is creating me right now. That's the reason you're gonna try to land this plane. You know you can land this plane.

JEFF: Yes, I can land the plane.

CHILD: Take my hand. Take me back into the cockpit. After that, I'm gonna disappear. But if you do the right things, I promise to come back to you as your real child. Will you kick a soccer ball with me? Will you love me? Will you love my mother? Maybe I'll have a brother and a sister. Will you do your best to make me happen?

JEFF: I promise. I prom-ise. I know what I want now. Let's go back to the cockpit.

> JEFF walks the CHILD very affectionately back into the cockpit, where the CHILD exits and JEFF, taking his seat, resumes flying the plane.

JEFF: Sea–Tac control. Talk me down. This was all a mistake. There's more than one kind of horizon, and I just got a peek at a horizon that I can believe in. I think I can settle myself. It won't be easy, but I'm ready for self-discipline.

OFFICER: Do we understand you want to land the plane and that you'll let us talk you down?

JEFF: That's right. That's what I want.

CHIEF: *(To OFFICER.)* We can't take a chance with this guy. He's still a psycho flying twelve tons of metal and fuel. He made a terrorist threat and nearly carried it out. At any moment he could change his mind and kill a lot of people. It's too bad. Seems like an OK guy. But he's going down. Not much left to that 90 seconds.

OFFICER: McChord pilots. Hold off! Hold off for now.

CHIEF: What are you doing? I give the orders here. You know that . . . I can't take a chance with this guy . . .

RED DOG 1: This is Red Dog 1. We're awaiting further orders.

OFFICER: No, wait. We can land him at Whidbey Naval Air Station. Bring him around from the northwest. He'll come in with nothing but water below him. We'll have the F-15s right over him. Almost no risk.

RED DOG 1: This is Red Dog 1. Repeat. We're awaiting further orders.

CHIEF: If this goes bad, my career is over . . . But . . . OK, I'll do it.

OFFICER: Jeff, we're gonna guide you in. But it won't be Sea–Tac. You're gonna land at Whidbey Island Naval Air Station. Because you buzzed the

Space Needle, we can't fully trust you. Any crazy idea, any divergence from our instructions, and you're an instant gonner.

JEFF: I'm good with that. Thank you.

OFFICER: McChord pilots, you copy this?

RED DOG 1: Yes, we copy. It works on our end.

OFFICER: OK, Jeff, you ready to come home?

The End

Luke Meets the Revenue Man

Written by Arthur Hopkins in 1919. Adapted by David K. Farkas.

Version 12-31-20

Arthur Hopkins' play "Moonshine," from which "Luke Meets the Revenue Man" has been adapted, is in the public domain. I place my modifications to "Moonshine" in the public domain. Anyone is welcome to distribute, perform, modify, or expand upon the script of this play.

– David K. Farkas, 2020.

"Moonshine" is available in B. Roland Lewis, *Contemporary One-Act Plays*. New York: Charles Scribner's Sons, 1922. (www.gutenberg.org/ebooks/37970).
An audio recording is available in Librivox.org, One Act Plays, volume 007. 14:05 minutes.
https://librivox.org/one-act-play-collection-007-by-various

Characters:

> **Luke Hazy:** Moonshiner.
> **A Revenue Officer.**

> Deep in the mountains of North Carolina, moonshiner Luke Hazy sits at a crude table in his one-room cabin. There is a second chair, a cupboard with a jug of moonshine whiskey, and perhaps other items. On a wall is a faded newspaper photograph of a well-dressed man. LUKE holds an old-style revolver.

> A commotion is heard outside the cabin.

LUKE: *(Looking offstage.)* It's all right, boys . . . Jist leave him to me. Git in here, Mister Revenue Man.

The REVENUE MAN is shoved roughly through the doorway. He wears city attire but has no hat. His clothes are dusty. He speaks as a Northerner and is educated. LUKE, a lanky, ill-dressed Southerner, motions with the barrel of his pistol for the stranger to take a seat. (It may be necessary for LUKE to close the door.)

LUKE: You must excuse the boys for gettin' a little rough. You see they don't come across you revenue fellers very often, and they kinda got excited.

RM: I understand.

More commotion and a gunshot.

LUKE: *(Barely reacting.)* That was quite a handsome firearm they took from you. Boys are probably tryin' to determine who's gonna keep it.

RM: I would hate to be the cause of any dissension . . . uh . . . trouble . . . among the boys.

Another gunshot.

LUKE: *(Again barely reacting.)* Well, that just can't be helped. Won't yer sit down?

RM: *(Sitting.)* Thank you.

LUKE: *(Going over to cupboard and taking out jug.)* We wus hopin' you might be Jim Dunn. Have a drink?

RM: *(Starts slightly at mention of JIM DUNN.)* No, thank you. Your mountain liquor is too rough for me.

LUKE: *(Draining cup.)* Rough? T'ain't rough. Ye just don't like the flavor of liquor that hain't been stamped.

RM: Maybe so.

LUKE: It's bad manners to drink alone when you got company. Please have some.

RM: Very well, my friend. I suffer willingly.

Drinks a little and chokes.

RM: It's not so bad.

LUKE: The last revenue man that sat in that chair got good and drunk on my hooch.

RM: That wouldn't be difficult.

LUKE: No, but it wuz awkward.

RM: Why?

LUKE: I had to wait till he sobered up before I give him his bullet. Don't like the idea of sending a man to meet his maker while he's drunk.

RM: Thoughtful executioner.

LUKE: I'm mighty sorry you ain't Jim Dunn. But I reckon you ain't. You don't answer his likeness.

RM: *(Again starts slightly at the mention of JIM DUNN.)* Who's Jim Dunn?

LUKE: You ought to know who Jim Dunn is. He's just the most notorious revenue man that ever hit these parts. *(Points to newspaper photograph on back wall.)* He's a smart one. Put a lot of moonshiners in jail. And when the occasion calls fer it, he's good with a gun too. We figure he's due here sooner or later, and we got a little reception all ready for him.

RM: *(Looking at photograph.)* That's Jim Dunn?

LUKE: Yep.

RM: *(Rising, examining picture.)* Doesn't look much like anyone.

LUKE: That's cause the picture's been up on that wall a long time . . . I'm mighty sorry you hain't Jim Dunn.

RM: I'm sorry to disappoint you.

LUKE: Oh, it's all right. I reckon one revenue man's about as good as another.

RM: What makes you sure I'm a revenue officer?

LUKE: Well, since we ketched ye climin' trees an' snoopin' round the stills, I reckon we won't take no chances that you hain't.

RM: Oh. Well, you do have pretty good evidence. I'll say that myself.

LUKE: So, what's your name, Mr. Revenue Man?

RM: I'm "Diego Oscuro." Pleased to get better acquainted with you.

LUKE: Dee-egg -oh? O-scrur-o.

RM: Sorry about those unfamiliar sounds. I'm from New York City. My father was Spanish. "Diego" is like "James." I won't trouble you about "Oscuro." My father had a business importing wine. But in New York City everyone pays the tax.

LUKE: How 'bout that! *(Laughing.)* Not here. In these parts, payin' the tax isn't just an expense, it's an embarrassment. Yeh, know, I'm just gonna trip over "Dee-egg-oh," so I'm gonna just say "Mister Revenue" . . . for the duration of our acquaintance. Luke Hazy is my name. Please do call me "Luke." I want you to feel like you had a friend with you at the end.

RM: *(Starting as though interested.)* Not the Luke Hazy that cleaned out the Crosby family?

LUKE: *(Startled and draws revolver.)* How'd you hear about that?

RM: Hear about it? Why, your name's been in every newspaper in the United States. Every time you kill another Crosby the whole feud is told all over again. Why, I've seen your picture in the papers twenty times.

LUKE: Hain't never had one took.

RM: Don't you ever read the newspapers?

LUKE: Me read? I hain't read nothin' fer thirty years. Reckon I couldn't read two lines in an hour.

RM: You've missed a lot of information about yourself.

LUKE: How many Crosbys they say I killed?

RM: I think the last report said you had just removed the twelfth.

LUKE: It's a lie! I only killed six . . . that's all they wuz growed up. I'm a-waitin' fer one now that's only thirteen.

RM: When'll he be ripe?

LUKE: Jes as soon as he comes a-lookin' fer me.

RM: Will he come?

LUKE: He'll come if he's a Crosby.

RM: A brave family?

LUKE: They don't make 'em any braver—they'd be first-rate folks if they wuzn't Crosbys.

RM: If you feel that way, why did you start fighting them?

LUKE: I never started no fight. My granddad had some misunderstandin' with their granddad. I don't know jes what it wuz about, but I reckon my granddad wuz right, and I'll see it through.

RM: You must think a lot of your grandfather.

LUKE: Never seen 'im, but I ain't goin' agin my own kin . . . Won't ye have another drink?

RM: No—no—thank you.

LUKE: Well, Mr. Revenue Man, I reckon we might as well have this over.

RM: What?

LUKE: Well, you know. The killin' part. I mean I gotta kill you.

RM: That's OK. That's why I'm here.

LUKE: What do yu mean?

RM: I mean that I've been trying to commit suicide for the last two months, but I haven't had the nerve.

LUKE: *(Startled.)* Suicide?

RM: Yes. Now that you're willing to kill me, the problem is solved.

LUKE: Why, what d'ye want to commit suicide fer?

RM: I just want to stop living, that's all.

LUKE: Well, yu must have a reason.

RM: No special reason—I find life dull, and I'd like to get out of it.

LUKE: Dull?

RM: Yes—I hate to go to bed, and I hate to get up. My work is a farce. I chase around these hills lookin' for moonshiners but nothin' really comes of it. There's always going to be more to take their place. I see by the fate of my friends that love brings only disappointment and sadness. Injustice is everywhere. The crafty schemer gets the money and the glory, while the fair-minded dealer is humiliated in the bankruptcy court. In the name of the law every crime is committed; in the name of religion every vice is indulged; in the name of education the greatest ignorance is rampant.

LUKE: I don't git all of that, but I reckon you're some put out.

RM: I am. The world's a failure, and I'm just aching to get out of it . . . And you, my friend, are my opportunity.

LUKE: Yes, I reckon you'll get your wish now.

RM: Good . . . if you only knew how I've tried to get myself killed.

LUKE: Well, why didn't you kill yerself?

RM: I was afraid.

LUKE: Afreed o' what—hurtin' yourself?

RM: No, afraid of the consequences.

LUKE: Whad d'ye mean?

RM: Do you believe in another life after this one?

LUKE: I kan't say ez I ever give it much thought.

RM: Well, don't—because if you do you'll never kill another Crosby, or even a revenue officer.

LUKE: 'Tain't that bad, is it?

RM: Worse. Twenty times I've had a revolver to my head—crazy to die— and then as my finger rested on the trigger, I'd get a terrible dread—a dread that I was plunging into worse terrors than this world ever knew. If killing were the end, it would be easy, but what if it's only the beginning of something worse?

LUKE: Well, you gotta take some chances.

RM: I'll not take that one. You know, Mr. Luke, life was given to us by someone who probably never intended that we should take it, and that someone probably has something ready for people who destroy his property. That's what frightens me.

LUKE: You do too much worryin' to be a regular suicide.

RM: Yes, I do. That's why I changed my plan. I'm going to make someone *else* responsible for my dying. I've been exposing myself to every danger I could think of.

LUKE: What ye mean by that?

RM: Well, did you ever see an automobile?

LUKE: No.

RM: They go faster than steam engines, and they don't stay on tracks. Did you ever hear of Fifth Avenue, New York?

LUKE: No.

RM: Fifth Avenue is jammed with automobiles, eight deep all day long. People being killed every day. I crossed Fifth Avenue every day for weeks, never once trying to get out of the way, and always praying I'd be hit.

LUKE: And couldn't yu git hit?

RM: *(In disgust.)* No. Automobiles only hit people who try to get out of the way. *(Pause.)* When that failed, I frequented the lowest dives on the Bowery, flashing a roll of money and wearing diamonds, hoping they'd kill me for them. They stole the money and diamonds, but never touched me.

LUKE: Couldn't you pick a fight?

RM: I'm coming to that. You know Two Gun Jake that keeps the dive down in Henderson?

LUKE: I do . . . Jake's killed enough fellers to git attention.

RM: He's a bad man, ain't he?

LUKE: He's no trifler.

RM: I wound up in Jake's place two nights ago. I elbowed my way up to the bar and announced to everyone in the place that Jake's wife has been with every man in town. And she does it because Jake can't do nothin' in bed.

LUKE: That shudda got Jake mad enough to kill yu.

RM: Well, he might still get around to it, but he went off and killed his wife instead. So he's in jail now.

LUKE: That's just plain bad luck.

RM: I decided that you moonshiners were my best chance. So I scrambled around in the mountains until I found your still and waited until your boys showed up.

LUKE: *(Pause.)* Ah, so ye want us to do yer killin' fer ye, do ye?

RM: You're my last hope. If I fail this time, I may as well give it up.

242

LUKE: *(Takes out revolver, turns sideways and secretly removes cartridges from the chamber.)* What wuz that noise?

Lays revolver on table and steps outside the cabin. The REVENUE MAN looks at revolver, apparently without interest. LUKE quickly re-enters and expresses surprise at seeing that the REVENUE MAN made no attempt to secure the revolver. Feigning excitement, he goes to the table and picks up the gun.

LUKE: I reckon I'm gettin' careless, leavin' a gun layin' around here that-a-way. Didn't you see it?

RM: Yes.

LUKE: Well, why didn't ye grab it?

RM: What for?

LUKE: To git the drop on me.

RM: Don't you understand what I've been telling you, Luke? I don't want the drop on you.

LUKE: Well, doggone if I don't believe yer tellin' me the truth. Thought I'd just see what ye'd do. Ye see, I emptied it first.

Opens up revolver.

RM: That wasn't necessary.

LUKE: Well, I reckon ye better git along out o' here, Mister Revenue.

RM: You don't mean you're weakening?

LUKE: I ain't got no call to do your killin' fer you if ye hain't sport enough to do it yerself.

RM: But one murder more or less means nothing to you. You don't care anything about the hereafter.

LUKE: Mebbe I don't, but there ain't no use my takin' any more chances than I have to. And what's more, mister, from what you been tellin' me, I reckon there's a charm on you, and I ain't goin' to take no chances goin' agin charms.

RM: So, you're going to go back on me?

LUKE: Yes, siree.

RM: Well, maybe some of the other boys will be willing. I'll wait till they come.

LUKE: The other boys ain't even gonna see you. You're a leavin' this here place right now. Ye ain't got no right to expect us to bear yer burdens.

RM: Damn it all! I've spoiled it again.

LUKE: Come on, I'll let you ride my horse to town. It's the only one we got, so yu can leave it at Two Gun Jake's, and one o' the boys'll go git it.

RM: I suppose it's no use arguing with you.

LUKE: Not a bit. Come on.

RM: Well, I'd like to leave my address so if you ever come to New York you can look me up.

LUKE: 'Tain't likely I'll ever come to New York.

RM: Well, I'll leave it, anyhow. Have you a piece of paper?

LUKE: Paper what you write on? Never had no paper.

REVENUE MAN takes Jim Dunn's picture from the wall.

RM: If you don't mind, I'll put it on the back of Jim Dunn's picture. *(Places picture on table.)* I'll print it for you, so it'll be easy to read.

REVENUE MAN prints on the back of the picture.

LUKE: All right—come on now.

Both go to doorway. LUKE extends his hand. REVENUE MAN takes it.

LUKE: Good-bye, mister—cheer up. There's the horse.

RM: Good-bye. *(Shaking LUKE'S hand.)*

LUKE watches for a while as the REVENUE MAN rides down the mountain. Then he hears loud laughter.

RM: *(Laughing still louder and calling.)* Farewell, my friend. Perhaps we'll meet another day.

LUKE: *(To himself.)* Now what does he mean by that?

RM: *(Shouting louder)* Lu-uke, loook aht the pict-tuure!

LUKE pauses for a moment, then returns to the table, takes a drink, picks up the picture, and turns it around several times before noticing the writing on the back. Then he begins to study. Attempting to make out the name, he slowly traces in the air with his index finger a capital "J"—then mutters "J-J-J"; then traces the letter "I"—mutters "I-I-I"; then a letter "M"—muttering "M-M-M, J-I-M—J-I-M—JIM." In the same way he traces and mutters D-U-N-N."

LUKE: Jim Dunn! By God! Ha! Ha! Whatta feller. Well, the joke's on me today. But mebbe we'll meet again. I'll have no trouble recognizin' him next time.

The End

Nordstrom Shopping Zombies

A 10-minute play by David K. Farkas

Version 12-31-20

I place this play in the public domain. Anyone is welcome to distribute, perform, modify, or expand upon the script of this play. – David K. Farkas, 2020.

Characters:

Henry Peck: Shopping, under protest, with his wife. He is at least 45 years old.

Priscilla Peck: Henry's wife, frustrated and impatient with Henry.

Gerri: A sales trainer working in the Men's Clothing department of a Nordstrom department store.

Darlene: A sales associate.

Suzie: A sales associate.

GERRI is standing and addressing a group of Nordstrom sales associates working in the Men's Department of a store. DARLENE and SUZIE are seated and attentive. Two or more audience members may be recruited to sit with them and react to the action. All sales associates have identical loose-leaf binders and a pen. Also on stage are PRISCILLA and, standing directly behind her, HENRY. They are mostly frozen and oblivious. He is slouched and dispirited, rather like a zombie that doesn't know what to do next.

GERRI: I hope you all enjoyed your lunch break. This afternoon, we will continue our examination of Men's Department shopper profiles. Just a reminder: Our research shows that sales associates who understand the eight shopper profiles enjoy 35% higher sales than those who have not taken this training. So, listen up, everyone! *(Beat.)* We will begin the afternoon with a discussion of the Male Shopping Zombie—or MSZ. Keep in mind that MSZs have a higher disposable income than most of the other categories of shoppers, and, as I will explain, they are often big spenders. Male Shopping Zombies may be annoying to deal with, but it's worth it—especially if you can form an alliance with their wife. MSZs, by definition, always shop with their wife. *(Beat.)* Let me introduce our "real life" MSZ and his wife: Mr. Henry Peck and Priscilla Peck. Let's give them a warm welcome. *(Gestures for applause, and the couple unfreezes slightly.)* This morning we examined the Bargain Hunter, the Dandy, and the Hipster. The MSZ is very different from these or any of the other categories that make up our Men's Department shopper profiles. In fact, MSZs are very easily recognizable.

The PECKS come fully to life. He follows her zombie-like across stage.

GERRI: Notice the slouch, the glazed eyes, the unkempt hair. The MSZ has been married to the same woman for decades, and no longer pays even the slightest attention to his appearance. Often you will hear, whining. Like this:

HENRY: I have a stomach ache. We need to go home.

GERRI: Or . . .

HENRY: I think I'm having a heart attack. You'd better call 911.

GERRI: Ignore this stuff. That "heart attack" is almost always fake, and, anyway, we're here to sell. You will notice that the wife always ignores this whining. You will also hear this:

HENRY: Why can't you just order some pants on Amazon?

PRISCILLA: You're between sizes. Also, your butt is too large *[Or too small.]*. We need the tailor to make alterations.

HENRY: *(In despair.)* The tailor?!

GERRI: The MSZ has no thoughts or opinions about the clothing his wife is picking out for him. His only thought is getting home as soon as possible, where he will recover with a long nap or, in some cases, a stiff drink.

HENRY: Or, in some cases, a stiff drink *and* a long nap.

GERRI: *(Brightly.)* Thank you, Henry . . . Now, how do we approach the MSZ? Suzie, want to give it a try?

SUZIE approaches the couple and focuses on HENRY.

SUZIE: Hello, Sir. I'm Suzie. Great day today! Can I help you?

HENRY: *(Miserable.)* You can't.

SUZIE: Well, what brings you to the Men's Department today?

> HENRY just points to his wife and pays no further attention to SUZIE, who returns to her seat.

GERRI: Can you all see Suzie's mistake? Darlene, what would you do?

> DARLENE stands and approaches PRISCILLA.

DARLENE: Do you know his size? We can take care of this very quickly. *(To HENRY.)* We have some very comfortable chairs, right over there. (*Pointing.*) I'm Darlene. If I can do anything to make you more comfortable, just let me know.

HENRY: *(With obvious gratitude.)* Thank you. I think I'll be OK in that chair.

> DARLENE returns to her seat. HENRY sits comfortably in the chair and returns to his zombie state. During GERRI'S next speech, HENRY, as actor, will inconspicuously leave the chair so that he can appear at the periphery of the stage following DARLENE'S next speech.

GERRI: MSZs have a habit of slipping away. You're talking to him, trying to explain what a "pleat" is, and he just disappears. It's remarkable how they can do that. Even their wives can't find them. Now, let's imagine that there are no chairs or that all of the chairs are occupied by other MSZs. Your MSZ has somehow disappeared mid-sentence. Where might he be hiding?

SUZIE: In the bathroom?

GERRI: No, men don't do that. So, where might you find your MSZ?

DARLENE: You can often find them near a speaker, trying to listen to the music . . .

> We see HENRY, at the periphery of the stage, with his ear cocked toward an imaginary speaker somewhere high on a wall.

GERRI: Yes. Yes. Very good, Darlene.

DARLENE: Or . . . *(DARLENE strikes the appropriate pose.)* Checking out the butt on a mannequin.

HENRY shows embarrassment. GERRI now addresses all the sales associates.

GERRI: Sad, but true. Now, sales associates, here's a little quiz.

HENRY tries to slip away, but PRISCILLA reigns him in harshly.

HENRY: We need to go home. I have a cold.

PRISCILLA: No you don't.

HENRY: I'm having a heart attack. We need to go home.

PRISCILLA: No! *(Addressing GERRI.)* Sorry for the interruption.

GERRI: That's OK . . . So, let's get back to our quiz. When the wife picks out a pair of slacks, shows it to the MSZ, and says, "I think we'll take the beige one," what is the MSZ likely to say? Anyone?

DARLENE: He says . . .

HENRY: *(Steps in to finish DARLENE'S speech but in a petulant voice.)* I want one of every color.

PRISCILLA: You don't need five pairs of slacks.

HENRY: Yes, I do.

GERRI: Now, why is Henry saying this? You really need to understand your MSZ—and the other Men's department shopper profiles. That's what this training seminar is all about. Remember, 35% higher sales. So, why did Henry say, "I want one of every color"?

SUZIE: Because he thinks this will make his wife cut short the shopping trip?

GERRI: *(Tactfully.)* That's poss-ib-ble.

DARLENE: Because Henry is thinking the more pairs of slacks Priscilla buys, the longer it will be before she takes him out shopping again.

GERRI: That's right! Money is no object to MSZs. They are way too miserable and too desperate to care about money. That's why they are often bigger spenders than much better dressed men. Do you see the opportunity here?

DARLENE: I do indeed see opportunity. Shouldn't we talk about "fetish objects"?

GERRI: Yes, I was getting to that . . . Many male customers, in all of the groups, have a deep attachment to some fetish object, some *favorite* article of clothing—a Levi's jean jacket, a hat, a pair of sneakers, very often a belt. You can usually spot the fetish object. Let's look at Henry . . . Henry has been wearing that belt *(Points.)* every single day of his life for 27 years—except for two weddings and three funerals. It was made by Joe, of Joe's Shoe Repair, in Ely, Minnesota, from elk hide brought in by a hunter. That is one sturdy belt. It could easily last 100 years. Priscilla hates it. So, how do we deal with a situation like this. Suzie?

SUZIE: I'd form an alliance with the wife.

PRISCILLA: Henry, you can't keep wearing that belt. It's falling apart.

HENRY: It isn't! It's rock solid, like the day I bought it.

SUZIE: Let me show you folks some of our leather belts. These are very fashionable . . .

HENRY: *(Baring his teeth and growling fiercely.)* Grrrr!!!!

SUZIE jumps back and, still facing HENRY, slowly returns to her seat.

GERRI: Do not call Security in these situations. Unless cornered, the MSZ is not actually dangerous.

HENRY: *(Again baring his teeth but growling more softly.)* Grrrr!!!!

GERRI: This is a tricky situation. Darlene, how would you handle it?

DARLENE stands, approaches HENRY, and speaks in a very soothing voice.

DARLENE: That's a *nice* belt. Lots of character. It would go great with some flannel shirts we have. Looks like you're a . . . Large. We can walk right over there and just grab a few of those shirts.

Contentedly, HENRY follows DARLENE offstage, totally ignoring PRISCILLA.

GERRI: Market researchers have studied the male shopper's attachment to fetish objects. However, the reasons for this attachment are not fully understood. Marketing departments at several business schools have performed experiments that suggest different explanations. One hypothesis is that . . .

HENRY and DARLENE re-enter. HENRY displays focus and energy we have not seen before.

HENRY: Darlene, do you like working here?

DARLENE: Not really.

PRISCILLA, GERRI, and SUZIE take notice.

HENRY: You do know that us Male Shopping Zombies generally have high disposable incomes?

DARLENE: Yes, I learned that in training.

HENRY: Well, I have a *very* high income.

PRISCILLA, GERRI, and SUZIE are amazed.

HENRY: Darlene, do you understand what John Prine meant when he sang "To believe in this living is a hard way to go"?

DARLENE: Yes, I do. I love John Prine.

HENRY: Do you understand what Bruce Springsteen meant when he sang, "I can't tell my courage from my desperation"?

DARLENE: Yes, I've felt that way sometimes.

HENRY: Darlene, would you leave this place with me?

DARLENE: Yes!

She follows a purposeful HENRY Offstage. His trailing arm is holding her hand.

SUZIE: *(Recovering herself.)* Far out!

PRISCILLA: *(To GERRI.)* I'm suing Nordstrom's!

GERRI: It's your own damn fault.

HENRY and DARLENE suddenly appear at the periphery of the stage, showing affection and joy.

HENRY: That's right, Gerri. Definitely nothing to blame on Nordstrom's!

They exit.

The End

The Expulsion from Eden

A 10-minute play by David K. Farkas

Version 12-31-20

I place this play in the public domain. Anyone is welcome to distribute, perform, modify, or expand upon the script of this play. – David K. Farkas, 2020.

Dedicated to Professor Katherine Koller Diez.

Characters:

Major roles are indicated in boldface.
Adam, Eve, Raphael, Cain, Enoch, Narrator, Messenger.

Suggested minimal casting:

Adam (young, mature, old)/Enoch.
Eve (young, mature, old).
Raphael/Narrator/Messenger/Cain (young and mature).

> **OR:**

Adam as young man (Scene 1) and mature man (Scene 2)/Enoch (Scene 4).
Eve as young woman (Scene 1) and mature woman (Scene 2).
Adam as old man (Scene 3).
Eve as old women (Scene 3).
Raphael/Narrator/Messenger/Cain as young man (Scene 2)/Cain as mature man (Scene 4).

[Scene 1]

ADAM and EVE enter from opposite sides of the stage and confront each other. RAPHAEL watches from upstage, but gradually steps forward and into their view.

ADAM: Why are you covered?

EVE: I did not want you to see me naked. And you?

ADAM: Yes, the same.

EVE: Everything is changing.

ADAM: Yes . . . Raphael, what do we call these coverings we now wear?

RAPHAEL: You will call them "garments." Adam, Eve, you will no longer need to ask me such questions. Your minds are now filling with new thoughts and words.

EVE: Like death?

RAPHAEL: Like death. You now know sin, and shame, suspicion, discord, and more. You will soon see death in many forms—including murder. You will know toil, pain, and illness. And you will need to find your own answers, for when you leave Eden, you will see me no more.

ADAM: This will happen soon?

RAPHAEL: Yes, very soon. You have just minutes to absorb the meaning of what has happened and to ready your minds for a world far more complex and threatening than what you have known. Adam, the beasts are no longer your friends, especially at night. You must cut a stout branch and sharpen one end so that you can ward off predators.

ADAM: Woman, you have caused all this woe!

EVE: I did nothing.

ADAM: You ate of the apple. Is that nothing?

EVE: The serpent was subtle. He lied.

ADAM: Why did that matter? We were given one prohibition, just one. "Eat not of the Tree of Good and Evil." That's all you needed to know.

EVE: The serpent tempted me. He spoke of knowledge like it was something I should want. The apple had a bright glow like no other fruit I'd ever seen. That glow made me hunger for its taste. Then, after I ate, I was so afraid, and I could not stand to be alone in my fear and dread. So, I offered the apple to you in order to join our fates.

ADAM: Stop! . . . Oh fatal deed! We needed only to obey that one prohibition and Paradise was ours forever. Now we must suffer and die, and our children must suffer and die. They will curse us—especially they will curse you.

EVE: Yes, they will curse me. I have caused great harm, never to be equaled. Adam, do you still love me? Am I not still lovely to look upon?

ADAM: You are less so. You are now mortal, and this can be seen. But that is not the point. Oh, Eve! Mother of sin and sorrow. I hate and despise you for what you have done.

EVE: Adam, I would gladly take the full weight of God's punishment upon myself alone. *You* might remain in Paradise.

RAPHAEL: No such thing is possible. Adam ate. He could have refused, but he did not.

EVE: *(To RAPHAEL.)* But I brought the temptation to him. I told him how the taste opened my mind, expanded my vision.

RAPHAEL: If Adam had refused, there would have been no Fall, no punishment—just a warning and further instruction. To Fall, you needed to fall together, and you did.

EVE: Adam, though you did eat, it was I that tempted you. And not just with my words. My golden hair, waving softly in the breeze, has led you always to comply with my desires. No different this time. Adam, I would take upon myself the full weight of God's punishment.

ADAM: *(Softening.)* You would. I know that.

EVE: I would . . . die. I would see *you* still in Paradise with *another* woman—a second Eve, a better Eve. I would have you take her to bed. You would say, "Once I had a woman named Eve, but she was evil."

ADAM: These thoughts are too terrible to speak of.

RAPHAEL: Is Eve entirely to blame? Think, Adam.

ADAM pauses and is stricken.

ADAM: Eve, I was commanded to watch over you. For our mutual safety, we were not to be long apart, and I let you stray far enough from me that I could not hear the serpent speak to you. I am also at fault for what has happened.

RAPHAEL: Yes, Adam. Yes. Think *further*, Adam.

ADAM: *(Looking closely at EVE.)* I am sorry for casting blame as I did. You are Eve still, and I love you. Whatever may befall us, I will cherish you.

RAPHAEL: Yes, Adam. *(To both ADAM and EVE.)* Time is very short, and I must help you prepare for life outside Eden. Adam, you have learned the most important lesson: Forgiveness. Eve has learned it too. In Eden, before you fell, love was easy. You loved each other, you loved the animals who greeted you each morning. They loved you. But forgiveness is much harder than love. Forgiveness comes after you've been hurt, and you *will* hurt each other in word and in deed. So too will the future generations. Therefore, you must always practice forgiveness and teach forgiveness to your children.

ADAM: Forgiveness quells anger. I understand. And I understand more. If I see a young deer caught and sinking in deep mud, and I pull it out, that is kindness. If an animal tries to steal our food, and I set down my spear, that is mercy. But forgiveness is hardest, for it comes when I have been injured.

RAPHAEL: Forgiveness comes hardest. But it heals.

EVE: Adam, I know some things you do not. I tell you that forgiveness comes more easily to women than to men. Someday I will joyfully forgive my new babes for the pain of childbirth. And my daughters will forgive their babes, even as they lie bleeding to death on the bed of childbirth. The woman, in her last moments, will ask to hold her babe. In her last moments she will ask her husband to forgive the child for the loss of his wife. In their last moments together, the woman will instruct her husband to love the babe and teach it well. And men shall heed.

ADAM: Raphael, what more can you tell us in the short time we have left?

RAPHAEL: Evil has been set loose upon the world. There is evil within you, and evil is now part of Nature. Your descendants will know pestilence, wildfire, and floods. They will know envy and cruelty, crime and plunder. The future generations will be born into a battle they can never win—but which they can easily lose—if they succumb to cruelty or despair. But you can push evil backwards and enlarge the precious space in which good flourishes. Adam, Eve, history now begins. The world lies all before you.

ADAM and EVE turn toward RAPHAEL, then toward each other.

RAPHAEL: *(Gesturing.)* You must go now. This way.

ADAM and EVE take each other's hands. They exit.

Freeze.

[Scene 2]

ADAM, looking older, holds a farming implement. EVE, looking older, carries a basket. CAIN holds a weapon.

Action.

ADAM: Cain, I cannot understand *why* you have killed your brother. Not understanding makes forgiveness much more difficult. But I can do this, must do this. In a world of terrible evil, we are doomed to incinerate ourselves without forgiveness.

CAIN: Father, why was Abel's sacrifice preferred before mine? Why?

ADAM: I do not know.

EVE: But was this cause for murder?

ADAM: It is not enough that we forgive you. You must learn to forgive yourself. You can earn this forgiveness through kindness and generosity and working to heal the world. And by teaching others what you have learned. Teaching, teaching our children, this is our greatest hope. It's our best way to grow the army that fights evil on the battleground of daily living. Do you understand me, Cain?

CAIN: Understanding does me no good, Father. Even now I have a strong impulse to slay you and possess Eve by force. I am deeply evil, so deeply evil! To keep my desires in check, I must run off to the desert and live alone.

ADAM: Then do so. You are evil only if you *carry out* your evil desires. Subduing the evil within you is virtue.

EVE: You have our love, Son.

Freeze.

[Scene 3]

The NARRATOR, reading from a Bible, enters upstage.

NARRATOR: And Cain spoke: "I shall be a fugitive and a vagabond on the earth. And anyone who findeth me shall slay me." But the Lord answered, "No" and set a mark upon Cain as a warning to all not to kill him. And Cain went out into the wilderness, and he settled east of Eden. And Cain knew his wife, and she conceived and bore Enoch. And Cain built a city in the desert.

The NARRATOR exits. EVE, now much older, enters. A MESSENGER enters.

MESSENGER: I bear a message from Cain, your son.

EVE: *(Astonished and joyful.)* Adam! Oh, Adam! Come here. Something wondrous. A messenger from Cain. *(To MESSENGER.)* Is he well? Where does he dwell? It has been many years.

ADAM, walking with a cane, joins EVE.

MESSENGER: Yes, Lady. Your son is well. He dwells in Nod, a city that he founded and governs. He is married to Trafelsa. His son is Enoch. I am Meraltic, Cain's trusted advisor and friend. He would have no ordinary messenger speak to you.

ADAM: Founded a city? How could this be?

MESSENGER: After many years of wandering, both through the desert and in his mind, he made peace with himself. Soon after, he found his goodness and his strength. He then gathered many followers. Nod is a populous city that has established many trade routes. It is guarded by walls, high and strong. Cain is much honored. But he has heavy responsibilities, so he could not take time for the long journey from Nod to where you dwell.

EVE: He waited all these years to send us news?

MESSENGER: He waited until he was sure you would be proud of him.

EVE: He was foolish. We would have rejoiced to receive any news—any news other than of his death.

MESSENGER: I understand. But those who've known great shame can be like that. He thanks you deeply for your forgiveness and for everything you taught him. All this he has imparted to his son, Enoch, and to many others. He governs with wisdom and always with mercy. Can you visit him in Nod?

ADAM: Alas, we are too old to travel.

MESSENGER: Perhaps a day will come when he can be absent long enough to visit you.

EVE: If we never see him, this is still a joyous day for us.

MESSENGER: I am very weary. Let me and my attendants withdraw to our tents. We will return in the morning. I will tell you much, and you will tell me much that I can relate to Cain.

ADAM: Yes. Please. Of course. Until tomorrow.

The MESSENGER exits.

EVE: Adam, what will be our last thoughts as we die? What *should* they be?

ADAM: That we have lived well . . . and would have been happy except for the memory of our original sin and of Abel's death. What the world will say of us, we cannot know.

EVE: We will be blamed. I especially.

ADAM: Sometimes I have strange thoughts. Sometimes I think, dare to think, that it was good we left Eden and struck out on our own. A baby sucking at his mother's breast is in Paradise. But is this living? Were we truly living? Perhaps our sin was a kind of birth, a birth into the adventure of life. Perhaps God was in league with the serpent. Perhaps God and the serpent are one and the same. Raphael was our teacher while we lived in Paradise, but the serpent truly opened our eyes. Perhaps this is how life should be lived.

EVE: These are indeed strange thoughts.

Freeze.

[Scene 4]

CAIN is seated on a chair that suggests authority and respect. ENOCH is standing.

Action.

ENOCH: Father, there is unrest. Some say that your mercy toward the Cimmerians is weakness, the softness of a woman, not acceptable in one who governs a city and leads an army.

CAIN: They must learn otherwise, Enoch. We must show mercy. We must forgive the Cimmerians their foolish attempt to conquer Nod. We must teach them to live in peace with us, to join our trading caravans.

ENOCH: Of those who govern cities and nations, few think as you do. Is this because of Abel? Is this your atonement?

CAIN: This is what the angel Raphael taught my parents, it is what my parents taught me—and Abel also. As Abel died from the blow I struck, he forgave me. So, how can I not extend mercy and forgiveness to others? How can I not teach these things?

ENOCH: I understand, Father.

The End

The Spaghetti Crisis

A 10-minute play by David K. Farkas

Version 12-31-20

I place this play in the public domain. Anyone is welcome to distribute, perform, modify, or expand upon the script of this play. – David K. Farkas, 2020.

Characters:

Chef Henri
Maître d' Simone

CHEF HENRI presides imperiously over a small gourmet restaurant in Paris. Seated in the restaurant is an American family, who will not be seen or heard. Maître d' SIMONE has left the dining area for the kitchen, where she will consult with HENRI. Later she will speak with Hisham, the sous-chef, who will also remain unseen and unheard.

[Scene 1]

CHEF HENRI, facing upstage, is sautéing with a skillet and cooking utensil. SIMONE enters.

SIMONE: Chef Henri . . . A problem. I seated a couple. They did not have a reservation, but we had an empty table that I wanted to fill. They have a child.

HENRI: This is not good . . . But, is the child causing trouble? How old is this child?

SIMONE: She is a little girl. Very pretty. Maybe seven years old. She is quiet.

HENRI: And the parents? They must be Americans. They are OK?

SIMONE: They seem OK. Yes . . . Americans.

HENRI: It would be Americans who would do this thing—bring a child. They want a fine dinner—good. But they should have arranged with their hotel for someone to look after the child. But, we will get through this. *(With sardonic laughter.)* They think we have a children's menu here?

SIMONE: They did not ask for a children's menu.

HENRI: Have they ordered?

SIMONE: Yes, Chef, that is the problem.

HENRI: What is the problem?

SIMONE: The little girl. She wants a plate of plain spaghetti. Nothing else.

HENRI: Why, we can do that. A little butter sauce. The girl will like it. This is a custom order, but we will charge the price of an hors d'oeuvre. We will be very fair to them.

SIMONE: Not quite so easy. The little girl was very specific—and very definite. She said "plain . . . spaghetti."

HENRI: OK. Just a little olive oil. We can get through this.

SIMONE: I whispered this to the mother. She said olive oil will not work. The girl—Madelynn—she can tell when there is oil or butter. It must be absolutely plain, totally plain, from the boiling water to the plate. The mother says the girl will refuse the spaghetti if it is anything but absolutely plain.

HENRI: This I cannot do. The parents, what did they order?

SIMONE: They ordered adequately. The man wants the chicken cordon bleu. The woman wants the duck à l'orange. They chose the wrong wine. Didn't ask, just chose badly, but we are used to that.

HENRI: The little girl. She is sitting quietly? . . . I will *do* this. *(Gazes upward.)* I hope my Father is not looking down on me tonight from Heaven.

SIMONE exits.

Freeze.

[Scene 2]

Action.

HENRI beating the contents of a bowl with a whisk. SIMONE enters.

SIMONE: Chef Henri. I am so sorry. They are back!

HENRI: What do you mean? Who is back?

SIMONE: The Americans, with the little girl, who were here last evening. They are back! And the girl is with them.

HENRI: How could this be? All the fine restaurants in this city. So many memorable dining experiences! And they are *back here* a second time?

SIMONE: They said last night's meal was delicious, so they wanted to come back.

HENRI: And the girl? She wants plain spaghetti?

SIMONE: Yes, she wants plain spaghetti. That is what she wants—nothing else. I told the Americans I would ask if you will do this. The man said, "You did it *last* night. What's the problem?"

HENRI: Mon Dieu! He thinks he is back at home. At a Denny's! I do not serve plain spaghetti—not twice—not for *anyone!* They should have known better. You tell them that. If they want to eat here, I will put some oil, some butter, some tomato sauce—something!—on the girl's spaghetti. Or they must leave. And another thing: we do not allow children to "nibble" from their parents' plates.

SIMONE: I don't think this is a nibbling child. She ate her whole plate of spaghetti last night.

HENRI: They must leave. That is all.

SIMONE: No. You own the back of the house. I own the front of the house. If I tell them to leave, there may be a ruckus. If not the little girl, then the father. Maybe the mother too.

HENRI: I own the back of the house. I also own the entire restaurant. Remember that, Simone. They leave!

CHEF HENRI turns abruptly and exits. SIMONE takes a few steps and looks offstage to address Hisham.

SIMONE: Hisham, I need a favor. Get ready to serve up a plate of plain spaghetti. Plain. No butter. No oil. Nothing at all. I'll come back and tell you when I will need it. Hide what you're doing. If Chef Henri comes by, he cannot see the spaghetti . . . Merci, Hisham.

SIMONE turns away from Hisham and exits to the front of the house.

[Scene 3]

CHEF HENRI stands alone at his chef's station, holding a slip of paper.

Action.

SIMONE enters in a leisurely manner and approaches CHEF HENRI.

HENRI: *(Waives the slip of paper with an accusatory air.)* Simone! Something is very suspicious. Yesterday, the Americans—with the girl— they ordered a grated carrot salad and a green salad with Dijon vinaigrette dressing. Tonight the exact same salad orders. Also, one of the entrees, the duck a à l'orange, is the same as last night. There is no little girl in my restaurant—you promise? I can go out and see for myself!

SIMONE: No, no, Chef. No little girl, no Americans. They are gone. Just as you instructed. This couple is from New Zealand. It is just a coincidence.

HENRI: A couple from New Zealand. OK.

SIMONE: Chef Henri, when will you plate their entrees?

HENRI: Seventeen minutes. We run just a little slow tonight. That is OK?

SIMONE: That is OK.

CHEF HENRI turns and exits. SIMONE approaches where Hisham is working offstage.

SIMONE: Hisham, I'll need the spaghetti in 17 minutes. Put it on a plate. Nothing else. That's right. Nothing else, just spaghetti on a plate. And remember: Do not let Chef Henri see any of this. I'll just swoop by and grab the plate . . . Thank you, Hisham. Je t'aime, mon ami!

SIMONE steps away from Hisham and walks toward where the American family is seated offstage. We hear SIMONE addressing the American couple.

SIMONE: *(Smiling graciously.)* Yes, your order is in. Chef Henri is happy to prepare "plain spaghetti" for the little girl.

SIMONE abandons her normal professional demeanor.

SIMONE: You do not know, but we had *quite* a "spaghetti crisis" in the kitchen tonight. If you are in Paree tomorrow night, please . . . please . . . do not come back to this restaurant!

The End

Appendix D

References and Resources

The first section of this appendix provides the complete bibliographic information for the works cited in the text. Because this is not a scholarly book, I depart from scholarly conventions of bibliographic referencing. The second section of the appendix consists of supplemental resources not cited in the text.

References

Abbott, H. Porter. (2002). *The Cambridge Introduction to Narrative.* Cambridge University Press.

Allen, Laurie. (2019). *22 Comedy Ten-Minute Plays: Royalty-free Plays for Teens and Young Adults*. Meriwether Publishing.

Chernow, Ron. (2017). *Grant.* Penguin.

Coghill, Nevill; Starkie, Martin; Hawkins, John; and Hill, Richard. (1968). *Chaucer's Canterbury Tales.* www.guidetomusicaltheatre.com/shows_c/canterbury_tales2.htm

Cold Reads International. (2020). Reading from tablets www.coldreads.wordpress.com/how-it-happens/library

Dean, Alexander and Carra, Lawrence. (1989). *Fundamentals of Play Directing.* 5th edition. Waveland Press.

Farkas, David K. (forthcoming 2022). *Writing the 10-Minute Play.*

Glassman, Joshua and Vuranch, Karen. (2020). *A How-To Guide for Virtual Theatre: For when the show must go on . . . line!* (Free download). Pioneer Drama Service. https://www.pioneerdrama.com/pdf/VT_Howto.pdf

Hishon, Kerry. (2017). All about transitions: 5 tips for success.
www.theatrefolk.com/blog/all-about-transitions-5-tips-for-success

Maio, Alyssa. (2020). How the best method actors prepare for their roles.
www.studiobinder.com/blog/what-is-method-acting

May, Elaine. (1996). *Hotline.* In the collection *Death Defying Acts.* Samuel
French.

Montano, Fran. (2019). Play reading vs staged reading – Part II.
https://nohoartsdistrict.com/play-reading-vs-staged-reading-part-ii/

Newcomer, Carrie. (2005). "Angels unaware," in the CD *Regulars and
Refugees.*
www.carrienewcomer.com/store/regulars-and-refugees

Newman, John. (2019). *Playwriting in Schools: Dramatic Navigation.*
Intellect/University of Chicago Press.

Oz emag. (2013). How to analyze a script? The professionals method.
www.ozemag.com/2013/03/26/how-to-analyze-a-script

Pace, Chelsea. (2020). *Staging Sex: Best Practices, Tools, and Techniques for
Theatrical Intimacy.* Routledge.

Rogers, Barb. (2001). *Costumes, Accessories, Props, and Stage Illusions.* MMI
Meriwether Publishing.

Sapio, George. (2017). *Workshopping the New Play: A Guide for Playwrights,
Directors, and Dramaturgs.* Applause Theater and Cinema Books (Hal
Leonard LLC).

Synge, J. M. (1904). *Riders to the Sea.*
www.gutenberg.org/ebooks/994

The Pulp Stage: Live storytelling for fans of science fiction fantasy, and
suspense (2020).
www.thepulpstage.weebly.com/submissions-call.html

Wilson, Mary Louise. (2011). "Deer Play." In *Theatrical Haiku: Seven Short
Plays by Mary Louise Wilson.* Dramatists Play Service.

Supplemental Resources

Cleveland Playhouse Drama Club

The Cleveland Playhouse offers extensive educational materials (text and
videos) covering such topics as play selection, securing rights, script
analysis, auditions, casting, creating a rehearsal schedule, and more.
Although developed for use in schools, the content is definitely useful for
adults with an interest in theater.
www.clevelandplayhouse.com/education/in-school/drama-club

Copyright Alliance

The Copyright Alliance maintains a highly informative, responsibly written
website on all aspects of copyright and licensing. Visitors should, however,
be aware that the Copyright Alliance represents the interests of copyright
holders.
www.copyrightalliance.org/policy/amicus-b

Books

There are a great many books and periodicals—far too many to list and
describe—on all aspects of theater.

Made in the USA
Las Vegas, NV
14 June 2022